Communications
in Computer and Information Science 54

T0238365

Luo Qi (Ed.)

Applied Computing, Computer Science, and Advanced Communication

First International Conference
on Future Computer and Communication, FCC 2009
Wuhan, China, June 6-7, 2009
Proceedings

 Springer

Volume Editor

Luo Qi
Wuhan Institute of Technology
Wuhan Hubei, China
E-mail: witluo@ieee.org

Library of Congress Control Number: Applied for

CR Subject Classification (1998): C.2, D.4.4, E.4, C.3, H.4

ISSN 1865-0929
ISBN 978-3-642-02341-5 Springer Berlin Heidelberg New York

springer.com

© Springer-Verlag Berlin Heidelberg 2009

Typesetting: Camera-ready by author, data conversion by Scientific Publishing Services, Chennai, India
Printed on acid-free paper   SPIN: 12691494   06/3180   5 4 3 2 1 0

Preface

The International Conference on Future Computer and Communication was held in Wuhan, China, June 6–7, 2009. The following topics are covered by FCC Conference: agents, knowledge-based technologies, bioinformatics engineering, computer architecture and design, computer networks and security, data mining and database applications, high-performance networks and protocols, multimedia and web services, network reliability and QoS, neural networks and intelligent systems, software engineering and agile development, antennas and propagation, information theory and coding, multiple access techniques, optical communications and photonics, RF and microwave devices, satellite, space and wireless communications, signal and image processing, 3G, 4G mobile communications, communications IC Design, instrumentation and control, and VLSI design.

The purpose of the FCC conferences is to bring together researchers and practitioners from academia, industry, and government to exchange their research ideas and results and to discuss the state of the art in the areas covered by the conference

The conference included invited talks, workshops, tutorials, and other events dedicated to this area. FCC 2009 provided a forum for engineers and scientists in academia, university and industry to present their latest research findings in any aspects of future computers and communication. The conference was co-sponsored by the Engineering Technology Press, Hong Kong, IEEE SMC TC on Education Technology and Training, and the Intelligent Information Technology Application Research Association, Hong Kong. Much work went into preparing a program of high quality. We received 110 submissions. Every paper was reviewed by 3 Program Committee members, and 32 were selected as regular papers, representing a 29 % acceptance rate for regular papers.

In addition, the participants of the conference had a chance to listen to renowned keynote speakers. We thank the production supervisor of Springer, who enthusiastically supported our conference. Thanks also go to Leonie Kunz for her wonderful editorial assistance. We would also like to thank the Program Chairs, organization staff, and the members of the Program Committee for their hard work. Special thanks go to Springer CCIS.

June 2009   Qi Luo

Organization

The 2009 International Conference on Future Computer and Communication was co-sponsored by the Engineering Technology Press, Hong Kong, IEEE SMC TC on Education Technology and Training, and the Intelligent Information Technology Application Research Association, Hong Kong

Honorary Chair

Chin-Chen Chang	IEEE Fellow, Feng Chia University, Taiwan
Jun Wang	The Chinese University of Hong Kong, Hong Kong
Chris Price	Aberystwyth University, UK

General Co-chair

Qihai Zhou	Southwestern University of Finance and Economics, China
Junwu Zhu	Yangzhou University, China
Zhitian Xian	Wuhan University of Science and Technology, Zhongnan Branch,. China

Program Committee Chairs

Bin Chen	Nanjing University of Aeronautics & Astronautics, China
Wei Li	Southeast University, China
Yun Yang	Yangzhou University, China
Jun Wu	Yangzhou University, China
Dehuai,Zeng	Shenzhen University, China

Publication Chair

Luo Qi	Intelligent Information Technology Application Research Association Chair, Hong Kong

Program Committee

Shao Xi	Nanjing University of Posts and Telecommunication, China
Xueming Zhang	Beijing Normal University, China
Peide Liu	ShangDong Economic University, China
Dariusz Krol	Wroclaw University of Technology, Poland
Jason J. Jung	Yeungnam University, Republic of Korea

Paul Davidsson	Blekinge Institute of Technology, Sweden
Cao Longbing	University of Technology Sydney, Australia
Huaifeng Zhang	University of Technology Sydney, Australia
Qian Yin	Beijing Normal University, China

Hosted by:

Engineering Technology Press, Hong Kong
IEEE SMC TC on Education Technology and Training
Intelligent Information Technology Application Research Association, Hong Kong

Supported by:

Wuhan University of Science and Technology, Zhongnan Branch. China
Wuhan Institute of Technology, China

Table of Contents

The Model of the Statistical Geography Information System in Grid

Xincai Wu[1], Ting Wang[1,2], and Liang Wu[1]

[1] Faculty of Information Engineering, China University of Geosciences,
Wuhan 430074
[2] China GIS Software Research and Application Engineering,
Center of the Ministry of Education, Wuhan 430074
wuliang@hb165.com

Abstract. Nowadays many statistical geography information systems (SGIS) have been developed with different languages and platforms. The various origin and diverse structure of the statistical resources make users share them and operate these systems mutually difficultly. To solve these problems, we should take into account many aspects, such as operating the database mutually, compatible operating systems and balancing the internet load and so on. While the traditional GIS technology can not solve these problems perfectly, the grid can do it well. Based on OGSA structure, a SGIS model using grid middleware technology is proposed. This paper discusses its infrastructure characteristics and explains how this model solves the problems. Then a specific example is proposed and discussed its implementation process .Considering several key problems needed to be solved in the construction of the system, this paper gives its resolvents. It points out that SGIS based on grid is the best way for digital statistical information.

Keywords: grid; middleware; SGIS.

1 Introduction

The application of GIS in statistical industry is an important research direction and application field. But there are some common problems existing in statistical GIS all long. Although some experts have made many researches about them, the problems can not be solved well. These problems are as follows:

1) The heterogeneous structure and origin of the statistical data

Due to the variability of the statistical data structure and a lack of common standard for sharing the resources, it is hard to get data from different departments or at different times together for a comprehensive analysis. A large number of data are left unused, many of which contain the discipline of related industry [1]. So if we do not make full use of these resources, they will reduce their values.

2) incompatible platforms

For the SGIS are developed with different languages and platforms, when we visit different systems, we should consider the data structure and the computing standard of their own [2]. It is very inconvenient.

L. Qi (Ed.): FCC 2009, CCIS 34, pp. 1–7, 2009.

3) One computer's computing capability is limited

When a great many clients visit one system at the same time, the server will over load.For that one computer's computing capability is very limited, the maximal number of clients it can support is also very limited. In order to solve this problem, we can distribute the statistical resources over several computers and it is feasible. But it will bring complex management and dispatch problems [3].

4) Repeating purchases of the hardware and software increase the cost badly

Capital scarcity is always the bottle-neck in SGIS. The statistical department begins to use computers to deal with statistical data in 20th century. For 20 years, many SGIS have been developed and many hardware and software have been purchased. But the time when they are left unused is much more than they are in use. In that case, if they can be used by other departments, their utilization rate will be raised. Meanwhile these departments can cut down cost of purchasing hardware and software.

While the traditional GIS technology can not solve these problems above, the grids can do it well.

2   The Statistical Geography Information System in Grids

2.1   The Infrastructure of the Statistical Geography Information System in Grids

"Statistical grid" regards internet as a "virtual super computer". Each computer is considered as a computing node. These nodes are worked together to assure all the statistical resources can be shared thoroughly. The statistical resources include investigation resources, data resources, method resources, model resources, manpower resources, expert resources, facilities resources, software resources and storage resources. Based on OGSA structure, this paper put forwards a SGIS model [4,5,8], as showed in Figure 1.

This system employs grid middleware technology, and is divided into four layers. From bottom to top, they are: resource layer, grid middleware layer, grid service layer, grid application layer.

Resource layer: resource layer contains physical resources (e.g. computers and internet) and logical resources (e.g. software and experts), which are the foundation of the whole system and form an abstract resource layer apt to the visitation of the upper layers. When user requests resources, the grid middleware layer will search the resource layer for the required resources and return them to the user. The users do not need to know where the resources are.

Grid middleware layer: this layer is substantively a series of agreements and tools. It is located between grid service layer and grid resource layer. It is the ties of them. The grid services obtain resources through the grid middleware. There can be multifarious grid middleware according to different functions, e.g. task assignment middleware, data conversion middleware.

Grid services layer: this layer is made up of the mainly statistical functions, such as statistical analysis, statistical information query, map display, print and so on. Grid service layer packs these functions as services and administrate their scheduling, dispatch process and so on.

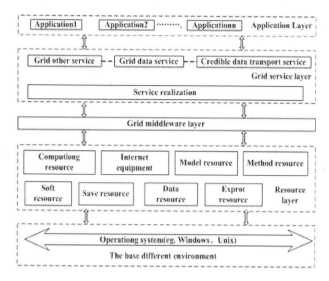

Fig. 1. The infrastructure of the statistical geography information system based on grid

Grid application layer: it is the final user. It offers an accessing interface for the users or the application procedures to visit.

2.2 The Ways Solving the Problems

2.2.1 The Various Origin and Diverse Structure of the Statistical Resources

XML is a marking language. It can describe all the resources and it has self-description and cross-platforms characteristics [6,7,9,13]. Moreover, the grid service has advantages of cross-platform, cross-language, and high-effectiveness [10]. So if we can combine them together, the problems of heterogeneous structure and origin can be settled perfectly. The concrete process is as follows: when a user asks for a grid service, the data conversion middleware is called to convert the original data into XML format as a interim data format in order to generate various different structure data finally, realizing integration of heterogeneous structure data. After that, the grid service continues to carry out the task. When the service requests resources, a resource management middleware is called to search for the resources and return them to the service. When the task is accomplished, the data conversion middleware is called again to convert the results (XML data) to the form required by the user.

2.2.2 Irrespective Platforms and Operating Systems

Grid middleware also belongs to the common middleware. So it has the characteristics of common middleware. Grid middleware is located above the operating system and below the grid application layer [11,12], as it is showed in Figure 1. It provides a group of common programming abstract interfaces and solves the heterogeneous structure in distributed systems effectively. Besides, the grid middleware offers running and developing environment for the grid application layer. So it can accept different operating system and platforms.

2.2.3 Balance Internet Load

Grid middleware has functions of managing resources and dispatching tasks. It can dispatch the task dynamically according to the load of the system currently. Concretely speaking, it can distribute the tasks to every computing node in the grid. When one node receives tasks, it becomes the core node and the center of the grid. Then it can pass its tasks to other nodes in a radiation form according to the complexity of its own tasks [14], as it is showed in Figure 2. So hundreds of thousands of unused computers in the internet are connected to work together It not only improve the computing speed but also make full use of the internet resources and balance the internet load.

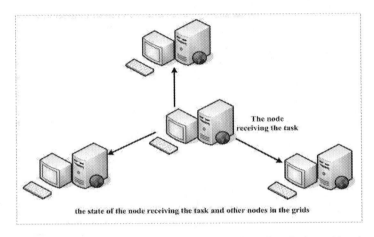

Fig. 2. The work state of the grid node receiving the task and other grid nodes

3 Application Instance and Key Problems

According to the four-layer structure systems above, we give a SGIS application instance. Then we give its implement process. Considering several key problems needed to be solved in the construction of the system, this paper gives its opinions. The system is on the base of grid computing and the physical structure is made up of grid nodes and various middleware. They are connected by the internet. The main functions of the system are carried out by the grid nodes and grid middleware, as showed in Figure 3.

3.1 Concrete Flow

As it is showed in Figure 4, when the user login in a grid node and submit a task (e.g. querying the population increasing percentage in the year 2008), the data conversion middleware is called to convert the original data to the XML format. Then resource

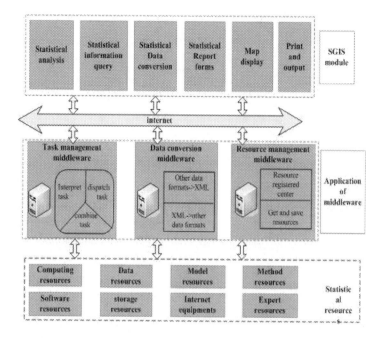

Fig. 3. The infrastructure and the flow chart of the statistical geography information system based on grid

management middleware begins to search the registered usable resources in the resource register center, including computers, software and other statistical resources. With these usable computers (computing nodes), the task management middleware assign the task to them. After the task is accomplished separately, the results (including task start time, task end time, and final result and so on) are returned to the task management middleware. Finally, the task management middleware combine these results (XML data) together and use the data conversion middleware to convert them to the form user required.

3.2 Several Key Problems and Solutions

3.2.1 Safety Problems

For the grid nodes are located at different places, how to share the resources safely and how to assure the integrity of the data are the urgent problems to be solved in grid SGIS. Because the SGIS is open to the public and the statistical information is apt to spread, not only can the data be easily disturbed, abused, lost but also can be stolen, juggled and destroyed. To solve this problem, we can add a safety management middleware. The user's identity must be validated before he or she can obtain the resources.

3.2.2 The Contradiction between the Ownership of the Statistical Resource and the Multilevel Authorization of the Statistical Resource

Although many statistical resources are open to the public, some very important and confidential data can not be shared by all the people. But the statistical grids require

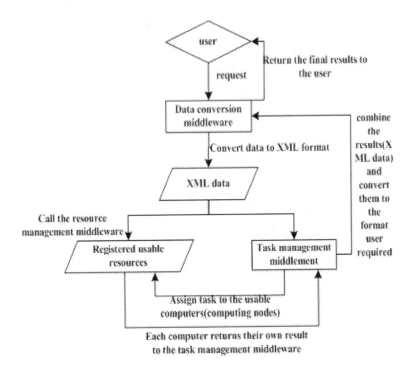

Fig. 4. The flow chart of the system

that all kinds of statistical resources can be shared. So it is very vital for statistical grids to give consideration to both autonomy and multilevel management. While the owner can manage his data on his own, the resource must be in the charge of the statistical grids. We can solve this problem by means of authorization. We can also add a safety management middleware. The user's identity must be validated before he or she can obtain the resources. It assures that the important and confidential data not only can be visited only by the authorized person but also in the charge of the grids.

3.2.3   Dynamic Statistical Resources and Extendable Statistical Grids

Statistical resources are various and heterogeneous. Some data or hardware may breakdown at a certain time, or some data and hardware that did not exist before may be added in the future. So the dynamic characteristic of the statistic data should be taken into consideration. The statistic grids should be expanded easily and can absorb new resources at any time. For the dynamic decrease of the resources and the bug occurring during the process, the statistic grids should shift the tasks automatically to avoid or reduce the loss of users. For this purpose, we can add an error management middleware. If an error occurs during the process of implementing the task, the error management middleware will record the error information (including the time, the error content and so on) and then give its solutions.

4 Conclusion

The SGIS model this paper proposed is based on the grid middleware. When a great deal of statistical data should be computed and analyzed at the same time, the SGIS based on grids is the best choice. For the statistical resources relate to many images and tables, how to treat with these images automatically is a problem we should still attempt to solve. It is also the important index weighing the intelligence of the SGIS in grids. It concerns the development of the grids in SGIS.

Acknowledgments. Financial supports from The 11th Five-Year Plan of 863 Projiect" The SoftWare Platform and Vital Application Of Grid GIS" (No. 2007AA120503) and National Natural Science Foundation of China (No. 40771165) are highly appreciated.

References

1. Xianzuo, Q.: Search:statistics innovation and modernization. China Statistical Publisher (2002)
2. Lingyun, W., Qi, L., Wencheng, Y.: Web Service and operationg geography information mutually. Mapping Science 29(1), 38–40 (2004)
3. Jiancheng, L., Chenhu, Z., Shaohua, C.: The structure of the web GIS based on the middleware technology. Earth information science 4(3), 17–25 (2002)
4. Jinyun, F., Jianbang, H.: The structure of the grid GIS and its realization technology. Earth Information Science 4(4), 36–42 (2002)
5. Zhihui, D., Yu, C., Peng, L.: Grid computing. Qinghua University Publisher (2002)
6. Zhaoqiang, H., Xuezhi, F.: Geography information system spatial heterogeneous data integration research. china image graphic transaction 9(8), 904–907 (2004)
7. Qin, Z., Jianxin, L., Jihong, C.: Heterogeneous data exchange technology based on XML and its Java realization. Computer Application Software 21(11), 52–53 (2004)
8. Zhiwei, X., Baiming, F., Wei, L.: Grid computing technology, vol. 6(1), pp. 44–47. Electron Industry Publisher, Beijing (2004)
9. Weiwei, L., Deyi, Q., Yongjun, L.: The heterogeneous data integration model based on grid. Computer Project 4(3), 24–32 (2006)
10. Foster, I., Kesselman, C., Nickj, M.: The Physiology of the Grid-An Open Grid Services Architecture for Distributed Systems Integration (2002),
    http://www.Globus.org/research/papers/ogsa.pdf
11. Humphrey, M.: From Legion to Legion-G to OGSI, NET: object-based computing for grids. In: Proceedings of the International Parallel and Distributed Processing Symposium, pp. 207–214. IEEE Computer Society, Washington (2003)
12. Grimshaw, A.S., Legion, N.A.: lessons learned building a grid operating system. Proceedings of the IEEE 93(3), 589–603 (2005)
13. Beaumout, O., Legand, A., Robert, Y.: Scheduling strategies for mixed data and task parallelism on heterogeneous clusters and grids. In: Proceedings of the 11th Euromicro Conference on Parallel, Distributed and Network-Based Processing, pp. 209–216. IEEE Computer Society, Washington (2003)
14. Subranunani, V., et al.: Distributed Job Scheduling on Computational Grids Using Multiple Simultaneous Requests. In: Proceedings of the 11th IEEE International Symposium on High Performance Distributed Computing, pp. 359–367. IEEE, Los Alamitos (2002)

Line-Scan Camera Control Pavement Detection System Research

Zhao-yun Sun[1], Ai-min Sha[2], Li Zhao[3], and Chang-rong Xie

[1] College of information engineering, Chang'an University, Xi'an 710064, China
zhaoyunsun@126.com
[2] College of road, Chang'an University, Xi'an 710064, China
[3] College of information engineering, Chang'an University, Xi'an 710064, China

Abstract. The paper designs the pavement detecting system, which is based on GPS and the serial port communication technology of the SCM (single-chip microcomputer) used to control the line-scan camera. The paper focuses on GPS and the serial port communication as well as the control programs of single-chip microcomputer .By comparing and analyzing large amounts of experiments' data and the serial images which are obtained in the high-speed vehicle moving by using this system, it shows that this system design satisfies the requirement of external trigger control in real-time line-scan camera for the pavement detection system. The result shows that the images obtained in high speed are much clearer.

Keywords: GPS; single-chip microcomputer; serial communication; crack detection.

1 Introduction

Because of the overweight of vehicles, rain erosion, climate change, the pavement may be destroyed. Using traditional crack detecting methods may lead to low efficiency, high cost, insecurity and poor consistency of detecting results. With the development of computer hardware and software technology, automatic pavement detection technology becomes possible. It not only greatly improves the detection rate, shortens the detecting cycle, but also overcomes the subjectivity of the detecting. It has great significance in the automatic pavement detection field. At present, there is still a wide gap between China's road detecting technology and the developed countries'.

In the pavement crack detection system, the line-scan camera first captures high-speed real-time images about the road, then sends it to the main image processor computer, at last processes it with image analysis software, get the crack's place, length and area so as to give reference to the road maintenance. Detection system is composed of the vehicle, line-scan camera, GPS, computer, image processing software, SCM control system. Detecting the asphalt pavement by use of the system can find the crack which is more than two millimeters, including its width, length and locations. By using the speed of GPS [1] and SCM control algorithms, it realizes the real time control for line-scan camera according to every two millimeters to give a

L. Qi (Ed.): FCC 2009, CCIS 34, pp. 8–13, 2009.

triggering signal. The detecting results meet the requirements of the system, meanwhile, obtain much clearer pavement moving images.

The design structure of line-scan camera control system is shown in Fig 1.

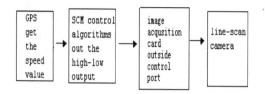

Fig 1. Line-scan camera control system design structure

2 GPS and SCM Serial Port Communication as Well as Control Realizing Method

By using GPS, the system is mainly used to obtain the crack location and the speed of the vehicle. The link between GPS and SCM depends on the RS232 serial interface standard. RS232 defines the physical interface standards between the data terminal equipment (DTE) and the data communications equipment (DCE) [2].

SCM serial port initializes programming finished by the special function register PCON and power control SCON register. SCON serial port is used to set the working modes, accept or send the control / state signal. The serial port has four working modes. This system uses working mode 2. Because the GPS 4800 baud rate is fixed, there is no need to calculate it. Communication mode adopts 8-N-1. GPS locating method has two modes. One is a single point locating mode. The other one is differential locating mode. Single-point approach is using a GPS receiver to receive three or four satellite signals so as to determine the location of receiving points. But its error is larger relatively, even up to 5 ~ 15 m. GPS has several kinds of data formats, typically we use $ GPRMC at the beginning of the data, set it as the standard receiving data format. GPS uses the RS232 to transfer data, so we should plus a MAX232 between GPS and SCM to finish logic level conversion. After the conversion data can be directly transmitted to the SCM, the system can obtain the speed value of the vehicle. The circuit design is shown in Fig.2.

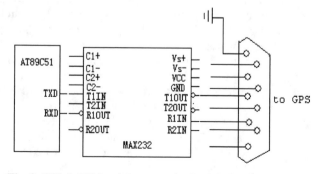

Fig. 2. GPS & SCM serial communication interface circuit design

The system adopts com1 to transfer data. The baud rate is 4800. SCM serial port adopts the mode 2 to work. Part of the realizing program is as follows:

```
TMOD=0x20; //timer1 working mode 2 (mainly used for timing)
TL1=0xf3;11
TH1=0xf3; SCON=0x50; PCON=0x00; IE=0x90;//serial port interrupt permitting
 TR1=1; }    serial () interrupt 4 using 1 //Serial port interrupt service function
{RI=0;                              //software clear interrupt index
 if (SBUF==0x24)
 {num++;record=1;i=0;k=0;r=1;igps=0;// variables Recording number of charac-
ters speed data
 numbercoma=0; if (record==1)    // Begin to judge whether the data received
GPRMC format
{ s="GPRMC";string[k]=SBUF;
k++;r=strcmp(string,s);if(r==0)
       {        if(SBUF==0x2c) {numbercoma++;}//record the numbers of comma
  if(numbercoma==2)
{if(SBUF==0x41)// if the second judge is A, then the data is valid
{if (numbercoma==7)  //the character followed the seventh comma is speed signal
{stringgps[igps]=SBUF; //put the character into the string "stringgps "
igps++;}}} // the first command is over when receive the second $, Variable given
the initial value
 if (num==2){stringgps[igps]='\0';  // The end of the data presented at the end of the
string
    numbercoma=0; num=0; Record=0; igps=0;   //restart receiving speed data when
Variable get zero.
```

3 SCM Control the Line- Scan Camera in Real-Time

SCM controls the line-scan camera in real-time by using SCM 89 C51 [3] microcontroller. Due to the need of every two millimeters to give a trigger signal to the camera, the system uses timer to control the trigger time in SCM, reads the vehicle's speed from the GPS by serial communication [4]. It uses the SCM T1 timer to time. The timing mode adopts mode1. It needs to calculate the interval time required by 2 millimeters to trigger according to the vehicle's speed value. In this method, the system presets time to be 12 seconds by using timers' T1, depends on the P20 port level output to realize the control for camera.

The system uses manner 1 to time .This mode can get much timing time and more timing cycles. The detection system can meetthe requirements of the camera's work frequency [5]. It can get the best timer input and output by using software to control TF1 and TR1, which means depending on the timers' time and timing cycles to control trigger signal. The system selects timer1's mode 1 to work. The crystal is 12 MHz. The machine cycle is 1μs. presetting time period is 12μs,then 12μs = (2 -Y)*1μs, next calculates the initial timing value Y as 65,524 and puts it into a 16 bits timer, then starts T1 to work . When the timing time12μs is over, TF1 = 1. According to the different speed values and formula: x=3000/v, calculate the cycle times and get to control for P20 high-low level so as to control the working frequency of the camera. Part of the realizing programs as follows:

```
{
int v=35;
int x;//adding the speed values, there is a Valuation
x=(3000)/(v); //calculate the cycle times
led_on();
time_lms(x);
led_off();
time_lms(x);
}
while(1);
}
time_lms(lms)
{TMOD=TMOD& (0x0f)|0x10;
TR1=1;          //start the timer
While (lms--)
   {TH1=65524/256;
 TL1=65524/256;
While (!TF1)
TF1=1;
}
TR1=0;

led_off(){P2_0=1;
}
led_on()
{P2_0=0;}
```

3 Image Analysis and Comparison

The system uses GPS to locate the beginning place and combines the road kilometer piles to mark the exact pavement cracks place [6]. Because the system needs to capture the pavement dynamic images in the vehicle moving, at the same time, meet the requirements two meters to give a frame image , thus the system needs to control the work frequency of line-scan camera to obtain real-time images. The system uses GPS to get the speed of the vehicle, and then sends it to the SCM control system by the serial communication, realizes the control for camera according to each two meters to capture a frame. Because the system adopts the linear array camera, it needs to give a trigger signal in each millimeter to meet the accuracy requirement of detecting two millimeters width pavement cracks [7]. If the system does not adopt real-time control for the camera work frequency, most of the moving images received by line-scan camera are not clear. Because the speed of the vehicle is always changing in the moving, using the control system designed in this paper will obtain much clearer road images [8]. Adopting fixed frequency acquisition method has no very good moving image effect. The system designed in this paper satisfies the pavement crack's detection acquisition requirement. Meanwhile it lays a good foundation for the following image processing. Two examples of capturing pavement detection images are Fig 3 and Fig 4.

Fig. 3. Real-time control capturing acquisition images

Fig. 4. Non- real-time capturing acquisition images

4 Conclusion

The system design realizing the functions are as follows:

(1) The system realizes the speed values measurement by designing hardware and software, programs to control GPS and SCM serial communication [9].

(2) According to the vehicle's speed value, programs control SCM P20 port output voltage to supervise the work frequency of the line-scan camera in real-time.

(3) The system finishes the pavement crack's detection accuracy requirement which is to recognize 2mm crack. It can obtain much clearer moving images and also run well in the highway detection.

(4) By comparing the acquisition image's quality and large amounts of outside experiments' data, it shows that the design system can obtain dynamic images clearly in high speed of vehicle moving.

References

[1] Le, X., Zhiqiang, L., Feng, Z.: The study and realize of GPS supervision system. Journal of East China normal university: natural science (3) (2005)

[2] Yali, W., Yong-ling, W., Jun, W.: C programming language tutorial. The People's traffic Press, Beijing (2002)

[3] Wentao, L.: SCM C51 microcontroller language typical application design. People's Posts and Telecommunications News Press, Beijing (2005)

[4] Quanli, L., Rongjiang, C.: SCM principles and interface technology. Higher Education Press, Beijing (2004)

[5] Huobin, D., Xin, X., Chunping, T.: The Application of SCM in the control of ice cold center air-conditions. Micro-computer information (3) (2005)
[6] Qiwei, Y.: SCM C51 procedure design and experiment. University of Aeronautics and Astronautics Press, Beijing (2006)
[7] Kun, J., Qingzhou, M.: Intelligence pavement acquisition system. Electron measurement technology (4) (2005)
[8] Jin-hui, L., Wei, L., Shoushan, J.: The study of road illness detection technology basing on CCD. Journal of Xi'an institute of technology (3) (2005)
[9] Kezhao, L., Jinaping, Y., Qin, Z.: The study of GPS document's decode and the realize of real time communication. Global positioning system (3) (2005)

Emergency Command System Based on Satellite Link

Wenbiao Peng, Junli Wan, and Chaojun Yan

College of Electrical Engineering and Information Technology,
China Three Gorges University, Yichang 443002, Hubei
pwb@ctgu.edu.cn

Abstract. In the project of monitoring, warning and geologic disasters prevention in the Three Gorges Reservoir Area, the emergency command system is an important part for it can provide a reliable technical guarantee. This paper describes a multimedia **emergency** command system based on satellite link. The characteristics include an on-the-spot information collection and transmission, an integrated emergency communications, an emergency commanding, an emergency dispatching and strategic decision analysis. The system can meet the need of emergency mobile command and is effective and practical. It enhances the efficiency of working for establishing interconnection of the discrete resources and realizing the commanding of emergency.

Keywords: satellite communications, emergency command, IP, geologic disaster.

1 Introduction

The Three Gorges Project, with comprehensive functions like flood prevention, power generation and shipping, is the largest project of nature reformation and utilization since the founding of New China. It has a landmark significance to the development of the Chinese nation. Right now, the Three Gorges Project has stored water in 156 meters, and it will reach 175 meters in 2009. According to the need of flood prevention in the Three Gorges Reservoir Area, the water level will change between 145 meters and 175 meters in the annual flood season when the Three Gorges project is completed. (The largest variation of the water level is 30 meters.) Due to rain frequently, the flow or raise the level of water and other factors, the Three Gorges reservoir area may has geological disasters inevitably. The State Council pays great attention to the prevention and control the geological disaster. In the beginning of 2001, entrusted with Immigration Development of Three Gorges Project Construction Commission of the State Council, the Ministry of Natural Resources assign the Ministry of Geologyand Environment Monitoring to layout a program. It called" program about the construction of geologic disaster engineering of monitoring and warning in the Three Gorges Reservoir Area". In the program, it contains the planning of landslide collapse in all 1302 which have been discovered. In July of 2001, controlling geological disasters in Three Gorges reservoir area are commenced on full scale by the State Council, and another program is Laid down. It called "the embodiment of

L. Qi (Ed.): FCC 2009, CCIS 34, pp. 14–20, 2009.

geologic disasters engineering of monitoring and warning and disaster prevention of the relocation and reconstruction to the immigration in the Three Gorges Reservoir Area" [1]. In the second program, it has more details about the control planning of the landslide collapse which from the first program that just be discovered. According to the implementation of the early warning monitoring project, the professional monitoring system, monitoring system of group and warning and command system will be built in the Three Gorges Reservoir Area.

Emergency Command System of geological disasters is an important part of monitoring the early warning project for prevention the geological disasters in Three Gorges reservoir area. The main function of the emergency monitoring is to help the leadership in the department of geological disasters prevention to make the decision. To find geological disasters in dangerous situations, to identify dangerous situations and to disposal of the dangerous situations. Providing real time information and sensitive information about geologic hazard immediately. It's easier for the decision-makers to have a good knowledge of the development about dangerous situations with this information. On this basis, leaders and experts can make scientific decision. Therefore, the emergency command system is the nerve center of emergency commanding in geological disaster monitoring. It's difficult to make for the high requirements of hardware and software.

In terms of the network, multimedia emergency command system can be divided into two categories. They are packet-switched and circuit-switched. In terms of the transmission platform, it can be divided into another two categories. They are the ground network (PSTN, GSM, microwave, etc.) and satellite network. The protocol [2] H.320 based on PSTN circuit switching and H.323 based on IP packet switching are frequently used in the emergency command system. The standards of H.261, H.263, H.263 + and so on which are from the ITU and compression standards of MPEG-1, MPEG-2 and MPEG-4 which are from the ISO are used in coding and decoding. The "air" transmission platform which is based on satellite network in the emergency command system can send all kinds of information flexiblly.With the specific function, the ground network (PSTN, GSM, etc.) is unapproachable when geological disasters suddenly happen and in a long distance [3–5].

2   The Function of Emergency Command System

According to the requirements of design, the system should have the following functions. Holding long distance conferences and emergency commanding. The date information of geological disasters can be added into the conference as soon as the monitoring workers get it. Decision makers who stay in 16 meeting place which are built around the command center---the headquarters of geologic disasters prevention in Yichang can participate in the meeting at the same time. The special line is used to transmist the audio and video date information between command center and other meeting place. Each one of the 16 meeting place can receive the information about the system from the moving worker through high-frequency wireless at first. And then, they communicate with the commanding center through satellite. Conference call can be used in the system when the network in one or several meeting place is out of order. In this circumstance, conference call is used instead of the video conference. The software terminal is directly installed in the office of Ministry of Natural Resources and environmental monitoring department. It is also installed in related conference rooms. So the decision makers in Ministry, department, meeting place and the Three Gorges reservoir area can have a good knowledge about the emergency and make decision together.

Therefore, in order to meet the requirement of warning geological disasters and transmission data information that is free from constraints of time and space about emergency commanding, and effectively guide the prevention of geological disasters, multi-media information transmission channel which is based on IP and satellite is set up in the emergency command system. The main characteristics of the channel include a input system which is supported by narrow band wireless network and also based on wireless network, and a multi-media information transmission channel which is based on IP and satellite communication is used to inspect the emergency of geologic disasters. Integrated the video and audio encoding technology, network communication technology, data conference technology and network storage technology efficiently which are based on advanced network communication technology. The scattered, independent image date and alarm detection are connected into a network. Realizing the monitoring and commanding at the same time although the decision makers stay in different place. Providing a best solution for the prevention geological disasters in Three Gorges reservoir area. The system can meet the requirements of emergency command for multilevel conference in a long-range. Establishing a strong technology foundation of holding conference for discussing and controlling geological disasters comprehensively in the future.

3   The System Composition and Operating Principle

The whole system contains several parts. They are amplifier circuit, video recorder, switching matrix, video conferencing, echo canceller etc, television transmitter, television surveillance, switch, satellite modem, antennas, cameras, data management and transmiting and receiving pictures. The composition diagram shown in Figure 1.

The signal processing is as follows. Multichannel signals of AV which include the output of the staff car and audio video signal received from the moving worker are send into the 8-24 amplifier circuit to get preprocessing. Then two new signals are obtained which the level and impedance are consistent, and they are exported from two ways. One signal is delivered into the video recorder to get storaged. So it is easier for worker to check it in the future. The other signal is delivered into the matrix switch circuit of AV. Switching matrix circuit is a much more flexible controlling circuit for it has other switching function besides supporting the video conference. One of output signals of matrix circuit is delivered into the television transmitter. The television transmitter can provides a range of the wireless signal and users living nearby can easily to watch through the TV. And most of the rest signals are delivered into the terminal of network video conference.

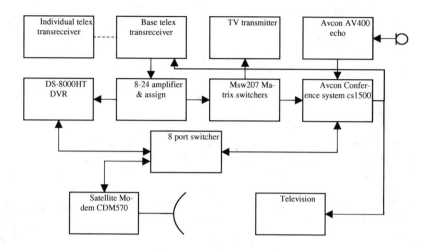

Fig. 1. Composition diagram

The terminal of network video conference is key equipment for the high requirements of software and hardware which used. The requirements are as followed. Advanced communications function for carrying out video conference, teleconference, instant message, monitoring, playing streaming media and data conferencing at the same time. Advanced error correction technology with high network adaptability. Powerful data transfer which supporting the transmission of multichannel video, audio signal and data. Besides sharing data, electronic white board, interacting text and transferring file, it has other date function of synchronous amendment and remote collaboration of documents. It cans dynamic display the data content and the frame rate is 25 per second. Powerful function of multipass encoding and multipass decoding. Multichannel image date can be encoded and sent to the remote by the multipass encoder. It meets the needs of multichannel image date transmission. Multichannel image date can be sent into the monitor by the multipass decoder. It meets the needs of multichannel image date display. The technology of high definition output and multifunction image are in the lead. It can be used in the conference with wide high definition for its terminal has a Full HD 1920 × 1080 decoder. Cooperated with MCU, each output of the terminal can display multipicture. Each output can display 16 images at the same time, and 64 images can be shown to the greatest extent.Multpicture displaying can ensure that each image's distinguish rate remain the same ,so it ensures the clarity of the subscreen.The conference can be recorded by the original function of conference recording and play sharing. Any one or more media sources of the conference, such as images, voice and data can be recorded. The video can be kept in the removable disk and U disk through the USB. The media resource and files which recorded in removable disk and U disk also can be played and shared. So it's easier for participants in other meeting place to watch the play. The function of dynamic meeting controlling is perfect. It has many advantages. Such as receiving, sending and broadcasting the video and audio message of the conference, calling a person to make a speech, asking questions, controlling remote video and audio message, controlling remote desktop and mute controlling. Conducting the list of staff who participate the meeting. Holding meeting in groups, so it's convenient for controlling meeting.

4 System Configuration and the Parameters

In order to save money, the main hardware equipments of the system are as follows. HDV-08, the moving wireless video transmission system of Beijing; DMDZ-8-24, the audio and video amplification distributor of Dima Electronics Corporation of Chongqing; MSW207 / AV0808 AV, the Matrix Switcher of the USA; CM9760 of Pelco, the Data Manager of the USA; DS-8000HT, the Video Recorder(DCIF) of the third generation of HaiKangWeiShi; AVCON CS1500-2200DC31500,the terminal of video conference of HuaPing; AVCON AV400, the echo canceller etc; CDM 570L,the satellite modem; TVV-3-V, the television transmitter of Chengdu; Pelco KBD300A, the Universal Keyboard and NJR2536LNB of Japan. The software about system of video conference is provided by Shanghai HuaPing Computer Technology corp. The relevant software about the system is as follows. Software about integrated management and dispatch; Software about the terminal of controlling system; Software about the terminal of printing reports; Software about the WEB inquisition and statistics server; Software about playing video record server; Software about conducting case server; Software about gateway service of GPS; Software about gateway service of data search by phone; Software about recording communication data server; Software about the terminal of conducting case server; Software about the terminal of system monitoring; Software about the system of conducting emphasis objection and software which is used by the chief.

The integrated equipments above all are installed in a converted car. The change of the car includes several parts. They are vehicle chassis, engine, suspension options, and the layout of the car, modification materials and processes of the car, folded tables and chairs, air-conditioning systems, power systems, lighting systems, cabinet designing and interface designing.

The key indicators of the systems are as follows.

Start up time is less than 5 minutes. The image distinguish is 720×576, 25 frame / s. The image compression pattern is based on MPEG-2. Broadband data transmission rate is 2 M (Images, data, voice). The range of view of moving worker is 3km to 5 km.

5 System Debugging and Application

When the system is in use, it is debugged for several times relevantly. The bottom layer code of the Video Conference System is also modified. The relevant equipments cooperate with each other very well. It has been carried out in practical application. Such as surveying the steep of Guojiaba of Zigui County in the Three Gorges Reservoir Area and surveying territorial resources of Huangshan in Anhui Province. The

(a) (b)

(c) (d)

Fig. 2. The condition of working field in geologic disasters, (a) Picture of the scene, (b) The road destroyed by landslide, (c)Two moving works shooting on location in two-way, (d) The interface of video conference system about the command car

experiment result is very good. It has high resolution ratio of picture and clear voice. Some pictures of the experiment shown in Figure 2.

6 Summarize

The system can transmit video, audio and data information of geological disasters at any time. So it's easier for members to communicate with each other though they are not stay on the spot. Based on the multimedia technology, workers can use the video conference to deal with a variety of information at the same time, such as sharing data and applications. To construct a virtual workspace that more than one workers share together. With the system, the working time is less and working efficiency is high. Video communication breakthrough the old form of "meeting", and develop into "office" integration in distance. It will be widely applied in the prevention and controlling the geological disasters.

In addition, the system can also be used in aid direction, fire commanding and traffic direction. It had been used in the Wenchuan earthquake to have long-distance meeting. It is effective and practical for it can meet the various needs of mobile commanding. The system can meet the need of emergency mobile command and is effective and practical. It enhances the efficiency of working for establishing interconnection of the discrete resources and realizing the commanding of emergency.

References

1. China to speed up prevention of geological disasters in the Three Gorges reservoir area, Rock and Soil Mechanics (5) (May 2008)
2. Li, Z.: A mobile Commanding Car System: Design and Application. Journal of Video Engineering (02) (February 2006)
3. Huang, Y., Zhu, Z., Pei, C.: Design and Implementation of MCU in Videoconferencing System Based on IP Network. Journal of Computer Engineering (14) (July 2004)
4. Li, C., Zhang, X.: IP/multicast video conferencing for distance learning, Journal of Tsinghua University (Science and Technology) (01) (January 2003)
5. Yurong, H., Li Victor, O.K.: Satellite-based internet:A tutorial. IEEE Communications Magazine 39(3), 154–162 (2001)
6. Ekici, E., Akyildiz, I.F., Bender, M.D.: A multicast routing algorithm for LEO satellite IP networks. IEEE/ACM Transactions on Networking 10(2), 411–424 (2002)
7. Nian, Y.D., Wanjiun, L.: On multicast routing using rectilinear Steiner trees for LEO satellite networks. In: Proc. IEEE Globecom, Hyatt Regency, Dalls,TX, pp. 2712–2716 (2004)
8. Wang, Z.-y., Hu, R.-m., Fu, Y.-m., Bian, X.-g.: Study on Video Coding Subsystem Design of H.323 Video Conference System. Journal of Electronics & Information Technology (07) (July 2007)
9. ITU. Packet -based multimedia communications systems 323, 12 (1997)
10. Peng, Z., et al.: On the trade-off between source and channel coding rates for image transmission. In: Proc.of the IEEE International Conference on Image Processing, Chicago,Illinois, pp. 118–121 (1998)
11. Worrall, S., Sadka, A.H., Sweeney, P., Kondoz, A.M.: Motion adaptive INTRA refresh for MPEG-4. IEEE Electronics Letters 36(23), 1924–1925 (2000)

SLA Monitoring Based on Semantic Web

Wenli Dong

Institute of Software, Chinese Academy of Science
No.4 South 4th Street, Zhongguancun , Haidian district, Beijing, China
wenli@iscas.ac.cn

Abstract. This paper proposes SLA monitoring based on Semantic Web to realize automatically service quality monitoring according to different services and consumes with syntactic information and necessary semantic description with explicit meaning and machines dealing with service level requirements. SLA monitoring ontology is constructed based on RDF Schema step by step based on SLA monitoring requirements, ontology theory, ontology knowledge for Semantic Web. Monitoring process is build based on OWL-S benefiting for automation, coordination, and collaboration between monitoring entities.

Keywords: Service Level Agreement, SLA Monitoring, Web Service, Semantic Web.

1 Introduction

SLA (Service Level Agreement) Monitor is one task of SLA management. SLA monitoring is a negotiation between service providers and service requestor. SLA monitoring provides the services runtime quality, compares the monitoring results with the customer's requirement according to SLA standards, and judges whether the system meets the initial requirements. So the service provider can take the next measure to provide services with specified quality. SLA Monitoring can report and notify latency, jitter, packet loss, network availability, and mean time to repair effectively. SLA monitoring provides the basis for ensuring that service provider is delivering what the requestor is promised.

Existing SLA monitoring focuses on performance of network level and network element level, lacking the enough support for monitoring performance of service level. With the various added value services appear, the demand for monitoring performance of service level is growing. Different consumers will have specific requirements surrounding their own applications, dynamical changed monitoring policy is needed to ensure that the service level requirements of the consumers are being met [1]. But existing SLA monitoring is designed and developed for specified services and scenario, and can not provide the fine-grain performance monitoring of various requirements. Resolving these types of issues includes being able to understand use -- consumer by consumer -- of the services on the network so that the organization can then prioritize how to use and allocate resources effectively, and designed, developed, deployed, and selected monitoring services flexibly and dynamically. SOA (Service Oriented Architecture) infrastructure software

L. Qi (Ed.): FCC 2009, CCIS 34, pp. 21–29, 2009.
© Springer-Verlag Berlin Heidelberg 2009

(Web Service defining an interoperable common platform supporting SOA) often assists in this process, as well.

Many researchers study the relationship between SLA and Web Service [2-6], including applying Web Service in SLA, and trustworthy Web Service based on SLA vice versa. In SLA monitoring, some researches mention the framework monitoring SLA using Web Services. But they are so simple that they cannot give enough information to understand the applying Web Service in SLA monitoring and cannot provide a strong basis for the applying Web Service in SLA monitoring. What's more, the above researches cannot provide enough systematic analysis. Lacking of enough systematic analysis will lead to the difficulty to grasp the applying Web Service in SLA monitoring and implement the applying Web Service in SLA monitoring. This paper proposes the applying semantic Web in SLA monitoring. With syntactic information and necessary semantic description with explicit meaning and machines dealing with service level requirements. And adapting the SLA monitoring system for Web Service/Web Service composition, the SLA monitoring system can have a common service interface enabling discovering, requesting, selection, using, and the interoperation of SLA monitoring system easily. As a universal technology, Web Service can fulfill almost all SLA monitoring tasks needing to be completed and meet the dynamical requirements.

The remainder of the paper is organized as follows. Section 2 analyzed the SLA monitoring motivations. The construction for the SLA monitoring based on Semantic Web is provided to illustrate the SLA monitoring based on Semantic Web in section 3. In section 4 the SLA monitoring process based on OWL-S is analyzed in details. Section 5 is the conclusion.

2 SLA Monitoring Motivations

The main motivations of the SLA monitoring based on Semantic Web are:

1) Providing a GUI (Graphical User Interface) for requestor to publish their requirements and forming SLA conveniently. SLA is used by both provider and requestor to form fixed service and performance agreement and create transparency for both parties in terms of performance and cost. SLA regulates business available class, service available class, performance class, operation class, price, maintenance, and remedies. Generally, SLA is described by technique of independent language, and need be translated into the language comprehended by Web Service composition based on SLA.

2) Designing the transformation from the consumer's requirements to WSLA (Web Service Level Agreement) [7]. WSLA proposed by IBM describes a novel framework for specifying and monitoring SLA for Web Services, which is targeted at defining and monitoring SLAs for Web Services. WSLA is a framework consists of a flexible and extensible language based on the XML Schema and a runtime architecture comprising several SLA monitoring services.

3) Mapping the service level requirements regarding the underlying transport network from the higher layer onto the actual underlying network technology at runtime in order to achieve an overall service level requirements support through the different layers in terms of the Internet model.

4) Monitoring the service level performance based on WSLA.

5) Comparing the monitoring results with consumer's requirements.

6) Reporting the comparing result to service manager.

The whole process is carried out around the service level requirement and the Semantic Web is employed to define a notation for specifying SLA monitoring process behavior based on Web Services to implement the monitoring flow control to enable task-sharing for a distributed computing automatically and effectively.

3 Construction for the SLA Monitoring Based on Semantic Web

In this section, the service level requirements and its parameters mapping based on RDF (Resource Description Framework)) [8] and Owl-S (Ontology Web Language For Services) [9] are analyzed.

3.1 Service Requirement Management

Service requirement management consisting of three conceptual layers: change instruction, reconfiguration management, and WSLA management. Each layer is constructed using multi-agent techniques [10] and it is a service.

For highly available system, where change is generally initiated by user proxy, change requests are simply submitted in the form of XML to the change instruction. In either case, the change instruction forwards change requests to the reconfiguration management, which is responsible for changing the running components based on requirements reconfiguration algorithm [11][12]. The WSLA management generate the corresponding WSLA specification.

3.2 Ontology Construction Process

The degree of coordination of distributed computation that occurs in Web service reconfiguration is high. The ontology analysis Based on OWL-S proposed by this paper has an emphasis on automated processing and thus also demands this kinds of coordination.

On one hand, each Web Service will provide interface specifying by WSDL (Web Service Definition Language) [13]. To look up a suitable service, the Web Service will be reasoned about their qualification based on WSDL. On the other hand, for the initial requirement set, the general strategy is a top-down approach: to identify a service that performs the required functionality. Both of these two depend on semantic analysis, and here, the semantic description of Web Service base on OWL-S will be provided.

OWL ontology

OWL ontology consists of individuals, properties, and classes.

The service, operation, message can be individual. Individuals represent the objects in the domain that we are interested in. It can be roughly correspond to an instance.

Properties are binary relations on individuals - i.e. properties link two individuals together. For example, the property hasSibling might link the individual Country to the individual China, or the property hasChild might link the individual Jack to the individual Smith. Properties can have inverses. For example, the inverse of hasOwner is isOwnedBy. Properties can be limited to having a single value –i.e. to being functional. They can also be either transitive or symmetric.

OWL classes are interpreted as sets that contain individuals. They are described using formal (mathematical) descriptions that state precisely the requirements for membership of the class. For example, the class Cat would contain all the individuals that are cats in our domain of interest. Classes may be organized into a super-class-subclass hierarchy, which is also known as taxonomy. Subclasses specialize ('are subsumed by') their super-classes. For example consider the classes Animal and Cat – Cat might be a subclass of Animal (so Animal is the super-class of Cat). This says that, 'All cats are animals', 'All members of the class Cat are members of the class Animal', 'Being a Cat implies that you're an Animal', and 'Cat is subsumed by Animal'.

Following, the ontology constructing process will be introduce to illustrated the relationship between services, operations and messages.

1) First, create the classed. The empty ontology contains one class, here, called owl: Thing. The class owl: Thing is the class that represents the set containing all individuals.

2) OWL Classes are assumed to 'overlap'. So that an individual (or object) cannot be an instance of more than one of these three classes, that is, to specify classes that are disjoint from the selected class.

3) The third step is the property definition. OWL Properties represent relationships between two individuals. There are two main types of properties, Object properties and Datatype properties. Object properties link an individual to an individual. Datatype properties link an individual to an XML Schema Datatype value or an RDF literal.

4) The last step is adding the restriction to the classes by specifying their properties.

Constructing ontology for the SLA monitoring

Giving a formal format to the data on the web, different domains have different data schemas that cannot be merged. A more powerful model is needed to provide mapping capabilities between divergent schemas. As a web ontology language, OWL-S meets this requirement. OWL facilitates greater machine interpretability of Web content than that supported by XML, RDF, and RDF Schema by providing additional vocabulary along with a formal semantics.

SLA parameters includes customer ID (Identification), service provide ID, customer SLA ID, service type, QOS (Quality of Service) lever, time period, product KOI (Key Quality Indicator), violation threshold, transformation algorithm, violation direction, sample period etc. The ontology constructing process should be executed using RDF based on the ontology constructing process analyzed above.

1) Creating the class

Basically, there are two kinds of classes to be created for SLA parameters. One is named SLA-parameter that is the parent of the detailed parameters class. The other is the detailed parameters class named customerID, serviceProvideID, customerSLAID, serviceType, QOSLever, timePeriod, productKOI, violationThreshold, transformationAlgorithm, violationDirection, samplePeriod. In RDF Schema, following section is created as shown in fig. 1.

```
<rdfs:Class rdf:ID="SLA-parameter"/>
<rdfs:Class rdf:ID="customerID"><rdfs:subClassOf rdf:resource="#SLA-parameter"/></rdfs:Class>
<rdfs:Class rdf:ID="serviceProvideID"><rdfs:subClassOf rdf:resource="#SLA-parameter"/></rdfs:Class>
<rdfs:Class rdf:ID=" customerSLAID"><rdfs:subClassOf rdf:resource="#SLA-parameter"/></rdfs:Class>
<rdfs:Class rdf:ID="serviceType"><rdfs:subClassOf rdf:resource="#SLA-parameter"/></rdfs:Class>
<rdfs:Class rdf:ID="QOSLever"><rdfs:subClassOf rdf:resource="#SLA-parameter"/></rdfs:Class>
<rdfs:Class rdf:ID="timePeriod"><rdfs:subClassOf rdf:resource="#SLA-parameter"/></rdfs:Class>
<rdfs:Class rdf:ID="productKOI"><rdfs:subClassOf rdf:resource="#SLA-parameter"/></rdfs:Class>
<rdfs:Class rdf:ID="violationThreshold"><rdfs:subClassOf rdf:resource="#SLA-parameter"/></rdfs:Class>
<rdfs:Class rdf:ID="transformationAlgorithm"><rdfs:subClassOf rdf:resource="#SLA-parameter"/></rdfs:Class>
<rdfs:Class rdf:ID="violationDirection"><rdfs:subClassOf rdf:resource="#SLA-parameter"/></rdfs:Class>
<rdfs:Class rdf:ID="samplePeriod"><rdfs:subClassOf rdf:resource="#SLA-parameter"/></rdfs:Class>
```

Fig. 1. RDF Schema for SLA Monitoring System Classes

2) Disjointing the class from one another

The sub-class of class SLA-parameter created for SLA parameters are disjoined from one another. Because the limited space, we take the class timePeriod as an example, illustrate the description disjointing timePeriod from the other sub-classes of class SLA-parameter as shown in fig. 2.

```
<rdfs:Class rdf:ID="timePeriod"><rdfs:subClassOf rdf:resource="#SLA-parameter"/>
<owl:disjointWith> <owl:Class rdf:ID="customerID"/></owl:disjointWith>
<owl:disjointWith> <owl:Class rdf:ID="serviceProvideID"/></owl:disjointWith>
<owl:disjointWith> <owl:Class rdf:ID="customerSLAID"/></owl:disjointWith>
<owl:disjointWith><owl:Class rdf:ID="serviceType"/></owl:disjointWith>
<owl:disjointWith> <owl:Class rdf:ID="QOSLever"/></owl:disjointWith>
<owl:disjointWith><owl:Class rdf:ID="productKOI"/></owl:disjointWith>
<owl:disjointWith> <owl:Class rdf:ID="violationThreshold"/></owl:disjointWith>
<owl:disjointWith><owl:Class rdf:ID="transformationAlgorithm"/></owl:disjointWith>
<owl:disjointWith><owl:Class rdf:ID="violationDirection"/></owl:disjointWith>
<owl:disjointWith><owl:Class rdf:ID="samplePeriod"/></owl:disjointWith>
</rdfs:Class>
```

Fig. 2. Description for Disjointing TimePeriod from the Other Sub-classes

3) property definition

Because of space limitation, we take the class timePeriod as an example, and illustrate the property definition of the class timePeriod too.

```
<rdf:Property rdf:ID="providedTo">
  <rdfs:domain rdf:resource="#serviceProvideID"/>
  <rdfs:range rdf:resource="#customerID"/> </rdf:Property>
```

4) adding restriction

With the limited space, the simple restriction allValuesFrom is defined to indicate the date type of the class timePeriod to illustrate the restriction definition.

```
<owl:allValuesFrom rdf:resource="http://www.w3.org/2001/XMLSchema# time "/>
```

4   SLA Monitoring Process Generation

SLA monitoring process and data flow based on Semantic Web are shown as fig. 3.

1) After consumer inputs service level requirements, the SLS treatment service (SLSTreatment) transforms the product qualitative KOI into product quantitative KQI.

2) The SLS (Service Level Specification) decomposition service (SLSDecomposition) decompose the productive KOI into service KQI

3) Based on service KQI, the measure service (MesureService) checks the services.

4) Collection service (CollectSevice) collect information from measure service periodically and provides the service KQI information to aggregation service (AggregationService) and performance degradation alarm service (PDegradationAService).

5) Aggregation service computes the product KQI based on the aggregation algorithm.

6) Performance degradation alarm service compares the service KQI provided by the collection service with the performance degradation threshold of service KQI and sends the comparing results to the SLA monitoring displaying service (SLAMonitoringDisplayingS) to display. If the performance of some service elements degrades, the alarm information is sent to SLA violation treatment service (ViolationTreatmentService).

7) Performance analysis service (PAnalysisService) compares the product KQI data with the corresponding product KQI threshold and analyzes the service quality. The analysis result is send to the SLA monitoring displaying service to display.

8) SLA violation treatment service locates the involved corresponding service element, and notifies the provider to take measures to ensure the service quality, and send violation information to the SLA monitoring displaying service to display. 9) SLA report generation service (SLAReportGenerationS) and SLA accounting service (SLAAccountingS) collects the service performance analysis and generate the SLA report and SLA accounting periodically.

During to the space limitation, not complete, but typical parts of the OWL-S specification describing the above process are shown as fig. 4.

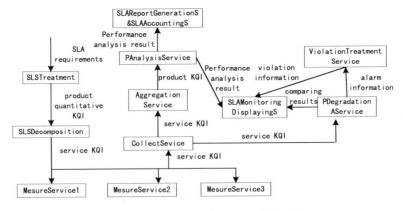

Fig. 3. SLA Monitoring Process and Data Flow

```
<!-- Service description -->
<service:Service rdf:ID="SLAMonitoringService">
        <service:presents rdf:resource="#SLAMonitoringProfile"/>
        <service:describedBy rdf:resource="#SLAMonitoringProcessModel"/>
        <service:supports rdf:resource="#SLAMonitoringGrounding"/></service:Service>
<!-- Profile description -->
<profile:Profile rdf:ID="SLAMonitoringProfile">
        <service:isPresentedBy rdf:resource="#SLAMonitoringService"/>
        <profile:serviceName xml:lang="en">SLA Monitoring</profile:serviceName>
        <profile:textDescription xml:lang="en">Returns the SLA report and accounting or
violation treatment.</profile:textDescription>
        <profile:hasInput rdf:resource="#ServiceLevelRequirement"/>
        <profile:hasOutput rdf:resource="#SLAReport"/></profile:Profile>
<!-- Process Model description -->
<process:ProcessModel rdf:ID="SLAMonitoringProcessModel">
        <service:describes rdf:resource="#SLAMonitoringService"/>
        <process:hasProcess rdf:resource="#SLAMonitoringProcess"/></process:ProcessModel>
<process:CompositeProcess rdf:ID="SLAMonitoringProcess">
        <process:hasInput rdf:resource="#ServiceLevelRequirement"/>
        <process:hasOutput rdf:resource="#SLAReport"/>
        <process:composedOf>
                <process:Sequence>
                        <process:components rdf:parseType="Collection">
                        <process:AtomicProcess rdf:about="file://d:/owl-s/
SLSTreatment.owl#SLSTreatmentProcess"/>
                                <process:AtomicProcess rdf:about="file://d:/owl-s/
SLSDecomposition.owl#SLSDecompositionProcess"/>
                                <process:CompositeProcess rdf:about="#MesureServiceGroup"/>
......
                        <process:AtomicProcess rdf:about="file://d:/owl-s/SLSTreatment.owl/
SLAReportGeneration.owl#SLAReportGenerationProcess"/>
<process:sameValues rdf:parseType="Collection">
                        <process:ValueOf>
                                <process:theParameter rdf:resource="#ServiceLevelRequirement"/>
                                <process:atProcess rdf:resource="#SLAMonitoringProcess"/>
                        </process:ValueOf>
                        <process:ValueOf>
                                <process:theParameter rdf:resource="#SLSSLAInput"/>
                                <process:atProcess rdf:resource="#SLSTreatmentProcess"/>
                        </process:ValueOf></process:sameValues>......</process:components>
                </process:Sequence></process:composedOf></process:CompositeProcess>
        <process:CompositeProcess rdf:ID="MesureServiceGroup">
        <process:hasInput rdf:resource="#serviceKQIInputingString"/>
        <process:hasOutput rdf:resource="#FserviceKQIOutputString"/>
        <process:composedOf>
                <process:Split-Join>
                        <process:components rdf:parseType="Collection">
                                <process:AtomicProcess rdf:about="file://d:/owl-s/
MesureService1.owl#MesureService1Process"/>
                                <process:AtomicProcess rdf:about="file://d:/owl-s/
MesureService2.owl#MesureService2Process"/>
                                <process:AtomicProcess rdf:about="file://d:/owl-s/
MesureService3.owl#MesureService3Process"/></process:components></process:Split-Join>
                </process:composedOf>......
```

Fig. 4. OWL-S Specification for SLA Monitoring Process

5   Conclusion

SLA monitoring based on Semantic Web= is proposed to realize automatically service
quality monitoring according to different services and consumes. SLA monitoring
ontology is constructed based on RDF Schema by providing additional vocabulary

along with a formal semantics. The SLA monitoring process is generated based on OWL-S and monitoring ontology. Specifying workflow specification for Web Service composition invocation based on OWL-S to manage the SLA monitoring management can benefit for automation, coordination, and collaboration between monitoring entities, and so optimizing service process, advancing the efficiency, implementing the service flow control, improving service quality etc.

The SLA monitoring based on Semantic Web is analyzed based on the SLA monitoring requirements, ontology theory, ontology knowledge for Semantic Web. The SLA monitoring based on Semantic Web proposed in this paper is practical. The SLA monitoring based on Semantic Web can be automatic base on existing OWL-S engine. The tool based on the SLA monitoring based on Semantic Web proposed by this paper has been designed and developed based on Protégé [14], OWL-S Editor [15], Graphviz [16], OWL-S API [17]. The tool is used in SLA monitoring system, and the application has proved the SLA monitoring based on Semantic Web is practical.

Acknowledgment

This work is supported by the National High-Tech Research and Development Plan of China under Grant No. 2007AA01Z190.

References

1. Dong, W., Jiao, L.: QoS-Aware Web Service Composition Based on SLA. In: The 4th International Conference on Natural Computation, pp. 247–251. IEEE Press, New York (2008)
2. Aihua, S., Guoqing, Z.: Framework of Service Quality Monitoring Based on SLA and Web Services. Computer Engineering and Applications 42, 157–160 (2006)
3. YuGang, W., JunWen, Z., Gang, D.: Application of Web Services based on Axis in Service Management System of Service Level Agreements. Applications of the Computer Systems 9, 72–74 (2006)
4. Guarantee your Web service with an SLA,
   http://www-106.ibm.com/developerworks/webservices/library/ws-sla/
5. Nepal, S., Zic, J., Chen, S.: WSLA+: Web Service Level Agreement Language for Collaborations. In: 2008 IEEE International Conference on Services Computing, pp. 485–488. IEEE Press, New York (2008)
6. Hua, X., Brian, C., Ying, Z., Benayon, W.J., Bill, O., Elena, L., Jen, H.: A Framework for Verifying SLA Compliance in Composed Services. In: IEEE International Conference on Web Services, pp. 457–464. IEEE Press, New York (2008)
7. Web Service Level Agreement (WSLA) language specification,
   http://www.research.ibm.com/wsla/WSLASpecV1-20030128.pdf
8. Resource Description Framework (RDF): Concepts and Abstract Syntax. W3C Recommendation, February 10 (2004)
9. OWL-S: Semantic Markup for Web Services. W3C Member Submission, November 22 (2004)

10. Foundation for Intelligent Physical Agents, http://www.fipa.org/
11. Dong, W.: Dynamic Reconfiguration Method for Web Service Based on Policy. In: International Symposium on Electronic Commerce and Security, pp. 61–65. IEEE Press, New York (2008)
12. Dong, W.: QoS Driven Service Discovery Method Based on Extended UDDI. In: The 3rd International Conference on Natural Computation, pp. 317–321. IEEE Press, New York (2007)
13. Web Services Description Language (WSDL) 1.1. W3C Note, March 15 (2001)
14. Protégé, http://protege.stanford.edu/
15. OWL-S (ed.), http://owlseditor.semwebcentral.org/index.shtml
16. Graphviz, http://www.graphviz.org/
17. OWL-S API, http://www.mindswap.org/2004/owl-s/api/

Research and Application on Bloom Filter

Jing Chi

Hebei University of Engineering, School of Information & Electronic Engineering,
Handan 056038, China
hdchijing@126.com

Abstract. A Bloom filter is a simple space-efficient randomized data structure for representing a set in order to support membership queries and has a false prediction. Bloom filters and their generalizations, weighted Bloom filters and compressed Bloom filters have been suggested as a means for sharing web cache information. In this paper, a summary about the current research and application on Bloom filter will first be given, and then Bloom filter was tested via simulation. The simulation results showed that Bloom filter is useful for space savings and it is easy to implement. The results also showed that the optimal number of hash function minimizes the false prediction.

Keywords: Bloom Filter, Web Cache, False Prediction.

1 Introduction

Bloom filters are an excellent data structure for succinctly representing a set in order to support membership queries [1]. Bloom filters have been around for ages and are commonly used in Databases and Linguistic applications. Bloom filters are described in detail in section 2; here, simply note that the data structure is randomized (in that uses randomly selected hash functions), and hence has some probability of giving a false prediction; that is, may incorrectly return that an element is in a set when it is not. For many applications, the probability of a false prediction can be made sufficiently small and the space savings are significant enough that Bloom filters are useful. In fact, Bloom filters have a great deal of potential for distributed protocols where systems need to share information. In [2], it is described that how Bloom filters can be used for web cache sharing. To reduce message traffic, proxies do not transfer URL lists corresponding to the exact contents of their caches, but instead periodically broadcast Bloom filters that represent the contents of their cache. If a proxy wishes to determine if another proxy has a page in its cache, it checks the appropriate Bloom filter. In the case of a false prediction, a proxy may request a page from another proxy, only to find that proxy does not actually have that page cached. In that case, some additional delay has been incurred. The small chance of a false prediction introduced by using a Bloom filter is greatly outweighed by the significant reduction in network traffic achieved by using succinct Bloom filter instead of sending the full list of cache contents. This technique is used in the open source web proxy cache

L. Qi (Ed.): FCC 2009, CCIS 34, pp. 30–35, 2009.

Squid, where the Bloom filters are referred to as Cache Digests [3][4]. Cache Digest allows cooperating caches exchange digests of their contents. Cache A that has a digest of cache B knows what documents are likely to be (or not to be) in cache B. Consequently, cache A can decide whether to fetch an object from cache B without contacting cache B first. One may think about Cache Digest as a zero delay ICP with somewhat less precise information. Cache Digest eliminates the need for per-client "Do you have it?" queries and network delays associated with them. The client response time improves. Network bandwidth requirements may improve. Cache Digest is implemented as two virtually independent modules or algorithms described below. A cache maintains its local digest as a variation of a Bloom filter. Bloom filter is a bit array with bits turned on the positions corresponding to hash values of the data. In short, whenever an object gets cached, a few bits based on object's URL are turned on. Later, to know if certain URL is cache, it is needed to perform the same hashing sequence and check that all the corresponding bits are "on". Note that due to collisions, a digest may return a "hit" when object is not in the cache. This phenomenon is called false-hit. In its pure implementation, Bloom filter can never return a "miss" for a cache object (no false-misses). Local digests are stored as ordinary objects on disk and could be requested by other cache. There is also a memory-resident copy that keeps track on current updates. Disk copy of a local digest is synchronized periodically with the up-to-date in-memory copy.

Bloom filters have also been suggest for other distributed protocols, e.g. [5][6][7]. Some generalized Bloom filters were introduced recently. The weighted Bloom filter was mentioned in the web cache scheme [8]. The idea of weighted Bloom filter came from the paper [9]. In that paper, a variation of the signature file access method for text and attribute retrieval was studied. The study allowed special treatment to words with high discriminatory power, high query frequency and low occurrence frequency.

2 Bloom Filter

Bloom filters will be introduced as follows [1].

A Bloom filter for representing a set $S=\{s_1, s_2, ..., s_n\}$ of n elements is described by an array of m bits, initially all set to 0. A Bloom filter uses k independent hash functions $h_1, h_2, ..., h_k$ with range $\{0, 1, ..., m-1\}$. Suppose that these hash functions map each item in the universe to random number uniform over range $\{0, 1, ..., m-1\}$ for mathematical convenience. For each element $s \in S$, the bits hi(s) are set to 1 for $1 \le i \le k$. A location can be set to 1 multiple times, but only the first change has effect. To check whether an item x is in S, it should be checked that whether all hi(x) are set to 1, suppose that x is not a member of S, if all hi(x) are set to 1, suppose that x is in S, although that is wrong with some probability. Hence a Bloom filter may yield a false prediction, where it suggests that an element x is in S even though it is not. For many applications, this is acceptable as long as the probability of a false prediction is sufficiently small. The probability of a false prediction is then

$$f = (1-(1-\frac{1}{m})^{kn})^k = (1-e^{-\frac{kn}{m}})^k.\qquad(1)$$

Let

$$p = e^{-\frac{kn}{m}}, \tag{2}$$

Then

$$f = (1 - e^{-\frac{kn}{m}})^k = (1 - p)^k. \tag{3}$$

Note that the asymptotic approximation p and f is used to represent respectively the probability a bit in the Bloom filter is 0 and the probability of a false prediction from now on for convenience.

Although it is clear form above discussion, it is worth noting that there are three fundamental performance metrics for Bloom filters that can be traced off: computation time(corresponding to the number of hash functions k), size(corresponding to the array size m), and the probability of error(corresponding to the false prediction rate f).

To be given m and n, it is wished to optimize the number of hash functions k to minimize the false prediction rate f. There are two competing force: using more hash functions gives more chances to find a 0 bit for a element that is not a member of S, but using fewer hash functions increases the fraction of 0 bits in the array. The optimal number of hash functions that minimizes f as a function of k is easily found taking the derivative. More conveniently, note that

$$f = e^{k \ln(1 - e^{-\frac{kn}{m}})}. \tag{4}$$

Let

$$g = k \ln(1 - e^{-\frac{kn}{m}}). \tag{5}$$

Minimizing the false prediction rate f is equivalent to minimizing g with respect to k. It is found that

$$\frac{dg}{dk} = \ln(1 - e^{-\frac{kn}{m}}) + \frac{kn}{m} \frac{e^{-\frac{kn}{m}}}{1 - e^{-\frac{kn}{m}}}. \tag{6}$$

It is easy to check that the derivative is 0 when

$$k = (\ln 2)(m/n); \tag{7}$$

Further more efforts reveal that this is a global minimum. In practice, of course, k must be an integer, and smaller k might be preferred since they reduce the amount of computation necessary. For comparison with later results, it is useful to frame the optimization another way. Letting f be a function of p, it is found that

$$f = (1-p)^k = (1-p)^{(-\ln p)(m/n)} = (e^{-\ln(p)(\ln(1-p))})^{m/n}. \qquad (8)$$

From the symmetry of this expression, it is easy to check that p=1/2 minimizes the false prediction rate f. Hence the optimal results are achieved when each bit of the Bloom filter is 0 with probability 1/2. And the minimized false prediction is

$$F_p = e^{-(\ln 2)^2 (m/n)}. \qquad (9)$$

Note that Bloom filter are highly effective even if $m = cn$ for a small constant c, such as c=8. An alternative approach if more bits are available is to simply hash each item into $\Theta(\ln n)$ bits and send a list of hash values. Bloom filters can allow significantly fewer bits to be set while still achieving very good false prediction rates.

Since the contents of the cache will be updated, in practice a generalized Bloom filter is used, i.e., counting Bloom filter. This is done by maintaining for each location l in the filter a count $c(l)$ of the number of times that the bit is set to 1(that is the number of elements that hashed to 1 under any of the hash functions). All the counts are initially 0. When a element a (i.e., the URL of a document) is insert or deleted, the counts $c(h_i(a))$ is incremented or decremented accordingly.

3 Simulation Scheme

In practice, suppose that using MD5 (used in [2]) will be suitable. The Bloom filter and the weighted Bloom filter were tested via simulation. In the simulation, the cache size was set fixed, 1024*1024*256 bytes. Generally speaking, the object size is 8*1024=8k bytes. So suppose that the number of objects in the cache when the cache is full is D=32*1024=32k. The filters with sizes are F=2*D, 3*D, 4*D, 5*D, A6*D and 8*D were tested. In practice, since the size of the objects is vary a lot, in the simulation the number of the objects in the cache will be counted and F/D will be calculated for each case. The following is the simulation scheme.

Choose three trace logs which contain more than 100,000 URLs. For each trace log, do

1. Saturate the cache with LRU replacement scheme.
2. Initialize the filter: for each URL in the cache, W hash functions will be used.
3. Start simulation using the next URL in the trace log. If the filter indicates that the URL is in the cache, look through the cache. If found it, put it in the header of the cache as the LRU replacement scheme, else false prediction happened, put the new URL in the header of the cache and update the filter. If the filter indicates that the URL is not in the cache, just put the URL in the header of the cache and update the filter. When all the URLs are visited, calculate the rate of false prediction.
4. Stop the simulation.

4   Test Results and Discussion

The test results are summarized in the following tables. In the following tables, F is the size of the filters, D is the number of objects in the cache.

In test 1, the total number of URLs is 323925.

In test 2, the total number of URLs is 126525.

In test 3, the total number of URLs is 326675.

The simulation results showed that the optimal number of hash functions minimizes false positive.

Table 1. Test 1

F/D	W	False Positive
2	2	0.15
3	2	0.084
4	3	0.043
5	4	0.022

Table 2. Test 2

F/D	W	False Positive
2	2	0.082
3	2	0.046
4	3	0.022
6	4	0.0115

Table 3. Test 3

F/D	W	False Positive
3	2	0.207
5	4	0.143
6	5	0.088
8	6	0.0547

5   Conclusion

Bloom Filters are an excellent data structure for succinctly representing a set in order to support membership queries. Bloom filters have a wide range of application areas. For the future work, it would be interesting to research on search technology of P2P network based 0n Bloom filter.

References

1. Bloom, B.: Space/Time Tradeoffs in Hash Coding with Allowable Errors. Communications of the ACM 13(7), 422–426 (1970)
2. Fan, L., Cao, P., Almeida, J., Broder, A.: Summary Cache: A Scalable Wide-area Web Cache Sharing Protocol. In: Proceedings of SIGCOMM 1998, Extended version available as technical Report, p. 1361 (1998)
3. SQUID Frequently Asked Question, http://www.squid-cache.org
4. Pousskov, A., Wessels, D.: Cache Digests. Computer Network and ISDN Systems 30(2-23), 2155–2168 (1998)
5. Czerwinski, S., Zhao, B., Hodes, T., Joseph, A., Katz, R.: An Architecture for Secure Service Discovery Service. In: Proceedings of the Fifth Annual International Conference on Mobile Computing and Networks (MobiCOMM 1999) (1999)
6. Kubiatowicz, J., Bindel, D., Chen, Y., Czerwinski, S., Eaton, P., Geels, D., Gummadi, R., Rhea, S., Weatherspoon, H., Weimer, W., Wells, C., Zhao, B.: OceanStore: Architecture for Global-scale Persistent Storage. In: Proceedings of ASPLOS 2000 (2000)
7. Snoeren, A.C., Partridge, C., Sanchez, L.A., Jones, C.W., Tchakounito, F., Kent, S.T., Strayer, W.T.: Hash-Based IP Traceback, SIGCOMM (2001)
8. Liang, Z.: Transparent Web Caching with Load Balancing. Master Thesis in Queens University (2001)
9. Faloutsos, C., Christodoulakis, S.: Design of a Signature File Method that Accounts for Xnon-Uniform Occurrence and Query Frequencies. In: 11th International Conf. on VLDB, Stockholm, Sweden, p. 165 (1985)

Research on the DDS to Generate MSK Signal

Wenbiao Peng, Chaojun Yan, and Lihua Deng

College of Electrical Engineering and Information Technology,
China Three Gorges University,Yichang 443002, Hubei
pwb@ctgu.edu.cn

Abstract. This paper introduced the working principle of Minimum shift keying(MSK) and direct digital frequency synthesizer(DDS),and realized the MSK modulator by AT89C51 and AD9862,The result show that it's feasible to realize the digital modulation meeting the needs of phase requirement using DDS technology.

Keyword: MSK (Minimum shift keying), DDS (Direct Digital Synthesis), Digital modulation, AD9852.

1 Introduction

With the rapid development of communication technology, there is a sharp increase in the service of business, so the frequency resources is becoming more and more insufficient; at the same time, due to the bad spread conditions of electromagnetic waves, the impact of fast fading, the ratio of the received signal to noise make a sharp decline, so modulation technique and signal should have a strong anti-interference capability. by the way, the bandwidth of signal should be narrow in order to improve the spectrum efficiency, the system should be to transmit data as much as possible to improve the bit rate in the given limited channel, and should be to adapt to the require of high-speed transmission. Based on these two factors, the minimum frequency shift keying (MSK) and other modern digital modulation technology in digital communications systems have been widely used.

MSK (MSK) is a constant envelope, phase continuous digital signal modulation, and its spectral characteristics are that the main-lobe bandwidth is narrow and the side-lobe roll-off fast. The radiation of outside the passband is small, the interference to other channel is small, and anti-interference capability is strong, error rate is low. Conventional analog modulation methods are quadrature modulation, impulse response method and conversion method based on the surface acoustic wave devices [1], with the technology of device, as well as the emergence of large-scale integrated circuits, direct digital synthesizer (DDS) have been rapid development, and plays an important role in modern frequency synthesis because of its unique advantages and characteristics [2].

2 Principle of MSK Modulation

In digital modulation, minimum-shift keying (MSK) is a type of continuous-phase frequency-shift keying that was developed in the late 1960s. the modulated Signal expression is:

L. Qi (Ed.): FCC 2009, CCIS 34, pp. 36–41, 2009.
© Springer-Verlag Berlin Heidelberg 2009

$$S_{MSk}(t) = \cos[\omega_c t + \frac{\pi a_k}{2T_s}t + \phi_k] \tag{1}$$

Where, $a_k = \pm 1$, $kTs \le t \le (k+1)Ts$, Ts is the symbol width, $\theta_k(t) = \frac{\pi a_k}{2T_s}t + \phi_k$ is the instantaneous phase offset of the No. k-symbol signal waveforms.

To meet the continuous phase of MSK carrier signal at $t = kTs$, so

$$\phi_k = \phi_{k-1} + \frac{\pi k}{2}(a_{k-1} - a_k) = \begin{cases} \phi_{k-1}, when.a_k = a_{k-1} \\ \phi_{k-1} \pm k\pi, when.a_k \ne a_{k-1} \end{cases} \tag{2}$$

We have the instantaneous frequency of No. k-symbol signal waveforms:

$$f_1 = f_c + \frac{1}{4T_s}, f_2 = f_c - \frac{1}{4T_s} \tag{3}$$

The difference frequency value is: $f_1 - f_2 = \frac{1}{2T_s}$

MSK carrier signal:

$$S(t) = \begin{cases} A\cos(\omega_1 t + \phi_k), when..a_k = 1 \\ A\cos(\omega_2 t + \phi_k), when..a_k = -1 \end{cases} kT_s \le t \le (k+1)T_s$$

At $a_k = \pm 1$, Correlation coefficient of the two signal waveforms is:

$$\gamma = \frac{\int_0^{T_s} S_1(t) \cdot S_2(t)dt}{\int_0^{T_s} S_1^2(t)dt} = \frac{\int_0^{T_s} S_1(t) \cdot S_2(t)dt}{\int_0^{T_s} S_2^2(t)dt}$$

$$= \frac{\sin[(\omega_1 - \omega_2)T_s]}{(\omega_1 - \omega_2)T_s} + \frac{\sin[(\omega_1 + \omega_2)T_s]}{(\omega_1 + \omega_2)T_s} \tag{4}$$

If $\omega_c = \frac{\omega_1 + \omega_2}{2}$, and $2\omega_c T_s = (\omega_1 + \omega_2)T_s = n\pi$,(n=1,2,......),so

$T_s = \frac{n}{4}T_c$,we can have that the symbol cycle is multiple to 1/4 carrier cycle. At this point:

$$\gamma = \frac{\sin[(\omega_1 - \omega_2)T_s]}{(\omega_1 - \omega_2)T_s} \tag{5}$$

Only when $(\omega_1 - \omega_2)T_s = n\pi$ (n=±1,±2,......), $\gamma = 0$, That is, two signals is orthogonal. when n=1,we can find the difference frequency value is smallest, the index of modulation is $\rho = |f_1 - f_2| \cdot T_s = 0.5$ [1].

Conventional analog modulation methods are quadrature modulation, impulse response method and conversion method based on the surface acoustic wave devices. According to the principle of Orthogonal modulation, MSK signal can be seen as the superposition result in time period T_S of cosine and sine-weighted pulse, the impulse method is curing response to SAWF, then utilizing the δ pulse signals controlled by the base-band signal to inspire, you can output the required MSK signal. Conversion method is that PSK modulation first where the center frequency is f1, for the, and then through the impulse response filter which $h(t) = \sin \omega_2 t$ for MSK signal output.

Because of the difficulty to create ideal narrow pulse, a larger filter insertion loss,PSK modulation process is non-ideal, and symbol time error, the output MSK signal is parasitic AM, in order to obtain better MSK signal, it must to be dealed with limiter. Now, in order to overcome these two shortcomings of analog modulation method, we can use DDS modulation methods.

3 Principle of Direct Digital Synthesizers

Direct digital synthesizers (DDS) has developed rapidly in recent years, it's a new synthesis method, and its main advantages are: frequency agility speedy, high frequency resolution, the output phase continuous, programmable, all-digital to facilitate integration. At present, the most widely used synthesizer is to use high-speed memory where the M samples of the sine wave exist in, and then looking for the tables, output these data sample to the high-speed D/A converter a uniform rate, so the sine wave signal is generated. The basic principle as shown in Figure 1.

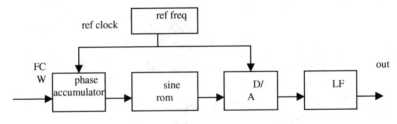

Fig. 1. Basic Structure of DDS

The reference frequency source in the fig 1 is a crystal with high stability, its output signal drive all parts of the DDS to work simultaneously. Phase accumulator steps with the given phase increment (frequency control word, FCW), and this phase can be used as the address to look for the sinusoidal shape memory table, resulting in the range of amplitude of output signal, the D/A convert the digital amplitude code into analog signals, so we can have the required signal waveforms after a low-pass filter smoothing.

When the frequency control words is FTW, reference frequency is f_{sc}, the phase accumulator is N-bit, the output signal frequency is: $f_{out} = FTW * f_{sc} / 2^N$.

In theory, the DDS maximum output frequency up to half of the frequency reference source. When FTW = 1, the output frequency is the DDS frequency resolution $\Delta f = f_{sc} / 2^N$.

4   Implement of MSK with AD9852

The AD9852 digital synthesizer is a highly flexible device that addresses a wide range of applications. The device consists of an NCO with a 48-bit phase accumulator, a programmable reference clock multiplier, an inverse sinc filter, a digital multiplier, two 12-bit/300 MHz DACs, a high speed analog comparator, and an interface logic. The innovative high speed DDS core of the AD9852 provides 48-bit frequency resolution (1μHz tuning resolution with 300 MHz SYSCLK). Maintaining 17 bits ensures excellent SFDR.This highly integrated device can be configured to serve as a synthesized LO agile clock generator and FSK/BPSK modulator. It is widely used in communications, radar, and many other applications. The internal structure shown in Figure 2.

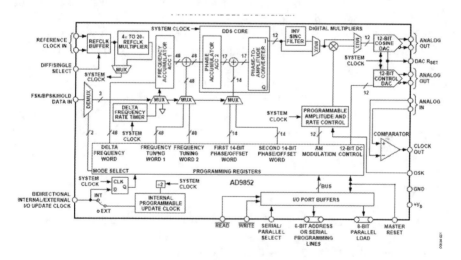

Fig. 2. Functional Block Diagram

From the resources and functions of AD9852, resulting in MSK signal is relatively easy. MSK is a special case of FSK, so AD9852 is set to FSK mode. In this mode, AD9852 output frequency is controlled by the frequency register 1,2 and FSK control input pin. When the FSK pin is low, the out frequency choose f1 (frequency control word 1), otherwise choose f2. Two frequencies should be in strict conformity with the requirements of MSK signal, and then we use the corresponding base-band signal to switch FSK input control pin. According to the characteristics of DDS, frequency changes are instantaneous in the switching time, the phase of phase accumulator at the new starting point is the phase of phase accumulator at the previous end point, so the phase of output signal is continuous at the switching time, it's matched with the required of MSK signal phase continue characteristics.

If the data rate is 5MHz, and fc= 50MHz, we have f1 = 51.25MHz, f2 = 48.75MHz. In order to reduce phase noise, the system clock frequency must up to to 3 times higher than the output frequency in general, it may be more than 150MHz. To ensure the quality of out waveform, set AD9852 system clock to 280MHz, it is multiplying the 20MHz external clock for 14 by internal PLL devices to achieve.

AD9852 power consumption is great, if all the functional modules to open and work at the highest frequency, the current consumption will exceed 1A,it will be far beyond the system load. To reduce the power consumption, we adopt some compromise in the design, and turn off the anti-sinc filter for the improvement of the broadband spectrum, and digital multiplier for amplitude modulation.

It should be noted that, in system design, it is important to pay attention to the following questions. Hardware: AD9852 using 3.3V power supply, and should be set up a conversion circuit between,MCU and DDS; reference clock can be single-ended input or differential input, when the DIFF / SINGLE SELECT (pin64) is high, it should use the differential input, when the DIFF / SINGLE SELECT is low, it should adopt single-ended input; AD9852 use high to reset MASTER RESET (pin71); when SERIAL / PARALLEL SELECT (pin70) is high, it work in parallel mode, When SERIAL / PARALLEL SELECT is low, it work in serial mode; I/O UPDATE CLOCK (pin20) can be internal generated, it can also be controlled by the external input, the update time is the rising edge. if pin20 internal generated, it can also be used as an external sync. Software programming: system power-on reset, the MCU initialization, followed by initialization of the AD9852, including SERIAL/PARALLEL SELECT, I/O UPDATE CLOCK (pin20) settings, control register, frequency control words, phase control settings and other characters.

5   Conclusion

It is feasible to generate MSK signal by DDS device, f1, f2 of generated MSK signal is corresponding to each other with base-band signal. The experimental results show that MSK signal by AD9852 parasitic AM is smaller, the ratio of the main-lobe to side-lobe is closer to the theoretical value. the advantages of this practical design is:flexible configuration, debugging convenient, change carrier frequency and frequency offset is easy and so on. In addition, the AD9852 can also be used in the realization of QPSK, PSK, FSK, AM, FM modulation by setting the work mode., particularly for higher-required phase modulation. The advantage of DDS devices is wide frequency range of a variety of modulation signal (including frequency hopping signals), if we adopt the high-speed DSP control, the DDS device will be very suitable for software radio and reconfigurable modulator applications.

References

1. Liu, J., Liu, J.: Spectrum characteristic analysis of DDS-based RF digital modulation Electrical and Electronic Technology, 2001. In: Proceedings of IEEE Region 10 International Conference on TENCON, vol. 2, pp. 588–591 (2001)
2. Jiaguo, L., Manqin, W., Xueming, J., Zhengxing, F.: Active phased array antenna based on DDS Phased Array Systems and Technology. In: IEEE International Symposium on October 14-17, 2003, pp. 511–516 (2003)
3. Wu, Y.-D., Lai, C.-M., Chou, C.-Y., Huang An, P.-C.: OPLL-DDS based frequency synthesizer for DCS-1800 receiver Circuits and Systems. In: Proceedings of IEEE International Symposium on ISCAS 2006, p. 4- (2006)
4. Liao, H., Yu, J., Wang, J., Chen, J., Liao, Y., Yi, J.: A Control and Acquisition System Design of Low-voltage Electrophoresis MicroChip Based on SOPC and DDS Embedded Software and Systems. In: International Conference on ICESS 2008, July 29-31, 2008, pp. 251–257 (2008)
5. CMOS MSPS Complete DDS AD9852, Analog Devices, Inc. (2002)
6. Jianhua, W., Min, X., Wei, W., Deyi, S.: Implementation of MSK Modulation with DDS Method. Telemetry & Telecontrol 26(3) (2002)
7. Liu, W., Huang, R.-G.: Design and Realization of Communication Signal Source Based on DDS Technology. Audio Engineering 3 (2004)

Establishment and Application of GIS Database in Urban Heritage Conservation[*]

Rui Li and Jinghua Song

School of Urban Design, Wuhan University, Wuhan, China
reallirui@126.com

Abstract. This paper is about the establishment and application of GIS database in urban heritage conservation. It first mines the needed data for database establishment from literature review. Then, a series of GIS database will be designed for urban heritage conservation, which integrates three parts: one is for Urban Heritage Inventory; another is for Urban Visual Management, and the other is for Evaluation of Historical District Renewal. Finally, a case of Hankou Historical District in Wuhan, China is applied to show the application result of the GIS database.

Keywords: GIS; database; urban heritage conservation.

1 Introduction

Rapid urbanization has made the inner city change quickly with the urban sprawl of the whole city. In China, a mass of urban renewal projects have been carried out for meeting the new need of people's life. However, the traditional means of total renewal has destroyed the urban heritage seriously, which especially led to the diminishing of historical district space. It is urgent to protect and reutilize the urban heritage effectively under the background of rapid urban renewal.

Application of GIS is considered as an effective means for urban heritage conservation. Because of GIS advantage on data management, data analysis and visualization, it is helpful in the filed of urban heritage conservation, with the aims of investigation on cultural relics or historical environment, foundation of database, evaluation of historical or cultural values, monitor management for influence factors, and planning formulation for urban heritage conservation. The famous foreign cases are the protection projects of Angkor Wat in Cambodia, Wanrong in Laos, Vietnam Hue, and some protection projects in Europe, Australia and North America [1].

For urban heritage conservation by GIS, the establishment and application of GIS database is the core. A series of GIS database will be designed for urban heritage conservation in this paper, which integrates three parts: one is for Urban Heritage Inventory; another is for Urban Visual Management, and the other is for Evaluation of Historical District Renewal. Then, a case of Hankou Historical District in Wuhan, China is applied to show the application result of the GIS database.

[*] Project supported by National Natural Science Foundation of China (No. 50608061).

L. Qi (Ed.): FCC 2009, CCIS 34, pp. 42–49, 2009.

2 Needed Data for Database Establishment

2.1 Needed Data for Urban Heritage Inventory

According to the administrative division, Wuhan city is made of 13 zones including Jiang'an Zone, Jianghan Zone, Qiaokou Zone and so on, with a zone made of several districts and a district made of several neighborhoods. Thus, district name and neighborhood name will be used to describe where the heritage is located.

About the data for historical building protection, some items have been listed, which contain building type (including architecture style and level for protection), protective status, architecture constituent factors (including garden, courtyard, enclosing wall, orientation and entrance), and environment constituent factors (including tree, water well, public aisle and characteristic paving) [2].

Referring from the Project of Beijing's Old and Dilapidated Housing Renewal [3], building function, building layer, building floor area, number of households and population in building and district, facilities, number of buildings in district, and lane arrangement are selected in historical building and Lifen[1] protection in this paper.

2.2 Needed Data for Urban Visual Management

Referring from the theory of urban imago of Kevin Lynch [4], three visual factors are defined for Urban Visual Management that are visual area, visual line and visual point, which can be in turn used to generate height control zone for urban heritage conservation and renewal.

At visual area level, Lifen and some characteristic public space, such as green area, square, and small plot for activity are included. At visual line level, street and corridor sight line are included. At visual point level, mark building (including its garden or courtyard), mark structure and important tree are all involved.

2.3 Needed Data for Evaluation of Historical District Renewal

As Buissink had defined six activities about urban heritage conservation and renewal that are maintenance, improvement, restoration, rehabilitation (upgrading), reconstruction, and redevelopment [5], the establishment of GIS database for evaluation of historical district renewal is to analyze which buildings can be maintained or improved, which buildings need be restored or reconstructed, and which buildings should be redeveloped. For above object, data about protection level, building age, building height, building physical and living condition, artistic value are needed especially.

---

[1] Lifen was called in the early Tang Dynasty but not only appeared in the modern history. In the ancient time residents inhabited a region as a group of families, it was called as a "Li". Different from Shanghai being called as "Li Nong", in Wuhan it is called as "Lifen". "Fen" is from local dialect of Wuhan, meaning as a little region of habitat. However, in this paper "Lifen" refers to the "new" style of dwelling houses appeared in the modern history, syncretizing the western style into Chinese traditional residential buildings.

3 GIS Database for Urban Heritage Conservation

3.1 GIS Database for Urban Heritage Inventory

The GIS database for urban heritage inventory reflects the general information about urban heritage that involves district, neighborhood, Lifen, historic building, lane, constituent factor and details of building from big to small. In Figure 1, yellow means entity part of database, while white and green represent attribute part of database, in which green part is the core of database including Lifen, historic building and lane. Generally, entity part can be used to reflect the spatial distribution directly and attribute part is useful for management, analysis and decision-making.

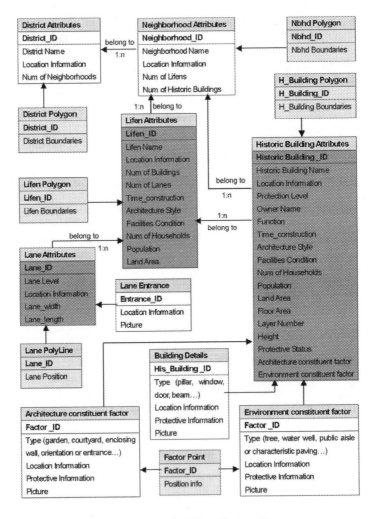

Fig. 1. GIS Database for Urban Heritage Inventory

3.2   GIS Database for Urban Visual Management

The GIS database for urban visual management focuses on visual elements, concluded as visual area, visual line and visual point, which includes Lifen, characteristic public space, street, corridor sight line, mark building, mark structure and important tree. In Figure 2,

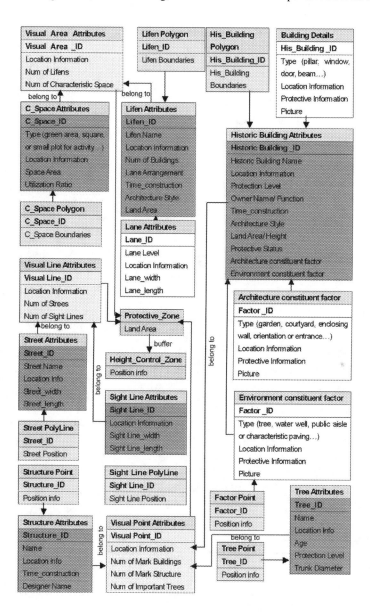

Fig. 2. GIS Database for Urban Visual Management

yellow means entity part of database, while blue, green and white represent attribute part of database, in which blue and green part is the core of database at different level, and red part means protective zone and height control zone generated at final for urban heritage conservation and renewal. The height control zone can be generated by the "buffer" function in GIS, according to different planning intention.

3.3   GIS Database for Evaluation of Historical District Renewal

As mentioned above, the main object of this database is to analyze the suitable renewal means to different buildings in historical district. Figure 3 is more like a flow chart of analyzing process, in which historic building and old building in good condition and with high artistic value can be renewed by means 1, old building in bad condition but with high artistic value can be renewed by means 2, while old building in bad condition and with low artistic and the new building exceeding limited height

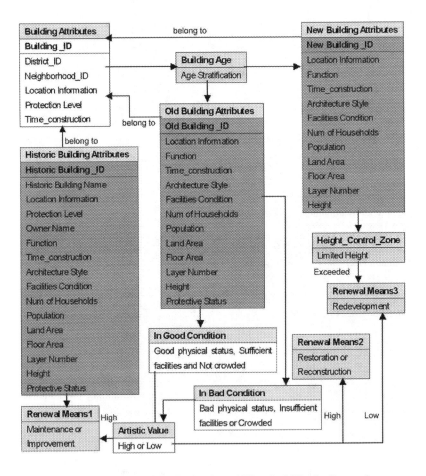

Fig. 3. GIS Database for Evaluation of Historical District Renewal

should be renewed by means 3. Because the historical district renewal is a giantproject and needs massive funds and time, old buildings in good condition but with low artistic value and new buildings under limited height are considered not to be so urgent to renew, which are defined to be maintained temporarily and renewed in future in this paper.

4 Application of GIS Database

4.1 Brief History of Case Study Area

As one of the three towns in Wuhan with Wuchang and Hanyang, Hankou is located at north of the junction of Yangtze River and Hanjiang River. After the Second Opium War (1856-1860), Hankou became the Concession District of British, German,

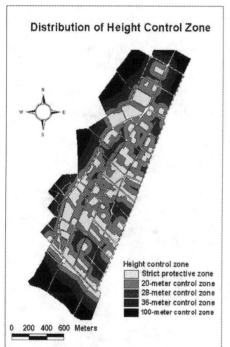

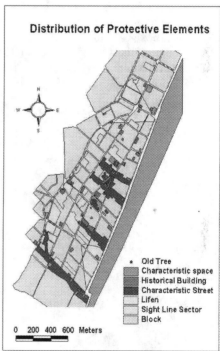

Fig. 4. Distribution of Height Control Zone   **Fig. 5.** Distribution of Protective Elements

France, Russia, and Japan as an open trading port. With the import of West Architecture Form, a "new" style of dwelling houses called as "Lifen" appeared in the Hankou Concession District at the end of 19th century, syncretizing the western style into Chinese traditional residential buildings.

At beginning, Lifen was built imitating the Lane of Shanghai, but for more interest, this part Lifen was done in worse living condition without independent kitchen and toilet in each unit, such as Sande Li, ChangQin Li and so on. From 1911 to 1937, a large number of Lifens boomed out with complete functions and in better environment, such as Kunhou Li, Xian'an Fang and so on. After then, the construction of Lifen came into recession period and stopped completely after Liberation in 1949 [6].

4.2 Case Study

According to the GIS database for urban visual management, visual area includes Lifen and characteristic public space; visual line includes characteristic street and corridor sight line; and visual point includes mark building, mark structure and important tree. Figure 5 shows the distribution of the protective visual elements.

In order to protect the traditional style of historical district, height control zones are defined in this paper, according to the distance from protective elements. First is the definition of strict protective zone, in which buildings cannot be constructed and demolished randomly. Second is the definition of height control zones, which include 20-meter control zone, 28-meter control zone, 36-meter control zone and 100-meter control zone in this paper. Figure 4 shows the distribution of strict protective zone and height control zones in historical district.

According to the GIS database for evaluation of historical district renewal, the result of evaluation has been made in Figure 6. After statistics, 482 buildings

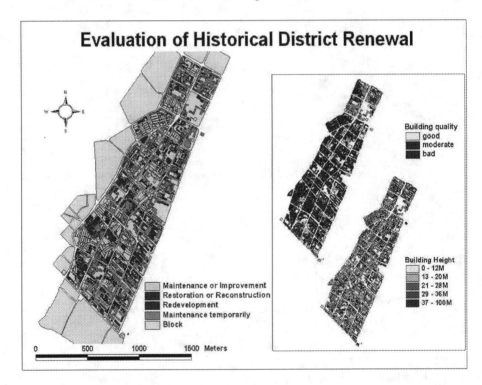

Fig. 6. Evaluation of Historical District Renewal

are involved in protective means of maintenance or improvement, 391 buildings are involved in protective means of restoration or reconstruction, 338 buildings are involved in means of redevelopment, and the rest 475 buildings can be maintained temporarily and renewed in future.

5 Conclusion

This paper focuses on designation of a series of GIS database for urban heritage conservation. The needed data are mined by literature review. A case study of Hankou historical district in Wuhan, China is used to show the application result of GIS database. Using the GIS database for urban heritage conservation, many other researches can be made, such as research on lane arrangement, protection of mark structure and building details etc.

References

1. Feng, M., Lingyun, W.: Application of New Technique in Historical Cultural Resources Protection. J. Beijing Planning Review. 4, 79–81 (2006)
2. Jian, Z., Kai, Z.: The Building Classification and Protection Measurements in the Preservation Planning for the Historical and Cultural Heritage. J. Planning Studies. 1, 38–42 (2001)
3. Junhua, L.: Beijing's Old and Dilapidated Housing Renewal (Phase I). J. China City Planning Review. 3, 27–35 (1993)
4. Lynch, K.: Urban imago. HuaXia Press, Beijing (2001)
5. Buissink, J.D.: Aspects of urban renewal: report of an enquiry by questionnaire concerning the relation between urban renewal and economic development. In: International Federation for Housing and Planning (IFHP), The Hague (1985)
6. Baihao, L., Yusu, X., Ling, W.: Research of Wuhan Modern Li-fen Residence. J. Huazhong Architecture 3, 116–117 (2000)

RFID Middleware Design Research

Xin Chen

Guangdong University of Foreign Studies

Abstract. The proliferation of RFID tags and readers will require dedicated middleware solutions that manage readers and process the vast amount of captured data. In this paper analyses the requirements and propose a design for such an RFID middleware. We argue that an RFID middleware should not only focus on the application needs, but must also consider the constraints imposed by passive RFID technology.

Keywords: RFID, middleware, RFID constraint, RFID tag, RFID application.

1 RFID Introduction

RFID stands for Radio frequency identification. The concept of using Radio Frequency to identify objects dates back to World War II when the RF was used to distinguish between returning English airplanes and the German ones. IFF or Identification Friend or Foe is another area where a device aboard an aircraft is queried by a ground based device. The returned reply contains a code which identifies the aircraft as a 'friendly' one.

If the code is wrong, the ground control system treats the intruding aircraft as potentially hostile. RFID technology captures data using tiny tracking chips that are affixed to products. RFID applications range from potential areas such as security, manufacturing, logistics, animal tagging, waste management, postal tracking to airline baggage and road toll management.

Find out how RFID tags are creating a revolution in tracking systems. RFID is not just for smart store shelves alone - they can also aid in locating children in amusement parks. Combined with GPS and active RFID technology they can be the wonder application of this century.

1.1 RFID Technology

A typical RFID system consists of an antenna and transceiver and transponder (RF tag). The transceiver reads the radio frequency and transfers information to a processing device. The transponder or RFID tag is an integrated circuit that contains information to be transmitted. RFID technology uses radio waves for identification. An RFID tag is made up of a chip and antenna. The antenna allows the chip to transmit the information that is used for identification. The reader sends electromagnetic waves, which are received by the tag antenna. RFID technology differs from bar code systems in that it is not a line of sight technology.

L. Qi (Ed.): FCC 2009, CCIS 34, pp. 50–56, 2009.
© Springer-Verlag Berlin Heidelberg 2009

Bar codes have to be seen and read by the scanner. Besides they do not uniquely identify each item. The RFID technology works on overcoming this shortcoming of line-of-sight technology. All types of RFID systems use non-contact and non line-of-sight technology. RFID tags can be read through snow, fog, ice, paint and other environmental conditions.

1.2 RFID Tag

RFID tags are helpful in tracking an individual item through the different locations it moves through. A case in example is the use of RFID systems to move cars through an assembly line. At different stages of the production process, it keeps the computers informed about the next step in the assembly line. An RFID tag can be either active or passive. Passive RFID tags use the electrical current induced in the antenna by the incoming radio frequency scan. This means that the response of a passive RFID tag is brief.

The commercially available RFID products using passive RFID tags are thinner than a sheet of paper. Active RFID tags have their own power source that enables longer range frequency as well as larger memory capacity. This allows it to store additional information. A typical RFID active tag has a battery life of several years. Passive RFID tags are more commonly available on account of their cheaper cost of manufacture. With passive RFID tags costing about $0.25, it is poised for wider commercial application. Varying levels of radio frequency give rise to different kinds of RFID tags:

- Low frequency tags (between 125 to 134 KHz)
- High frequency tags (13.56 MHz)
- UHF tags (868 to 956 MHz)
- Microwave tags (2.45 GHz)

Active RFID tags are used to track high-value goods that need scanning over long ranges. A read-only RFID tag does not allow for any change to the information stored on it. Read-write RFID tag allows additional information to be added on to it.

1.3 RFID Middleware

The widespread adoption of RFID requires not only low cost tags and readers, but also the appropriate networking infrastructure [4]. Such a supporting RFID infrastructure typically comprises a component – often referred to as RFID middleware – that is application-agnostic, manages readers, filters and aggregates captured RFID data and delivers these to the appropriate consumers. To facilitate application development even further, an RFID infrastructure can also feature another component that consumes the events delivered by the middleware, combines the RFID data with application logic, and generates application-level events. While the latter can be a standalone system that provides this service to an application, this functionality can also be integral part of an existing application as indicated on Fig. 1.

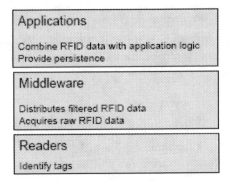

Fig. 1. Overview of functional components in an RFID system. The reader identifies tags using radio-frequency. The middleware acquires these raw tag reads, filters and delivers them to applications, where the RFID data are combined with application logic.

2 RFID Middleware Design

This section presents an RFID middleware design that addresses the requirements and constraints described in the previous two sections. We show how the restricted bandwidth available to RFID systems can be efficiently utilized given the application needs for filtered and aggregated data. Specific RFID aggregate types are presented that reduce the flood of elementary tag detection events. Characteristics of the messaging component of our RFID middleware design are discussed and we outline how these help to address the limitations of RFID. There is also dedicated support for the heterogenous reader landscape and the different memory structures on RFID tags. At the end of the section we discuss the challenge of meeting the requirements to integrate RFID readers into IT-service management. The design concept presented here was also the foundation for the implementation of the RFIDStack, a middleware platform, which is described in the following section.

2.1 Filtering and Aggregation

The removal of certain tag read events based on the reader which generated the event and the tag data captured is usually referred to as filtering. Table 1 shows the two most common filter types. In the design proposed here, we decided to carry out the

Table 1. Filter types

Filter by	Description
Reader Identifier	This filter type allows the application to specify that it is only interested data from a particular set of readers.
Tag Identifier and Data	The application can define the tag population that it is interested in, e.g., the restriction to tags attached to pallets.

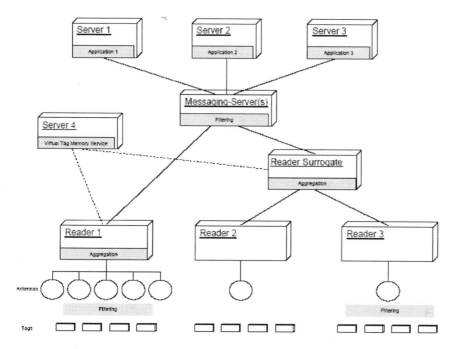

Fig. 2. Deployment diagram of the proposed RFID middleware design. The diagram shows how a event-based messaging systems decouples applications and readers. It also features the virtual tag memory system and the surrogate concept that address the limitations of tag memory and the heterogeneous reader landscape respectively. To utilize the scarce bandwidth effectively, the filtering is done on the air interface where possible or otherwise directly in the messaging system.

Table 2. Aggregate types

Aggregate types	Description
Entry & Exit	This aggregate type reduces a number of successful reads of a tag to the best estimate when the tag appeared and disappeared from the read range.
Count	Applications can prefer to receive information about the total number of items of a specific category detected rather than the individual ID of each object. Examples include the legacy warehouse management system in the above scenario.
Passage	When a tagged object passes a gate, applications would prefer receiving a passage event rather than being forced to interpret a sequence of entry and exit events from two individual readers.
Virtual readers	When an application does not distinguish between two readers, this aggregate type allows it to virtually join their read range.

filtering on the air interface for bandwidth considerations, whenever possible, or otherwise within the messaging service (cf. Fig. 2).

Aggregation is desired to reduce the flood of raw tag reads to more meaningful events such as the first appearance of a tag in the read range and its subsequent disappearance (cf. Fig. 3). Aggregation is also needed to address the problem of temporary false negative reads and to smooth the data accordingly [1].

The aggregation types that need to be supported are listed in Table 2. The aggregation functionality is currently realized via surrogates to which the readers are connected (cf. Fig. 2). In the future more powerful readers can carry out this functionality themselves, while less powerful readers will continue to rely on a surrogate to carry out the aggregation.

2.2 Messaging

Given the diverse set of applications that consume the captured RFID data and the networking limitations of readers, an eventbased middleware that decouples readers and applications is appropriate for RFID. Readers produce RFID events, deliver them to the messaging system and it is the responsibility of the messaging system to get the messages to their intended destinations (cf. Fig. 2). In such a publish/subscribe concept the producer, the reader, does not need to track which applications are supposed to receive a certain message. Likewise, applications consuming RFID data, do not need to maintain communication channels with individual readers, but can simply specify which events they are interested in by submitting subscriptions to the messaging system.

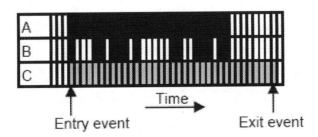

Fig. 3. Entry&Exit event illustration. The row labeled A shows the frames, in which the tag under test was present in the read range and should ideally have been detected (dark boxes). The row below shows the frames in which the tag was actually detected by the HF reader. Row C shows the assumed presence of the tag and the point of time, where the entry&exit events are generated.

2.3 Reading from and Writing to a Tag

The RFID middleware should ideally make writing to an RFID tag as easy as writing data to a hard disk of a computer. The virtual tag memory service (VTMS) proposed in our system design facilitates this by shielding the application from the particularities of RFID tag memory: limited memory size, different memory organizations, reduced write range. Applications simply provide key-value pairs that should be written to a set of tags. The RFID middleware then checks with the VTMS for the appropriate tag memory block and page to write to given the key. If the write succeeds, the RFID middleware will acknowledge this to the application and will store a backup copy of the data in the virtual representation of the tag in the VTMS. If the memory gets corrupted at a later stage or the application wants to access the tag's memory, while the tag is outside the range of any reader, the RFID middleware can make the data available via this virtual memory. If the write to the tag fails due to insufficient power, the key-value pair will be stored in the VTMS and flagged as "open". The RFID middleware will retry the write command at a later point of time. If there is insufficient memory space, the application will receive the appropriate error message and the key-value will be stored in the virtual tag memory only. The application can also indicate that the virtual memory of a tag can only be accessed, once the tag is in the read range of the particular reader. The VTMS service is a distributed infrastructure itself that is available to all RFID middleware instances (cf. Fig. 2).

2.4 Reader Integration in IT-Service Management

The desirable integration of RFID readers in an existing IT- service management concept that performs incident, change, release, and configuration management is straightforward from a technical perspective. It requires methods to query and modify the existing configuration of a reader, mechanisms to remotely update the software on a reader, and exception reporting functionality. The absence of a de-facto standard to date that fulfills these requirements seems to be more a matter of the reader vendors not agreeing on a common approach rather than technical challenges.

3 RFIDStack

The RFIDStack is a middleware platform that was developed in our research group and which is currently in use in various research groups to facilitate RFID application development. The messaging component relies on the content-based router Elvin [5]. Through its quenching functionality it provides the feedback mechanism we require to address the bandwidth limitations. The RFIDStack also benefits from the built-in security features, which prevent unwanted eavesdropping, unauthorized applications receiving notifications and unauthorized readers feeding false information to applications. A single instance of the above event router can process more than 10000 messages per second [2]. In the worst case this corresponds to 100 readers detecting continuously 100 tags per second and feeding the raw data non-aggregated to the messaging system. In a more realistic scenario, a single non-federated event router should thus be able to deal with at least 1000 readers. Likewise, a federation of event routers will be capable of processing the captured data within an RFID-enabled enterprise featuring more than 10000 readers.

The RFIDStack currently supports seven different types of readers from several different manufacturers. It also features the filter and aggregate types mentioned in the previous section. The support for disconnected applications is currently not realized, but has been shown to work in conjunction with the particular event router used [3]. There is also no support for IT service management yet.

4 Conclusion

This paper analyses the requirements RFID middleware solutions should meet in order to manage large deployments of readers and the amount of data these readers capture. We argue that the characteristics of passive RFID technology introduce constraints that are unique to the development of middleware for the RFID domain and present a design for such a middleware solution that addresses both application needs and the RFID constraints.

References

1. Brusey, J., Floerkemeier, C., Harrison, M., Fletcher, M.: Reasoning about uncertainty in location identification with RFID. In: Workshop on Reasoning with Uncertainty in Robotics at IJCAI 2003, Acapulco, Mexico (2003)
2. Mantara: Elvin router product datasheet (2005), http://www.mantara.com/
3. Peter Sutton, R.A., Segall, B.: Supporting disconnectedness - transparent information delivery for mobile and invisible computing. In: CCGrid 2001 IEEE International Symposium on Cluster Computing and the Grid, Brisbane, Australia (May 2001)
4. Sarma, S., Brock, D.L., Ashton, K.: The networked physical world – proposals for engineering the next generation of computing, commerce & automatic identification. Technical Report MITAUTOID-WH-001, MIT Auto-ID Center (2000),
   http://www.autoidcenter.org/research/MIT-AUTOID-WH-001.pdf
5. Segall, B., Arnold, D., Boot, J., Henderson, M., Phelps, T.: Content based routing with elvin4. In: Proceedings AUUG2K, Canberra, Australia (J une 2000)

RFID Applications of Consumer Perceptions and Privacy Concerns

Xin Chen

School of International Trade & Economics
Guangdong University of Foreign Studies

Abstract. This paper discussed the applications and implications for consumers of RFID, and focused on consumer perceptions and privacy concerns, including three fields: consumer survey results, RFID and consumer privacy, database security issues.

Keywords: RFID, consumer perception, consumer privacy, database security, RFID implication.

1 Introduction

Radio frequency identification technology, known as RFID, has been described as "tech's official Next Big Thing." [1] RFID is not actually a new technology, but it is being applied in new ways, spurred by technological advances and decreased costs. Once used during World War II to identify friendly aircraft, RFID is now being used in a variety of public and private sector settings, from hospitals to the highway.

In RFID systems, an item is tagged with a tiny silicon chip and an antenna; the chip plus antenna (together called a "tag") can then be scanned by mobile or stationary readers, using radio waves (the "RF"). The chip can be encoded with a unique identifier, allowing tagged items to be individually identified by a reader (the "ID"). Thus, for example, in a clothing store, each particular suit jacket, including its style, color, and size, can be identified electronically. In a pharmacy, a druggist can fill a prescription from a bottle bearing an RFID-chipped label confirming the authenticity of its contents. On the highway, cars with RFID tags on their windshields can move swiftly through highway tollbooths, saving time and reducing traffic congestion. At home, pets can be implanted with chips so that lost animals can be identified and returned to their owners more readily. In each case, a reader must scan the tag for the data it contains and then send that information to a database, which interprets the data stored on the tag. The tag, reader, and database are the key components of an RFID system.

RFID proponents believe that the ability of these systems to deliver precise and accurate data about tagged items will improve efficiency and bring other benefits to businesses and consumers alike. [2] One major retailer has already announced a mandate for its largest suppliers to begin tagging cases and pallets of merchandise. [3] Other companies in the U.S. and abroad reportedly are exploring similar directives.[4] Spending on RFID implementation in the retail supply chain alone has been estimated

L. Qi (Ed.): FCC 2009, CCIS 34, pp. 57–63, 2009.

at $91.5 million last year – an amount expected by some to exceed $1 billion by 2007. [5] Outside the retail sector, libraries across the country reportedly are already tagging books, [6] and the FDA has announced that it is actively encouraging pharmaceutical manufacturers to use RFID to fight drug counterfeiting. [7]

While these developments may offer significant benefits for industry and consumers, some applications have raised privacy concerns. The capacity to encode unique identifiers at the individual item level may have revolutionized thinking about inventory management, but it has also raised fears that this technology might be used to track individual products out of the store and into consumers' homes or otherwise monitor individual consumer behaviors. As with the Internet and other data-intensive technologies, these concerns must be addressed so that they do not hinder the development and deployment of RFID in the marketplace.

On June 21, 2004, the Federal Trade Commission explored these issues at a public workshop entitled "Radio Frequency Identification: Applications and Implications for Consumers." The Workshop brought together technologists, RFID proponents, privacy advocates, and policymakers to discuss the range of applications for RFID, the future of this technology, and its implications for consumers. [8] This staff report will summarize the discussion at the Workshop and offer some preliminary recommendations for addressing the privacy concerns raised by some participants. [9]

2   Consumer Survey Results

In addition to addressing how RFID works and can be used, Workshop participants discussed the implications of this technology for consumers. The Workshop included a presentation about the results of a study concerning consumer perceptions of RFID. According to a survey of more than 1,000 U.S. consumers conducted in October 2003, the majority of those polled were unfamiliar with RFID. [10] Over three-quarters of the sample – 77% – had not heard of RFID. Confirming the general lack of knowledge about this technology, nearly half of the group aware of RFID had "no opinion" about it. [11]

Consumers who did have an opinion about RFID expressed a variety of views about whether or how this technology would affect them. When asked to rank a set of potential benefits of RFID, 70% identified recovery of stolen goods and improved food and drug safety high on the list. The majority (66%) also placed cost savings toward the top of the list of benefits, although some consumers were also concerned that RFID use would instead raise prices. Consumers placed access to marketing-related benefits, like in-aisle companion product suggestions, at the bottom of the list. [12]

The most significant concerns expressed by consumers familiar with RFID related to privacy. In response to both open-ended and prompted questions (with pre-programmed answers to select or rank), privacy emerged as a leading concern. For example, approximately two-thirds of consumers identified as top concerns the likelihood that RFID would lead to their data being shared with third parties, more targeted marketing, or the tracking of consumers via their product purchases. These findings are consistent with the views of consumers who submitted comments to the Commission about RFID. [13] Many of those consumers voiced strong opposition to having RFID devices track their purchases and movements, with some citing as reasons for their position the potential for increased marketing or government surveillance.

A more recent consumer survey, conducted by two market research companies, revealed similar results. [14] Of more than 8,000 individuals surveyed, fewer than 30% of consumers were aware of RFID technology. Further, nearly two-thirds of all consumers surveyed expressed concerns about potential privacy abuses. [15] Their primary concerns centered around RFID's ability to facilitate the tracking of consumers' shopping habits and the sharing of that information among businesses and with the government. Like the study discussed at the Workshop, this survey also demonstrated that the great majority of consumers remain unfamiliar with RFID. Additionally, consumers who fell into the "RFID non-aware" category were more likely to be concerned about RFID's implications for their privacy than were consumers who were familiar with the technology. [16]

3 RFID and Consumer Privacy

Against the backdrop of survey data about consumer perceptions of RFID, Workshop participants discussed the nature of privacy concerns associated with some of the emerging uses of this technology. While there was some consensus among Workshop panelists that certain uses of RFID today – such as in the supply chain – may not jeopardize consumer privacy, [17] a number of consumer advocates voiced concerns about the potential impact of other RFID applications on consumer privacy. [18] According to these panelists, such concerns may arise when consumers interact more directly with tags and readers, particularly in the context of item-level tagging of retail goods.

The concerns articulated by these Workshop participants implicated issues specific to RFID technology as well as more general privacy issues. Some panelists discussed how RFID's unique or distinguishing characteristics may jeopardize consumer privacy. First, these participants cited as a key concern the "bit capacity" of Electronic Product Codes ("EPCs"), which enable the assignment of individual identifiers to tagged objects. [19] They argued that RFID's potential to identify items uniquely facilitates the collection of more – and more accurate – data. [20]

Other features of RFID that troubled these Workshop participants related to the devices' physical attributes. According to these panelists, the small size of tags and readers enables them to be hidden from consumers. [21] One Workshop participant explained that if a long read-range is not required, scanners can be smaller than a U.S. quarter. [22] Another Workshop participant focused on the privacy implications of the small size of RFID chips and how their shrinking dimensions facilitate their unobtrusive integration into consumer goods. [23] Some panelists highlighted the ability of RFID devices to communicate with one another through materials, without line-of-sight, and at some distance. [24] These technical characteristics, they argued, distinguish RFID from bar codes, which in order to be read must be visible on the outside of product packaging. [25] Some commenters pointed to these characteristics as evidence that RFID would allow surreptitious scanning to gather information about the products consumers wear or carry. [26] Participants also raised concerns about what they termed the "promiscuity" of RFID devices [27] – when tags can be accessed by multiple readers, it raises the specter of unfettered third-party surveillance. [28]

The combination of these factors, some Workshop participants asserted, will weaken consumers' ability to protect themselves from in-store tracking and surreptitious monitoring in public places, at work, and even at home. Certain panelists were especially concerned about RFID's potential to facilitate consumer tracking, by linking personally identifiable information in databases to the unique numbers on RFID tags. One participant described how a retailer could associate purchaser data with the uniquely identified product an individual buys. [29] According to the participant, this practice would be similar to what retailers can currently do with customer loyalty cards or credit cards. [30] However, a number of Workshop panelists maintained that RFID poses greater threats to consumer privacy because of the enhanced level of information it provides about each tagged item. They suggested that a tagged item carried by a consumer out of a store could be read covertly, and what it communicates could be more than just the presence of a particular item. If linked to purchase data, the identification of a particular product could also identify the individual who bought that item. [31]

Privacy advocates at the Workshop cited this latter potential as the basis for another privacy concern: consumer profiling. By tracking the movement of tagged goods and the people associated with them, more information can be gathered about the activities of those individuals. [32] That in turn could make it easier to predict the behavior of others who buy the same items, even without monitoring them. [33] Another concern raised at the Workshop relates to RFID's facilitation of "customer relationship management," whereby retailers customize pricing and service based on a consumer's potential profitability. [34] According to one Workshop participant, if RFID tags were embedded in customer loyalty cards, consumers could be identified as soon as they entered the store that issued the card. This could result in targeted marketing or customer service directed at the consumer, depending on his or her purchase history or other information linked to the loyalty card. [35]

Many of these fears are associated with item-level tagging. However, a number of Workshop participants representing retailers and other RFID users maintained that RFID was not being used in this manner on a widespread basis now and would not be in the near future. [36] Some panelists also argued that no real business case exists for the adoption of a network accessible to multiple users that contains information about these users' RFID-tagged goods. As one participant stated, "Wal-Mart doesn't want its competitors to read tags that are from Wal-Mart stores. Wal-Mart probably also doesn't want its suppliers to read information about its other suppliers. They want to control that information for competitive reasons." [37]

Even if and when item-level tagging is adopted on a widespread basis, some Workshop participants disputed that consumer privacy would be jeopardized as a result. They asserted that RFID's technological limitations will prevent its surreptitious use. For example, reading an RFID tag from a significant distance currently requires use of a sizable antenna ("about the size of a plate," according to one panelist) and significant energy. [38] Another argument advanced at the Workshop focused on how cost factors will continue to slow retailers' adoption of RFID, limiting the sophistication and proliferation of readers on the store floor. [39] One participant representing a retail chain argued that no business case exists for linking data collected via RFID to personally identifiable information about consumers, so fears about this potential are misplaced. [40] In addition, many panelists addressed the emergence of a variety of technological protocols and products, such as encryption and blocker tags, that may offer a means to address privacy concerns associated with these devices. [41]

4 Database Security Issues

Regardless of panelists' views regarding the existence or extent of many privacy concerns, many participants agreed that database security was an important issue, especially in the manufacturing and retail environment. Rather than concentrating on how information may be collected via RFID devices, these participants discussed security issues that focus on how such data is stored and whether it is adequately protected. [42] According to one panelist, database security is a critical aspect of any analysis of privacy concerns associated with RFID use, because the tags themselves may contain only limited data, such as a number in the case of EPC chips. [43] The panelist further explained that the information associated with that number will be stored on a server of the product manufacturer or other authorized user, where it can be linked to additional data. [44]

References

1. Jo Best, Cheat sheet: RFID, silicon.com, April 16 (2004)
2. See, e.g., Allen, Texas Instruments, at 67-75. Unless otherwise noted, footnote citations are to the transcript of or comments submitted in connection with the Workshop. The Workshop transcript, specific panelist presentations, and comments are http://www.ftc.gov/bcp/workshops/rfid/index.htm, Footnotes that cite to specific panelists cite to his or her last name, affiliation, and the page(s) where the referenced statement can be found in the transcript or appropriate comment. A complete list of Workshop participants can be found in Appendix A.
3. See Press Release, Wal-Mart, Wal-Mart Begins Roll-Out of Electronic Product Codes in Dallas/ Fort Worth Area (April 30, 2004), http://www.walmartstores.com
4. See Jacqueline Emigh, More Retailers Mull RFID Mandates, eweek, August 19 (2004)
5. See Boone, IDC, at 226
6. Tien, Electronic Frontier Foundation ("EFF"), at 97
7. Press Release, FDA, FDA Announces New Initiative to Protect the U.S. Drug Supply Chain Through the Use of Radiofrequency Identification Technology (November 15, 2004), http://www.fda.gov
8. Over the past decade, the FTC has frequently held workshops to explore emerging issues raised by new technologies. The Commission's earliest workshops on Internet-related issues were held in 1995, http://www.ftc.gov/opp/global/trnscrpt.htm More recently, the Commissions workshops have focused on such issues as wireless technologies, information security, spam, spyware, and peer-to-peer networks. For more information about each of these forums and the Commission's privacy agenda, http://www.ftc.gov/privacy/privacyinitiatives/promises_wkshp.html
9. This report was prepared by Julie Brof and Tracy Thorleifson of the FTC staff. It does not necessarily reflect the views of the Commission or any individual Commissioner

10. The survey discussed at the Workshop, "RFID and Consumers: Understanding Their Mindset," was commissioned by Capgemini and the National Retail Federation, Unless otherwise noted, references to survey results concern this study,
    `http://www.nrf.com/download/NewRFID_NRF.pdf`

11. The unfamiliarity with the concept of RFID extended even to those consumers who might be using it. For example, eight out of ten survey respondents did not know that the ExxonMobil Speedpass and the E-ZPass employ RFID technology

12. Other pre-programmed benefits consumers were asked to rank included improved security of prescription drugs, faster and more accurate product recalls, improved price accuracy, faster checkout times, and reduced out-of-stocks

13. Consumer comments are,
    `http://www.ftc.gov/bcp/workshops/rfid/index.htm`

14. BIGresearch and Artafact LLC released the results of their joint study, RFID Consumer Buzz (October 2004), `http://www.bigresearch.com`

15. The RFID Consumer Buzz survey broke respondents into two categories: "RFID-aware" and "RFID non-aware" consumers. Interviewers described how RFID works to the latter group prior to asking them about perceived benefits and concerns associated with the technology

16. According to an Artafact spokesperson, "The people [who] were aware of RFID were more practical about balancing the positives and the negatives. Those who were not aware seemed to be surprised to learn about the technology, and they gravitated more toward the potential negative impacts of RFID. We concluded from that that it's better to inform people about the positive applications than to wait for them to discover the technology on their own." Mark Roberti, Consumer Awareness of RFID Grows, RFID Journal, October 22 (2004)

17. See Albrecht, CASPIAN, at 228-29 (discussing a hypothetical manufacturer's internal RFID program); Stafford, Marks & Spencer, at 264

18. Privacy advocates at the Workshop collectively called for RFID to be subjected to a neutral, comprehensive technology assessment. For a discussion of this and other requests by these advocates, see infra Section V.B

19. Givens, Privacy Rights Clearinghouse ("PRC") at 145; CASPIAN, PRC, et al., Position Statement on the Use of RFID on Consumer Products ("Privacy Position Statement"), Comment, at 2. This capability distinguishes EPCs from typical bar codes, which use generic identifiers

20. Id. For example, using RFID devices to track people (such as students) or their automobiles (as with E-ZPasses) could generate precise and personally identifiable data about their movements, raising privacy concerns. As one ninth grader in the Texas school system that reportedly plans to use RFID explained, "Something about the school wanting to know the exact place and time [of my whereabouts] makes me feel like an animal." Matt Richtel, In Texas, 28,000 Students Test an Electronic Eye, N.Y. Times, November 17 (2004)

21. See, e.g., Givens, PRC, at 145; Parkinson, Capgemini, at 213-14

22. Fishkin, Intel, at 76. He also stated that he had recently seen a reader the size of a U.S. dime, but explained that the scanning range for such small readers would be less than an inch. These readers would be appropriate for hospital use, for example; they can be integrated into medical equipment "to make sure that when you stick RFID tagged object A into . . . RFID reader receptacle B, you did the right thing." Id. at 78

23. See Albrecht, CASPIAN, at 235

24. See id. at 232; Givens, PRC, at 145

25. Parkinson, Capgemini, at 213-14

26. Privacy Position Statement at 2

27. See Tien, EFF, at 96; Mulligan, Samuelson Clinic, at 156
28. See, e.g., Juels, RSA Labs, at 311. This access depends on whether RFID devices are interoperable. Currently, "existing RFID systems use proprietary technology, which means that if company A puts an RFID tag on a product, it can't be read by company B unless they both use the same vendor." See Frequently Asked Questions, supra note 15. This limitation may change, however, with the recent announcement by EPCglobal approving the second-generation EPC specification. The so-called Gen 2 standard will allow for global interoperability of EPC systems, although it is unclear when Gen 2-compliant products will be introduced or whether the initial round of these products will be interoperable. See Jonathan Collins, What's Next for Gen 2?, RFID Journal, December 27 (2004)
29. Albrecht, CASPIAN, at 231
30. See id.; see also Atkinson, Progressive Policy Institute ("PPI"), at 291 (explaining that "[e]very time I use a credit card, I link product purchases to [personally identifiable information]. We've been doing it for 30 years"). Cf. Constance L. Hays, What Wal-Mart Knows About Customers' Habits, N.Y. Times, Nov. 14, 2004 (describing the tremendous amount of customer data Wal-Mart maintains, but claims it currently does not use to track individuals' purchases)
31. Albrecht, CASPIAN, at 231
32. See Privacy Position Statement at 2
33. Mulligan, Samuelson Clinic, at 157 (asserting that such profiling may even be more "troublesome" where the tagged item is a book or other type of information good)
34. Albrecht, CASPIAN, at 239
35. Id. at 239-40
36. E.g., Hughes, Procter & Gamble ("P&G"), at 173 (asserting that P&G is "not doing item-level testing"); Wood, RILA, at 60 ("We see a little bit of testing going on in the item level. We do not see widespread item adoption . . . or use for at least ten years")
37. Boone, IDC, at 222-23; see also Maxwell, International Public Policy Advisory Councils, Auto-ID Labs and EPCglobal, at 257-58 (noting the alignment between the interests of retailers and consumers in protecting data generated by RFID systems)
38. Waldo, Sun Microsystems ("Sun"), at 248 (explaining that if a reader is trying to "read[] from very far away, you're not only going to get your stuff read, you're going to get a tan," because of the powerful amount of energy required)
39. Id. at 249-50
40. Stafford, Marks & Spencer, at 313 (advising the public to "[b]e clear, there isn't a business case about gathering customer information through RFID")
41. A number of technological proposals to resolve privacy issues are addressed in Section V.C., infra
42. As one commentator has observed: "RFID is one data-gathering technology among many. And people should be worried about how data related to them gets handled and regulated. That's much more important than how it's gathered, because it will be gathered one way or another." Thomas Claburn, RFID Is Not The Real Issue, InformationWeek, September 13 (2004)
43. Hutchinson, EPCglobal US, at 26. However, outside of the EPC and supply chain context, privacy concerns center on the security of communication between tags and readers. For example, the proposed biometric passports, see supra note 70, have been criticized as having inadequate privacy protections. This lack of security could enable the rogue scanning of biometric data embedded on RFID chips in passports. Under these circumstances, access to a database would not be necessary to interpret that information
44. Hutchinson, EPCglobal US, at 38; see also The EPCglobal Network §7.1, supra note 11

RFID Application of Addressing Consumer Privacy Challenges

Xin Chen

Electronic Commerce Department
Guangdong University of Foreign Studies

Abstract. This paper discussed the applications and implications for consumers of RFID, and focused on addressing consumer privacy challenges, including three fields: existing industry practices and standards, regulatory approaches, technological approaches.

Keywords: RFID, consumer perception, consumer privacy, industry practice, RFID implication, industry standard.

1 Introduction

Radio frequency identification technology, known as RFID, has been described as "tech's official Next Big Thing." [1] RFID is not actually a new technology, but it is being applied in new ways, spurred by technological advances and decreased costs. Once used during World War II to identify friendly aircraft, RFID is now being used in a variety of public and private sector settings, from hospitals to the highway.

In RFID systems, an item is tagged with a tiny silicon chip and an antenna; the chip plus antenna (together called a "tag") can then be scanned by mobile or stationary readers, using radio waves (the "RF"). The chip can be encoded with a unique identifier, allowing tagged items to be individually identified by a reader (the "ID"). Thus, for example, in a clothing store, each particular suit jacket, including its style, color, and size, can be identified electronically. In a pharmacy, a druggist can fill a prescription from a bottle bearing an RFID-chipped label confirming the authenticity of its contents. On the highway, cars with RFID tags on their windshields can move swiftly through highway tollbooths, saving time and reducing traffic congestion. At home, pets can be implanted with chips so that lost animals can be identified and returned to their owners more readily. In each case, a reader must scan the tag for the data it contains and then send that information to a database, which interprets the data stored on the tag. The tag, reader, and database are the key components of an RFID system.

RFID proponents believe that the ability of these systems to deliver precise and accurate data about tagged items will improve efficiency and bring other benefits to businesses and consumers alike. [2] One major retailer has already announced a mandate for its largest suppliers to begin tagging cases and pallets of merchandise. [3] Other companies in the U.S. and abroad reportedly are exploring similar directives.[4] Spending on RFID implementation in the retail supply chain alone has been estimated

L. Qi (Ed.): FCC 2009, CCIS 34, pp. 64–71, 2009.
© Springer-Verlag Berlin Heidelberg 2009

at \$91.5 million last year – an amount expected by some to exceed \$1 billion by 2007. [5] Outside the retail sector, libraries across the country reportedly are already tagging books, [6] and the FDA has announced that it is actively encouraging pharmaceutical manufacturers to use RFID to fight drug counterfeiting. [7]

While these developments may offer significant benefits for industry and consumers, some applications have raised privacy concerns. The capacity to encode unique identifiers at the individual item level may have revolutionized thinking about inventory management, but it has also raised fears that this technology might be used to track individual products out of the store and into consumers' homes or otherwise monitor individual consumer behaviors. As with the Internet and other data-intensive technologies, these concerns must be addressed so that they do not hinder the development and deployment of RFID in the marketplace.

On June 21, 2004, the Federal Trade Commission explored these issues at a public workshop entitled "Radio Frequency Identification: Applications and Implications for Consumers." The Workshop brought together technologists, RFID proponents, privacy advocates, and policymakers to discuss the range of applications for RFID, the future of this technology, and its implications for consumers. [8] This staff report will summarize the discussion at the Workshop and offer some preliminary recommendations for addressing the privacy concerns raised by some participants. [9]

2 Addressing Consumer Privacy Challenges: Best Practices and Principles

The Workshop concluded with a panel examining various approaches to addressing the privacy issues raised by RFID technology. As participants noted, these challenges are not insubstantial, in light of RFID's evolving nature and the uncertainty as to how various existing and potential uses may affect consumers. [10] Industry guidelines, legislative developments, and technological solutions designed to address privacy and security concerns were among the options discussed and debated. [11]

3 Existing Industry Practices and Standards

Panelists voiced a range of opinions as to what approach or combination of measures would be most effective at meeting the challenges posed by RFID. Many participants agreed that, at a minimum, businesses deploying RFID should take steps to protect consumer privacy. One self-regulatory model already in place is EPCglobal's "Guidelines on EPC for Consumer Products" ("EPCglobal Guidelines"). [12] According to a Workshop panelist, the Guidelines were developed with input from privacy experts and apply to all EPCglobal members. [13] The Guidelines call for consumer notice, choice, and education, and also instruct companies to implement certain security practices. [14]

The first element, consumer notice, requires that companies using EPC tags "on products or their packaging" include an EPC label or identifier indicating the tags' presence. According to a Workshop participant, EPCglobal has developed a template label that companies can use to inform consumers of the presence of EPC tags. [15]

Displaying a copy of the model identifier, the speaker explained that the template label discloses that a particular product's packaging contains an EPC tag, which may be discarded by a consumer after purchase. [16]

The Guidelines' second requirement, consumer choice, concerns the right of consumers to "discard or remove or in the future disable EPC tags from the products they acquire." The Guidelines explain, "for most products, the EPC tags [would] be part of disposable packaging or would be otherwise discardable."

Consumer education is the third prong of the Guidelines, which provides that consumers should have "the opportunity easily to obtain accurate information about EPC tags and their applications." The Guidelines task companies using RFID with "familiariz[ing] consumers with the EPC logo and . . . help[ing] consumers understand the technology and its benefits."

Finally, the Guidelines call for companies to ensure that any "data which is associated with EPC is collected, used, maintained, stored and protected" consistent with "any applicable laws." [17] They further instruct companies to publish "information on their policies regarding the retention, use and protection of any personally identifiable information associated with EPC use." [18] To help ensure compliance with these Guidelines, EPCglobal will provide a forum to redress complaints about failures to comply with the Guidelines. [19]

According to Workshop participants, some companies have already endorsed or implemented these practices as they test RFID systems. [20] Panelists discussed how Wal-Mart, which is currently operating a pilot program with EPC tags in a limited number of stores, has posted a "shelf-talker" disclosing the presence of EPC tags. [21] According to this tear-off notice reportedly made available to Wal-Mart shoppers, only cases of certain products or specific large items, like computer printers, include EPC tags and bear the EPCglobal logo. The disclosure further explains that the technology "will not be used to collect additional data about [Wal-Mart's] customers or their purchases." [22] Consistent with that commitment, Wal-Mart has stated that it has no readers on store floors, so consumers should not be exposed to any communications between tags and readers. [23]

Workshop panelists also discussed the privacy guidelines adopted by Procter & Gamble ("P&G"), another company involved in RFID trials both in the U.S. and abroad. [24] In addition to its global privacy policy, P&G has developed an RFID-specific position statement calling for "clear and accurate" notice to consumers about the use of RFID tags and consumer choice with respect to disabling or discarding EPC tags "without cost or penalty" as well as disclosure of whether any personally identifiable information about them is "electronically linked to the EPC number on products they buy." [25] Further, P&G stated at the Workshop that it will not participate in item-level tagging with any retailer or partner that would link personal information about consumers using RFID, "other than what they do for bar codes today." [26]

The Workshop also explored a case study of retail item-level RFID tagging in action. A representative of Marks & Spencer, one of the United Kingdom's largest retailers, described his company's in-store RFID pilot program, tagging menswear in select stores. Marks & Spencer's use of "Intelligent Labels," as it has designated its RFID program, is for stock control – a continuation of the supply chain management process. [27] With this limited purpose in mind, the Marks & Spencer official explained how his company incorporated privacy-protective measures into its Intelligent Label program. [28] According to the company, these considerations are reflected in the mechanics of its RFID deployment, which apply the notice, choice, and education principles advocated by EPCglobal and others. The hang-tags bearing the Intelligent Labels are large, visibly placed, and easily removable. [29] No data is written to the tags, and they are not scanned at the cash register, so there is no possibility of connecting the unique identifier on the tag to the purchaser. Indeed, the tags are not scanned at all during store hours, but rather are read for inventory control purposes when customers are not present. Finally, all of these practices are described in a leaflet that Marks & Spencer makes available to shoppers. [30]

Some Workshop participants stated that these industry initiatives represent effective ways to address consumer privacy concerns, but others maintained they are necessary, but insufficient, steps. Privacy advocates at the Workshop called for merchants to take additional precautions when using RFID tags on consumer items, including fully transparent use of RFID. [31] With respect to company statements disclosing the presence of in-store RFID devices, privacy advocates argued that such disclosures should be clear and conspicuous. [32] One participant stated that disclosures should contain specific information: that a product bears an RFID tag; that the tag can communicate, both pre- and post-purchase, the unique identification of the object to which it is attached; and the "basic technical characteristics of the RFID technology." [33] Another Workshop panelist urged that any such disclosures be "simple and factual," avoiding "happy face technology" that is essentially "marketing hype." [34] This panelist felt that by disclosing its RFID practices in a straightforward manner, a company will convey information in a way that consumers are more likely both to understand and trust. [35]

4 Regulatory Approaches

Privacy advocates at the Workshop also called for RFID to be subjected to a "formal technology assessment," conducted by a neutral body and involving all relevant stakeholders, including consumers. [36] This process could examine issues such as whether RFID can be deployed in less privacy-intrusive ways. [37] Until such an assessment takes place, these participants requested that RFID users voluntarily refrain from the item-level tagging of consumer goods. [38]

In addition, some Workshop panelists argued that government action to regulate RFID is necessary. [39] One panelist urged the Commission to implement a set of guidelines for manufacturers and retailers using RFID on consumer products [40]. According to this participant, other international standards that already apply to the use of RFID in this context support the need for comparable regulation in the U.S. Certain Workshop participants also endorsed specific restrictions on RFID use, including prohibitions on tracking consumers without their "informed and written consent" and on any application that would "eliminate or reduce [individuals'] anonymity." In addition, these participants called for "security and integrity" in using RFID, including the use of third-party auditors that could publicly verify the security of a given system. Similarly, one panelist argued that consumers should be able to file with designated government and industry officials complaints regarding RFID users' non-compliance with stated privacy and security practices.

Other Workshop panelists disputed the need for regulation at this point, contending that legislation could unreasonably limit the benefits of RFID and would be ill-suited to regulate such a rapidly evolving technology. According to one participant, the FTC's existing enforcement authority is adequate to address abuses of RFID technology, citing the Commission's ability to challenge misrepresentations by a company about its privacy and/or security practices. Therefore, this participant concluded that technology-specific privacy legislation is unnecessary at this juncture.

5 Technological Approaches

Workshop participants also debated the merits of various technological approaches to addressing consumer privacy concerns. In addition to the database security measures discussed above, these proposals include protocols protecting communications between readers and tags, such as encryption or passwords. These methods would restrict access to the tag itself by requiring some measure of authentication on behalf of the scanning device. Even if a reader could get a tag to "talk," encryption would prevent the reader from understanding the message. One commenter strongly urged that "[a]uthorization, authentication, and encryption for RFID . . . be developed and applied on a routine basis to ensure trustworthiness of RFID radio communications."

A related technical approach discussed at the Workshop involves "blocker tags," which prevent RFID tags from communicating accurately with a reader. With blocker tags, which are tags literally placed over or in close proximity to the RFID tag, consumers would be able to control which items they want blocked and when. This would allow consumers to benefit from any post-purchase applications of RFID that may develop, such as "smart" refrigerators.

Finally, Workshop participants discussed the "kill switch," a feature that permanently disables at the point-of-sale an RFID tag affixed to a consumer item. Such a function has been proposed as a way to provide "choice" to consumers in the context of item-level tagging. However, a number of Workshop participants disputed the effectiveness of this approach. Some privacy advocates found the options of killing or blocking tags both lacking because of the burden they could impose on consumers. For example, setting up a "kill kiosk," as one retailer abroad reportedly had done, contemplates that consumers first purchase an item and then deactivate an attached RFID tag. Some panelists argued that this process was cumbersome by requiring that consumers engage in two separate transactions when making a purchase. They argued that this process may dissuade consumers from exercising the option to disable tags on purchased items.

Another critique of these technological "fixes" raised at the Workshop focused on their potential to reward – and thus foster – RFID use. Some participants argued that if the only method of protecting consumer privacy was to disable tags at purchase, any post-purchase benefits would accrue only to those who kept their RFID tags active. As a result, these panelists suggested, consumers would be more likely to keep tags enabled. Conversely, another participant argued that giving shoppers this option could drive up costs for all consumers, even those who do not object to the presence of active RFID tags on items they purchase. According to this speaker, merchants would likely be reluctant to charge higher prices for consumers who elect to deactivate RFID tags prior to purchase. Finally, as one commenter pointed out, the effectiveness of tag-killing technology depends on whether the presence of RFID is effectively disclosed: no consumer will seek to deactivate a tag of which she or he is unaware.

References

1. Jo Best, Cheat sheet: RFID, silicon.com, April 16 (2004)
2. See, e.g., Allen, Texas Instruments, at 67-75. Unless otherwise noted, footnote citations are to the transcript of or comments submitted in connection with the Workshop. The Workshop transcript, specific panelist presentations, and comments are, http://www.ftc.gov/bcp/workshops/rfid/index.htm, Footnotes that cite to specific panelists cite to his or her last name, affiliation, and the page(s) where the referenced statement can be found in the transcript or appropriate comment. A complete list of Workshop participants can be found in Appendix A
3. See Press Release, Wal-Mart, Wal-Mart Begins Roll-Out of Electronic Product Codes in Dallas/ Fort Worth Area (April 30, 2004), http://www.walmartstores.com
4. See Jacqueline Emigh, More Retailers Mull RFID Mandates, eweek, August 19 (2004)
5. See Boone, IDC, at 226
6. Tien, Electronic Frontier Foundation (EFF), at 97
7. Press Release, FDA, FDA Announces New Initiative to Protect the U.S. Drug Supply Chain Through the Use of Radiofrequency Identification Technology (November 15, 2004), http://www.fda.gov
8. Over the past decade, the FTC has frequently held workshops to explore emerging issues raised by new technologies. The Commission's earliest workshops on Internet-related issues were held in 1995, http://www.ftc.gov/opp/global/trnscrpt.htm More recently, the Commissions workshops have focused on such issues as wireless technologies, information security, spam, spyware, and peer-to-peer networks. For more information about each of these forums and the Commission's privacy agenda, http://www.ftc.gov/privacy/privacyinitiatives/promises_wkshp.html
9. This report was prepared by Julie Brof and Tracy Thorleifson of the FTC staff. It does not necessarily reflect the views of the Commission or any individual Commissioner
10. See Maxwell, International Public Policy Advisory Councils, Auto-ID Labs and EPCglobal, at 260; Bruening, CDT, at 285-86
11. This panel focused largely on the privacy challenges facing private industry. The costs and benefits of RFID deployment by government, including current and proposed uses by the Department of Homeland Security, raise issues not addressed in depth at the Workshop or in comments submitted to the Commission
12. The Guidelines are posted at http://www.epcglobalinc.org/consumer/, under the public policy section of the EPCglobal Inc. Web site
13. Board, EPCglobal, at 271-72. EPCglobal currently has over 400 members
14. Id. at 272
15. Board, EPCglobal, at 272 and presentation slide. More information about the template label is available on the EPCglobal Web site, along with explanatory information for consumers about RFID technology, http://www.epcglobalinc.org/consumer/

16. Board, EPCglobal, at 272 and presentation slide
17. The significance of this provision and the protection it provides consumers obviously depends on the existence and rigor of applicable privacy laws or regulations
18. All quoted items are excerpts from the EPCglobal Guidelines, supra note 127
19. The Guidelines provide that "EPCglobal will monitor the proper use of these Guidelines," but details concerning enforcement or accountability mechanisms have not yet been announced
20. Board, EPCglobal, at 272; see also GMA, Comment, at 5 (stating that "[i]n January 2004, the GMA Board of Directors formally adopted privacy guidelines established by EPCglobal"). In addition, some industry members have endorsed self-regulatory principles similar to those embodied by the EPCglobal Guidelines. See, e.g., NRF, Comment; Microsoft, Comment, at 14-15. Another example is the 1,500-member Food Marketing Institute, which added RFID-specific provisions to its "Policy Statement on Consumer Privacy" in May 2004. In addition to calling for notice, choice, access, and security of consumer data, the FMI statement advocates legislation prohibiting the unauthorized access, interception, or receipt of an "EPC signal" (i.e., barring the rogue scanning of RFID tags), http://fmi.org/consumer/privpolicy.htm, Commission staff will continue to monitor compliance with the EPCglobal Guidelines and other industry self-regulatory standards
21. Board, EPCglobal, at 272; Langford, Wal-Mart, at 65-66. Wal-Mart's RFID announcement calls for its top 100 suppliers to place RFID tags on cases and pallets shipped to a regional distribution center in Texas. Readers will be installed at the dock doors of seven stores in the Dallas-Ft. Worth metropolitan area in order to track tagged cases or packages of goods. No readers are placed on store floors. Other company stores in the distribution center's region, which covers North Texas and parts of Oklahoma, may receive RFID-tagged cases and pallets, but no readers will be installed there as part of the pilot program. For more information about Wal-Mart's RFID plans, see the "Supplier Information" section of http://www.walmartstores.com
22. Wal-Mart's shelf-talker
23. See Langford, Wal-Mart, at 66
24. A list of current P&G trials using EPC technology, http://www.pg.com/company/our_commitment/privacy_policy/index.jhtml
25. P&G, Comment, http://www.pg.com/company/our_commitment/privacy_policy/index.jhtml
26. Hughes, P&G, at 172. However, some panelists asserted that retailers currently use bar code data to link customer identity to their purchases. Albrecht, CASPIAN, at 231; see also Atkinson, PPI, at 291
27. See Stafford, Marks & Spencer, at 265
28. Prior to implementing their program, company officials met with key privacy organizations in an effort to accommodate their concerns. See Marks & Spencer, Corporate Social Responsibility, Issue Two: Responsible Use of Technology, http://www2.marksandspencer.com/thecompany/
29. Consumers may detach the tags themselves post-purchase or may request that a cashier do so. The tags are not required for return, so may be discarded by consumers without further consideration. For a picture of what an Intelligent Label looks like, see Figure B, supra
30. Stafford, Marks & Spencer, at 266-68

31. Specifically, privacy advocates called for RFID users to make public their policies and practices involving the use and maintenance of RFID systems. Further there should be no "secret databases" or "tag-reading in secret." Privacy Position Statement at 3
32. See id.; Laurant, Electronic Privacy Information Center ("EPIC"), at 278
33. Laurant, EPIC, at 278
34. Givens, PRC, at 211
35. See id
36. The Privacy Position Statement, which forty-five consumer and privacy organizations have signed, endorses the need for such an assessment. Workshop participants representing some of these groups reiterated this recommendation. See Givens, PRC, at 150-51, Laurant, EPIC, at 279; Bruening, CDT, at 282–83
37. Givens, PRC, at 150-51. For example, RFID tags could be used effectively for recycling purposes without containing unique identifiers; instead, the chips could be encoded to communicate only the presence of certain toxins that recyclable materials may contain. A comment from a consumer made an analogous suggestion, recommending that tollway transponders (such as E-ZPass), be sold like phone cards in stores, where they could be purchased with cash and used anonymously. See Greenberg, Comment
38. Privacy Position Statement at 3-4
39. See Tien, EFF, at 100-01; Laurant, EPIC, at 279. In addition, although Workshop participants did not discuss state legislation, a number of bills have been introduced across the country, including California, Maryland, Massachusetts, and Utah. See Claire Swedberg, States Move on RFID Privacy Issue, RFID Journal, Apr. 30, 2004; Thomas Claburn, Privacy Fears Create Roadblocks for RFID, InformationWeek, Mar. 8, 2004. These proposals, which were not enacted, would have required notice and other measures in connection with a retailer's use of RFID on individual consumer items. Some observers believe that these or similar proposals are likely to resurface in next year's legislative sessions
40. Laurant, EPIC, at 279; see also EPIC, Comment, at 14

New Interleaving and Forward Error Correction Strategies for Streaming

Mahila Dadfarnia and Majid Noorhoseini

Amirkabir University of technology
Tehran, Iran
m-dadfarnia@aut.ac.ir, majinh@aut.ac.ir

Abstract. If the frame size of a multimedia encoder is small, Internet Protocol streaming applications need to pack many encoded media frames in each Real-time Transport Protocol (RTP) packet to avoid unnecessary header overhead. Forward Error Correction (FEC) can be used in order to minimize the probability of packet loss in bursty loss environments such as network congestions. FEC is one of the techniques used to tackle loss problem by adding redundant data to the flow and helping receivers to recover missed data. In this paper, we present an approach for interleaving packets optimized for different situation of networks. Considering time constraints in multimedia streaming, we change the number of redundant FEC packets according to the condition of network, so that the experienced frame loss rate does not vary greatly under different packet loss rates. We present the results of simulation using NS2 simulator.

Keywords: component; FEC; MDS; RS; MILD; MBL streaming, interleaving, multimedia.

1   Introduction

In recent years there has been an increasing trend towards personal computers and workstations becoming portable. Desire to maintain connectivity of these portable computers to the existing installation of Local Area Networks (LANs), Metropolitan Area Networks (MANs), and Wide Area Networks (WANs), in a manner analogous to present day computers, is fueling an already growing interest in wireless networks. Wireless networks will be needed to provide voice, video and data communication capability between mobile terminals and also to permit such terminals to have access to wire line networks. However, before wireless networks can be employed for packet voice, video, data, and other applications, it is important that appropriate communication protocols suited for the wireless environment are developed. Of specific interest are "physical", "link" and "network" layer protocols that take into account the characteristics of the underlying communication channel.

Wireless channels provide error rates that are typically around 10–2. Such high error rates result due to multipath fading which characterize mobile radio channels. However, many applications such as video and data transmissions require that the error rates be

L. Qi (Ed.): FCC 2009, CCIS 34, pp. 72–81, 2009.

significantly smaller. To increase the apparent quality of a communication channel there exist the following two distinct approaches:

1) Forward Error Correction (FEC)
2) Automatic Repeat Request (ARQ)

ARQ is simple and achieves reasonable throughput levels if the error rates are not very large. However, in its simplest form, ARQ leads to variable delays which are not acceptable for real-time applications. Real-time delivery requirements restrict the use of retransmissions to recover from packet loss. This is why streaming applications must often rely on reproducing missing data with purely receiver-based error concealment or redundancy-based transmission strategies, which are often known as forward error correction. In FEC redundant packets are transmitted along with source packets. If the number of lost packets is smaller than the number of redundant packets, data can be reconstructed without error. Although perfect recovery cannot be guaranteed by applying FEC, the human visual system can tolerate certain types of data errors better than others.

It is further possible to subdivide the set of channel coding techniques with forward error correction (FEC) and interleaving. Since the audio and speech frame size is typically much smaller than the maximum packet size, at least some frames can be packed together [4] and it possible to rearranges packets so that adjacent frames are not transmitted consecutively. In this paper, we propose a protocol used simple new interleaving and changed the redundant packets in the sender side according to the loss rate. This protocol increased redundant packets if the rate of burst error is too much in order to have more recovered frames and decrease the redundant packets if the burst loss is low. FEC schemes maintain constant throughput and have bounded time delay.

2 Sender Based Repair

We discuss a number of techniques which require the participation of the sender of an audio stream to achieve recovery from packet loss. These techniques may be split into two major classes: active retransmission and passive channel coding. It is further possible to subdivide the set of channel coding techniques with forward error correction and interleaving based schemes being used. This taxonomy is summarized in figure 1[12].

In order to simplify the following discussion we distinguish a unit of data from a packet. A unit is an interval of audio data, as stored internally in an audio tool. A packet comprises one or more units, encapsulated for transmission over the network.

Fig. 1. A Taxonomy of Sender Based Repair Techniques

3 Forward Error Correction Technique

A number of forward error correction techniques have been developed to repair losses of data during transmission. These schemes rely on the addition of repair data to a stream from which the contents of lost packets may be recovered. A common method for generating FEC data is to take a set of packet payloads and apply the binary exclusive or (XOR) operation across the payloads. This scheme allows the recovery of missing data in the case where one of the original packets is lost but the FEC packet is received correctly. There are also many other more complex error correcting codes such as Reed Solomon code which is has the optimal distance properties and is called maximum distance separable or MDS code. Reed Solomon codes provide optimal error correction capability given a fixed number of parity bits and there isn't any code that can recover lost symbols using smaller number of symbols [6].

The outline of FEC scheme using Reed-Solomon (RS) code is shown in Fig. 2[2]. At the sender, RS(n, k) coding k data packets are encoded and n − k redundant packets are generated . The data block of n packets is called an FEC block and each packet is called an RS packet. At the receiver, we can completely recover the n-k lost packets in an FEC block by checking the sequence number attached to the packet and specifying the position of the error. Obviously, it's need to buffer at the receiver for recovering loss packets.

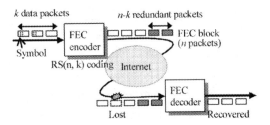

Fig. 2. FEC scheme using RS code

In practice, the media stream and the FEC stream are usually transmitted using the same transport medium. This is why we cannot expect packet losses to occur only in the media stream as both streams are likely to suffer from similar error characteristics. In the network perspective, it is realistic to assume the media stream and the FEC stream to form a single stream containing both media and FEC packets.

4 FEC Redundancy Control

To better understand the meaning of the MBL and MILD metrics, Fig. 4 illustrates their potential impact on adaptive FEC transmission [3]. Here, adaptive FEC-capable communication is affected by two loss bursts having a length of MBL = 3. The two loss bursts are separated by k (MILD) correctly received packets.

In order to reflect loss burst length, we use both MBL and MILD as parameters in FEC blocks. MBL is the mean loss run length defines mean loss based on the burst distribution and MILD is the mean inter loss distance describe the distance between packet loss events in terms of sequence number. According to [10] choosing the number of original data k = MILD and amount of redundancy h=MBL makes communications robust against the most likely expected clustered losses.

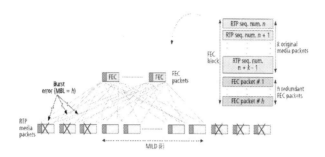

Fig. 3. Model-based FEC block allocation scheme

5 Interleaving

When the unit size is smaller than the packet size and end to end delay is tolerable, interleaving is a useful technique for reducing the effects of loss. Units are resequenced before transmission, so that originally adjacent units are separated by a guaranteed distance in the transmitted stream and returned to their original order at the receiver. Interleaving disperses the effect of packet losses. If for example unites are 5ms in length and packets 20ms (i.e. 4 units per packet), then the first packet would contain units 1, 5, 9, 13; the second packet would contain units 2, 6, 10, 14 and so on, as illustrated in figure 4 [12].

Frame sizes are highly dependent on the audio or video encoder being used. In video coding, there are typically many different types of frames, and the frame size varies much as well. Because there is an upper limit for transport unit (packet) size in IP networks, large frames must be fragmented. In audio and speech coding, fragmentation is not usually needed because the frame size is typically much smaller than the maximum packet size. This is why it is often necessary to pack several frames in one Real-Time Protocol (RTP) packet. In this case, we can use interleaving in packets to have better performance. It can be seen that the loss of a single packet from an interleaved stream results in multiple small gaps in the reconstructed stream, as opposed to the single large gap which would occur in a non-interleaved stream. If the loss is spread out so that small parts of several phonemes are lost, it becomes easier for people to mentally patch over this loss resulting in improved perceived quality for a given loss rate.

The major advantage of interleaving is that it does not increase the bandwidth requirements of a stream; however, it causes extra delay at the receiver due to the time needed for buffering.

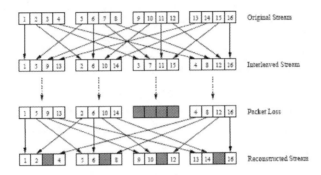

Fig. 4. Interleaving units across multiple packets

6   Interleaving and FEC

According to studies, bursty losses of multimedia frames or blocks (speech, audio, video and even still images) are much more harmful to perceived quality and more difficult to conceal than smaller gaps[11]. Assume that when there are frames x, y,... and a related parity FEC frame f(x, y,...), these data frames and the FEC frame form a group of mutually dependent frames. This definition is justified by the fact that a lost frame can be recovered by applying the XOR operation to all the remaining dependent frames. An example is shown in figure 5, where all mutually dependent frames are connected with lines. In general, when the XOR operation is applied to n frames, the total number of frames in the group (including the FEC frame) is n + 1. When n is small, error protection is strong but redundancy overhead is increased (1/n).

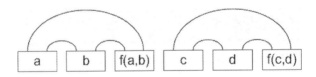

Fig. 5. Dependencies between data and FEC packets

In the following, it is assumed that there are a fixed number of slots, s, in every RTP packet payload to be occupied by frames. In practice, s must be chosen so that it is smaller or equal to the maximum packet payload size divided by the frame size. For simplicity, we assume that all frames are equal in size. If this is not the case, the length of each frame has to be increased within the additional data inserted in each packet.

Figure 6 shows arranging frames between packets spreading FEC frames. In this example, loss of two packets out of the first three packets would then always lead to loss of four frames.

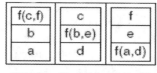

Packet 1   Packet 2   Packet 3

Fig. 6. FEC with even spread of FEC frames among packets

In [4] proposed a new packetization technique in that FEC frames are spread evenly among payloads for having better recovery. In this case, a longer interleaving cycle is involved to achieve better performance following basic guidelines for packetizing is considered:

First of all, frames that are mutually dependent must not be located in the same packet.

Second, redundant dependencies between the same packets should be avoided i.e. every group of dependent frames should be allocated in the packets so that there are no two groups with any more than one frames located in the same packet. Another important principle is to spread FEC frames evenly across payloads. This can be achieved if the number of slots s in each payload is a multiple of the number of frames per FEC group.

Assume P is the numbers of packets have interleaved frames and N is the number of FEC groups in the P packets. Also considered s is the number of slots in a packet and n is the number of data packets in one group of FEC (a FEC group is a group of dependent frames, such as {a, b, f(a,b)}. In an ideal situation, the number of frames and packets in an interleaving cycle cannot be selected arbitrarily, and they must fulfill certain conditions. First of all, P packets should accommodate exactly N FEC groups of packets. Since no slots should be left empty, condition (1) should be valid.

(1) $N(n+1) = Ps$

In addition, there should be exactly as many dependencies between packets as there are dependencies between the frames to be allocated in these packets. Every FEC group contains n media frames plus one FEC frame. Thus, there are $(n^2 + n)/2$ pairs of depending frames in each FEC group, resulting in $N(n^2 + n)/2$ pairs of dependent frames in total, where N is the number of FEC groups. Given P packets, there are $(P^2 - P)/2$ unique pairs of packets in total. In an optimal situation, $N(n^2 + n)/2$ pairs of frames can be allocated evenly among $(P^2 - P)/2$ pairs of packets. In this case condition (2) applies that all the variables should have integer values to fulfill the conditions.

(2) $N(n^2+n) = P^2 - P$

It is possible to calculate the optimal number of frames F, packets P and groups of frames N for each cycle with Eqs. 3–5. If these conditions are not met, frames cannot be allocated in packets optimally, i.e., some slots are left empty or parallel dependencies exist between packets.

(3) $P = sn + 1$

(4) $F = Ps$

(5) $N = F/(n+1)$

A packetization example is illustrated in figure 7. In this example, s = 3 and n = 2, when the resulting number of packets and frames are P = 7 and F = 21 (of which 14 are media frames and seven are FEC frames). Each of the groups of dependent frames has its own unique combination of packets not conflicting with any other packet combination. In this example, the packet combinations are (1,2,3), (1,4,5), (1,6,7), (2,4,6), (2,5,7), (3,4,7) and (3,5,6). Therefore, the first group containing frames a, b, and f(a,b) is allocated to packets 1, 2 and 3; the second group of frames c, d, and f(c,d) to packets 1, 4 and 5, etc. As we can see, there are no redundant dependencies between the same packet pairs as in the example in figure 7. Another advantage of the proposed scheme that can be seen in figure 7 is the interleaving effect. Because adjacent media frames are allocated in different packets, bursty frame losses are easier to avoid. Also, this facilitates the concealment of missing frames.

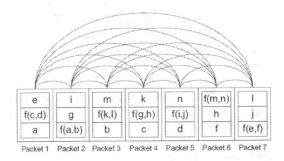

Fig. 7. A packetization example following the scheme

7 Adaptive Model Based Burst Loss

According to the changeable bursty losses of multimedia frames, using an optimal FEC redundancy is so important in any stream. Packetization scheme explained in section 5 break down the order of frames, so an extra delay is presented at sender and receiver side and the end to end delay is increased.

For this reason, we defined a simple interleaving method using data packets and FEC packets according to the loss burst in network. Our approach is to apply an appropriate amount of redundancy that uses FEC according to the current network burst

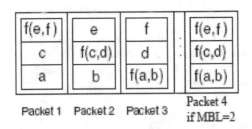

Fig. 8. A packetization example following the proposed scheme

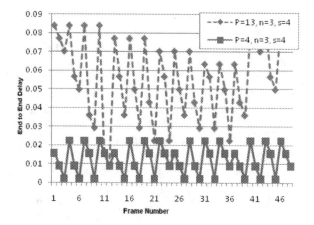

Fig. 9. End to end delay for packetizations

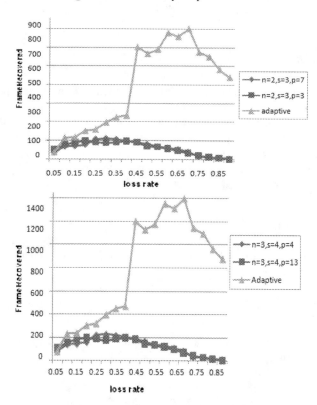

Fig. 10. Recovered frames using three methods of interleaving

rate. In this way, we measure the burst rate in a specific time and calculate the average MBL parameter; according to [10] choosing amount of redundancy h=MBL makes communications robust burst losses; so we change redundant packets based on the MBL in different network conditions. The example of 3 slots in a packet is shown in figure 8; if we have MBL=2 in a specific time, we will change the pattern of sent packets by adding packet 4 same as figure 8; also if we have MBL=3 in a time period, we add two packets of redundancy like packet 4 and so on. Nafaa in reference [3] shown most of the burst loss lengths in real traffic network are between 8 and 16; we add maximum number of redundant packets to 16 if there are bursty situation. It is easy to see the advantage of this simple interleaving for having a lower end-to-end delay in figure 9 which is shown end to end delay in sequential frames. Obviously, end to end delay for this proposed interleaving is significantly lower than a large interleaving in a group of packets.

The experiment runs with three different methods: one of them is the interleaving we introduce in section 3; another one is fixed interleaving like the first three packets in fig 8 and the other one is the method we proposed in this section. Figure 10 shows the result of these three methods; it is clear that recovered frames in our proposed method are more than other two methods in any situation when we change the loss rate gradually from 0.05 to 0.9. Using this result, our adaption shows benefit by changing redundant packets in different bursty situation.

8   Conclusion

In multimedia service reliability is a prerequisite which can be reach deploying error control techniques.

In this article, we present an adaptive protocol which can be used in multimedia applications. We research delay time in various interleaving strategies; the result shows adapting the redundancy to the network burst loss rates increase the recovered packets. According to the result of simulation, The experiment shows adapting FEC packets with the burst loss length have a good result in recovering the packets.

Acknowledgment

The author would like to thank Iran Telecommunication Research Center provided the financial backing for this research.

References

1. French, K., Claypool, M.: Repair of Streaming Multimedia with Adaptive Forward Error Correction. In: Proceedings of SPIE Multimedia Systems and Applications (part of TCOM), Denver, Colorado, USA (August 2000)
2. Mochizuki, K., Yoshimura, Y., Uematsu, Y., Suzuki, R.: Forward Error Correction for Visual Communication Systems Using VBR Codec. IEICE Transactions 89-B(2), 334–341 (2006)
3. Nafaa, A., Hadjadj-Aoul, Y., Mehaoua, A.: On Interaction between Loss Characterization and Forward ErrorCorrection in Wireless Multimedia Communication. In: IEEE ICC 2005, the IEEE International Conference on Communications (2005)

4. Korhonen, J., Huang, Y., Wang, Y.: Generic forward error correction of short frames for IP streaming applications. Multimedia Tools Appl. 305–323 (2006)
5. Konomi, M., Yasujiko, Y., Yoshihiko, U., Ryoichi, S.: Adaptive forward error correction for interactive streaming over the internet. IEICE transactions on communications 89, 334–341 (2006)
6. Liu, H., et al.: Error control schemes for networks: an overview. Mobile Networks and Applications, 167–182 (1997)
7. Kostas, T.J.: The effects of forward error correction on IP networks, Thesis (PhD.)– Northwestern University (2000)
8. Nafaa, A., Hadjadj-Aoul, Y., Mehaoua, A.: On Interaction between Loss Characterization and Forward Error Correction in Wireless Multimedia Communication. In: Proceedings of IEEE ICC 2005 (2005)
9. Nafaa, T.T., Murphy, L.: Forward Error Correction Strategies for Media Streaming over Wireless Networks. IEEE Communications Magazine: Feature Topic on New Trends in Mobile Internet Technologies and Applications 46(1), 72–79 (2008)
10. Yuan, Y., Cockburn, B.F., Sikora, T., Mandal, M.: Efficient allocation of packet-level forward error correction in video streaming over the internet. Journal of Electronic Imaging 16(2), 023-012 (2007)
11. Claypool, M., Zhu, Y.: Using interleaving to ameliorate the effects of packet loss in a video stream. In: Proc. Of the International Workshop on Multimedia Network Systems and Applications (MNSA), pp. 508–513 (2003)
12. Perkins, C., Hodson, O., Hardman, V.: A Survey of Packet Loss Recovery Techniques for Streaming, Audio. IEEE Network (1998)

Adjusting Forward Error Correction for Media Streaming

Mahila Dadfarnia[1] and Samaneh Khakbaz[2]

[1] Amirkabir University of technology, Tehran, Iran
m-dadfarnia@aut.ac.ir
[2] Iran University of Science and Technology, Tehran, Iran
samaneh.khakbaz@gmail.com

Abstract. Considering time constraints in multimedia streaming, multimedia applications use UDP protocol which does not guarantee data arrival. However, UDP flows often have a high data loss rate that needs to be dealt with. Forward Error Correction (FEC) is one of the techniques used to tackle this problem by adding redundant data to the flow and helping receivers to recover missed data. Another technique used is Interleaving improves the chance of recovery particularly during data burst; however it causes delay at the receiver side. This paper is proposing a new data transfer protocol that combines the two techniques in an adaptive fashion to improve data loss recovery by explicitly adapting the amount of redundancy and interleaving to the measured burst loss. a new parameter "recovery depth" is defined and controlled according to the transport media condition. Using higher recovery depth values in bursty loss increases the recovered. The adaptive scheme using the recovery depth parameter is discussed and the results of network simulations are demonstrated. We demonstrate that overall network performance for multimedia streaming application is improved using the new scheme.

Keywords: FEC; MDS; RS; MILD; MBL.

1 Introduction

Emerging new applications on the internet proposed lots of methods for streaming multimedia on the network. Since multimedia applications have timing constraints, TCP protocol is not used for transporting these applications and User Datagram Protocol (UDP) is commonly used. One of the important qualities of service parameter is packet loss. Since UDP does not provide any protection against loss and also the receiver does not understand data losses, this protocol suffers from data loss which can be repaired by the use of Forward Error Correction (FEC). The main idea behind FEC is for the server to add redundant data to a stream to help the client repair data loss. In fact, FEC is typically the best choice for real-time multicast applications or real time networking in general when round-trip times are long. A common method for generating FEC data is to take a set of packet payloads and apply the binary exclusive or (XOR) operation across the payloads. This scheme allows the recovery of missing data in the

L. Qi (Ed.): FCC 2009, CCIS 34, pp. 82–91, 2009.

case where one of the original packets is lost but the FEC packet is received correctly. There are also many other more complex error correcting codes such as Reed Solomon code which is has the optimal distance properties and is called maximum distance separable or MDS code. Reed Solomon (RS) codes provide optimal error correction capability given a fixed number of parity bits and there isn't any code that can recover lost symbols using smaller number of symbols [6].

Since the audio and speech frame size is typically much smaller than the maximum packet size, at least some frames can be packed together [4] and it possible to rearranges packets so that adjacent frames are not transmitted consecutively. In this paper, we propose a protocol used interleaving and changed the recover depth parameter in the sender side according to the loss rate and these loss packets are recovered in the receiver side. This protocol increased recover depth if the rate of burst error is too much in order to have more recovered frames and decrease the recover depth if the burst loss is low in order to have lower delay.

2 Fectechique

The outline of FEC scheme using Reed Solomon code is shown in Fig. 1 [2]. At the sender, RS(n, k) coding k data packets are encoded and n − k redundant packets are generated . The data block of n packets is called an FEC block and each packet is called an RS packet. At the receiver, we can completely recover the n–k lost packets in an FEC block by checking the sequence number attached to the packet and specifying the position of the error. Obviously, it's need to buffer at the receiver for recovering loss packets.

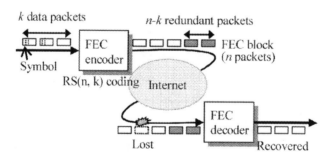

Fig. 1. FEC scheme using RS code

Figure 2 shows two different schemes using the generic FEC defined in RFC 2733. Function f(x, y,...) denote the resulting FEC packet when the XOR operation is applied to the packets x, y.... In example (a), every single packet loss in the original media stream can be recovered, and in example (b), every packet loss can be recovered, assuming that the FEC stream is received correctly in both cases. However, both schemes require more network bandwidth because of the redundancy overhead: 50% in case (a) and 100% in case (b).

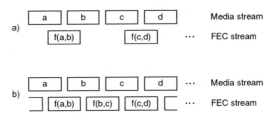

Fig. 2. Two sample schemes using generic FEC

In practice, the media stream and the FEC stream are usually transmitted using the same transport medium. This is why we cannot expect packet losses to occur only in the media stream as both streams are likely to suffer from similar error characteristics. In the network perspective, it is realistic to assume the media stream and the FEC stream to form a single stream containing both media and FEC packets.

3   Fec Performance Metrics

Some performance metrics is defined to determine the suitability of FEC code as follows:

A.   Redundancy ratio

The ratio n/k is usually referred to amount of redundancy with respect to the source data.

B.   Decoding inefficiency ratio

This represents the minimum number of packets required to recover an FEC block divided by the number of source packets. Typically, the inef_ratio is equal to one in MDS codes, while it is slightly higher in non-MDS codes. It is calculated as follows:

$$\text{inef\_ratio} = \frac{\text{Number of packets require for encoding}}{\text{Number of sending packets}} \tag{1}$$

C.   Encoding/decoding times and bandwidth

Measuring the time needed to encode/decode an FEC block is useful for computing the achievable bandwidth in a real time streaming system and the suitability of such codes for resource-constrained wireless terminals. This bandwidth is calculated as follows:

$$\text{BW} = \frac{\text{Size of packet} * n}{\text{Time}} \tag{2}$$

Also In order to reflect loss burst length; we use both MBL and MILD as parameters in FEC blocks. MBL is the mean loss run length defines mean loss based on the burst distribution and MILD is the mean inter loss distance describe the distance between packet loss events in terms of sequence number (see fig. 3) [3]. According to [10] choosing the number of original data k = MILD and amount of redundancy h=MBL makes communications robust against the most likely expected clustered losses.

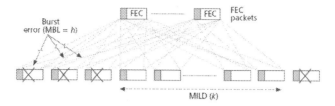

Fig. 3. Model-based FEC block allocation scheme

4   Interleaving

Assume that when there are frames x, y,... and a related parity FEC frame f(x, y,....), these data frames and the FEC frame form a group of mutually dependent frames. This definition is justified by the fact that a lost frame can be recovered by applying the XOR operation to all the remaining dependent frames. An example is shown in figure 4, where all mutually dependent frames are connected with lines. In general, when the XOR operation is applied to n frames, the total number of frames in the group (including the FEC frame) is n + 1. When n is small, error protection is strong but redundancy overhead is increased (1/n).

In the following, it is assumed that there are a fixed number of slots, s, in every RTP packet payload to be occupied by frames. In practice, s must be chosen so that it is smaller or equal to the maximum packet payload size divided by the frame size. For simplicity, we assume that all frames are equal in size. If this is not the case, the length of each frame has to be increased within the additional data inserted in each packet.

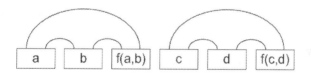

Fig. 4. Dependencies between data and FEC packets

Figure 5 shows dependencies between packets using the traditional generic FEC marked with lines. In this example, one packet loss can always be recovered entirely. However, the loss of two out of the first three packets could lead to loss of three or six media frames. If the FEC frames are spread evenly among payloads, the situation is changed.

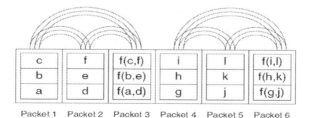

Fig. 5. Baseline generic FEC and the dependencies between packets

As shown in figure 6, loss of two packets out of the first three packets would then always lead to loss of four frames.

This is a clear improvement to the baseline generic FEC scheme. However, the interleaving effect is still limited due to the short interleaving cycle with three packets only. Performance improvement can be achieved if a longer interleaving cycle is involved.

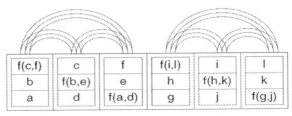

Fig. 6. Generic FEC with even spread of FEC frames among packets

Following basic guidelines for packetizing is considered:

First of all, frames that are mutually dependent must not be located in the same packet.

Second, redundant dependencies between the same packets should be avoided i.e. every group of dependent frames should be allocated in the packets so that there are no two groups with any more than one frames located in the same packet. Another important principle is to spread FEC frames evenly across payloads. This can be achieved if the number of slots s in each payload is a multiple of the number of frames per FEC group.

Assume P is the number of packets have interleaved frames and N is the number of FEC groups in the P packets. Also considered s is the number of slots in a packet and n is the number of data packets in one group of FEC (a FEC group is a group of dependent frames, such as {a, b, f(a,b)}. In an ideal situation, the number of frames and packets in an interleaving cycle cannot be selected arbitrarily, and they must fulfill certain conditions. First of all, P packets should accommodate exactly N FEC groups of packets. Since no slots should be left empty, condition (3) should be valid.

$$N(n+1) = Ps \qquad (3)$$

In addition, there should be exactly as many dependencies between packets as there are dependencies between the frames to be allocated in these packets. Every FEC group contains n media frames plus one FEC frame. Thus, there are (n2 + n)/2 pairs of depending frames in each FEC group, resulting in N(n2 + n)/2 pairs of dependent frames in total, where N is the number of FEC groups. Given P packets, there are (P2 - P)/2 unique pairs of packets in total. In an optimal situation, N(n2 + n)/2 pairs of frames can be allocated evenly among (P2 - P)/2 pairs of packets. In this case condition (4) applies that all the variables should have integer values to fulfill the conditions.

$$N(n^2 + n) = P^2 - P \qquad (4)$$

From Eqs. 2 and 3, it is possible to calculate the optimal number of frames F, packets P and groups of frames N for each cycle with Eqs. 5–7. If these conditions are not met, frames cannot be allocated in packets optimally, i.e., some slots are left empty or parallel dependencies exist between packets.

$$P = sn + 1 \tag{5}$$

$$F = Ps \tag{6}$$

$$N = F/(n+1) \tag{7}$$

Table 1 summarizes some useful parameter combinations and their overheads.

Table 1. Some useful parameter combinations

n	s	P	F	N	FEC overhead (in %)
2	3	7	21	7	50
2	4	9	36	12	50
2	6	13	78	26	50
3	4	13	52	13	33
3	8	25	200	50	33
4	5	21	105	21	25

A packetization example is illustrated in figure 7. In this example, s = 3 and n = 2, when the resulting number of packets and frames are P = 7 and F = 21 (of which 14 are media frames and seven are FEC frames). Each of the groups of dependent frames has its own unique combination of packets not conflicting with any other packet combination. In this example, the packet combinations are (1,2,3), (1,4,5), (1,6,7), (2,4,6), (2,5,7), (3,4,7) and (3,5,6). Therefore, the first group containing frames a, b, and f(a,b) is allocated to packets 1, 2 and 3; the second group of frames c, d, and f(c,d) to packets 1, 4 and 5, etc. As we can see, there are no redundant dependencies between the same packet pairs as in the example in figure 7. Another advantage of the proposed scheme that can be seen in figure 7 is the interleaving effect. Because adjacent media frames are allocated in different packets, bursty frame losses are easier to avoid. Also, this facilitates the concealment of missing frames.

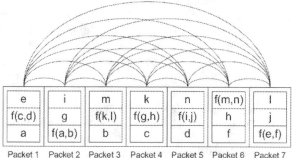

Fig. 7. A packetization example following the scheme

5 Proposed Protocol

According to the changeable bursty losses of multimedia frames, using an optimal FEC redundancy is so important in any stream. Our approach is to develop a new protocol that uses specific FEC according to the current network burst rate. In this way, we define a parameter called recovery depth equal to the inverse of n; where n is the number of data frames regardless of FEC frame in a packet, put in another words, this parameter shows one FEC frame is defined for how many frames. More value for the depth recovery shows more protection for each frame.

In addition, since a small s and a small frame size would cause header overhead; it is usually reasonable to choose s close to the maximum and if it is possible, s should be chosen so that it is a multiple of n + 1. This allows FEC frames and media frames to be spread evenly among all packets. So we should consider the s as much as possible.

Generally, we define recovery depth according to the burst loss rate. So if the burst loss is too much, we increase the recovery depth to have the better quality and if the burst loss rate is low, decreasing the recovery depth is a good solution for sending more packets in a lower time. Since the recovery rate is more for a low number of flows, lower recover depth is chosen when the number of flows is low and higher recovery depth is chosen when the number of flows is more.

6 Simulation Experiments

The analysis results are conducted on the NS2 network simulator which is an event driven simulator; some examples of events are packet arrival, packet transmission and packet loss. The simulation engine that controls the system is written in C++ and uses a version of TCL that is object oriented called OTCL. This program sends packets with a fixed rate.

D. Adaptive FEC

To verify the value of proposed protocol, we have compared Average recovery in different MBL and n. As shown in figure 8, decreasing recovery depth (increasing n) has better recovery results if MBL is low; while when there are lots of consequently packet loss, our protocol increase recovery depth (more redundancy) to have better recovery. It is easy to see the advantages of adaptive FEC in different network burst rate. Figure 8-B uses a set of table 1 for comparison.

Following our intuition, we implement our protocol using some combinations from table1 in a different number of flows. We changed the number of flows from 10 to 100. Flows from the sender send packets to the same number of flows in the receiver and then we measure loss packets and recovered packets. Figure 9 shows the percentage of perceived loss packets, i.e., percentage of lost packets could not be repaired at the receiver.

The percentage of packets that could not be recovered at 50 receivers is lower if n=2 while when 10 flows send packets it's better to choose n=3. With lower recovery depth, the experiments runs with few flows had most of the data recovered; while using higher recovery depth with a high number of flows saw a decrease in the number of lost packets. Using this result, our adaption is done by decreasing recovery depth when the number of flows is high and increasing recovery depth when the number of flows is low.

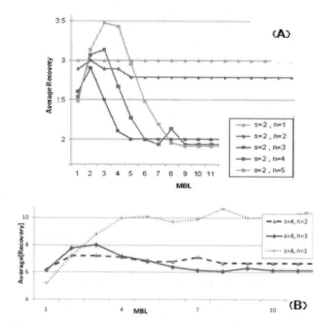

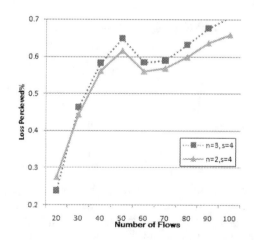

Fig. 8. Average Recovered frames in comparison with different MBL

Fig. 9. Effect of different recovery depth (1/n) in loss rate of different number of flows

E.   Increasing the number of slots in a packet

Figure 10 depicts the advantages of the higher value for (s). the program sends 630 packets and shows the recovered frames changing with the random loss rate model. If loss rate is high, many frames either FEC or data frames get lost, its why when we have high loss packets in 50% loss rate, recovered frame is low. Moreover, the result of examining for different packet size shows when s has more value, recovered frames is more. As a result, packetization more frames in one packet has better results.

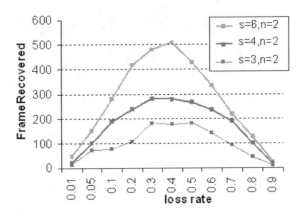

Fig. 10. Comparison of frame recovered considering different slot number

Figure 11 shows a comparison of various (s) with different burst lost rate. It's clear that having higher value for (s), increase the number of recovered packets.

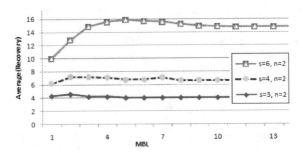

Fig. 11. Average recovery with different slot number

7   Conclusion

In multimedia service reliability is a prerequisite which can be reach deploying error control techniques. In this article, we present an adaptive FEC protocol which can be used in multimedia applications. We research recovery depth in various loss rate; the result shows adapting the redundancy to the network burst loss rates increase the re-covered packets. The experiment shows using lower recovery depth with a low number of flows and higher recovery depth with a high number of flows decrease number of lost packets. According to the result of simulation, choosing higher value for s also increase the number of recovered frames.

Acknowledgement

The author would like to thank Iran Telecommunication Research Center provided the financial backing for this research.

References

1. French, K., Claypool, M.: Repair of Streaming Multimedia with Adaptive Forward Error Correction. In: Proceedings of SPIE Multimedia Systems and Applications (part of TCOM), Denver, Colorado, USA (August 2000)
2. Mochizuki, K., Yoshimura, Y., Uematsu, Y., Suzuki, R.: Forward Error Correction for Visual Communication Systems Using VBR Codec. IEICE Transactions 89-B(2), 334–341 (2006)
3. Nafaa, A., Hadjadj-Aoul, Y., Mehaoua, A.: On Interaction between Loss Characterization and Forward ErrorCorrection in Wireless Multimedia Communication. In: Proceedings of IEEE ICC 2005, the IEEE International Conference on Communications 2005, Seoul, South Korea, May 20 (2005)
4. Korhonen, J., Huang, Y., Wang, Y.: Generic forward error correction of short frames for IP streaming applications. Multimedia Tools Appl., 305–323 (2006)
5. Konomi, M., Yasujiko, Y., Yoshihiko, U., Ryoichi, S.: Adaptive forward error correction for interactive streaming over the internet. IEICE transactions on communications 89, 334–341 (2006)
6. Liu, H., et al.: Error control schemes for networks: an overview. Mobile Networks and Applications, 167–182 (1997)
7. Kostas, T.J.: The effects of forward error correction on IP networks, Thesis (PhD.)–Northwestern University (2000)
8. Nafaa, A., Hadjadj-Aoul, Y., Mehaoua, A.: On Interaction between Loss Characterization and Forward Error Correction in Wireless Multimedia Communication. In: Proceedings of IEEE ICC 2005, the IEEE International Conference on Communications 2005, Seoul, South Korea, May 20 (2005)
9. Nafaa, A., Taleb, T., Murphy, L.: Forward Error Correction Strategies for Media Streaming over Wireless Networks. IEEE Communications Magazine: Feature Topic on New Trends in Mobile Internet Technologies and Applications 46(1), 72–79 (2008)
10. Yuan, Y., Cockburn, B.F., Sikora, T., Mandal, M.: Efficient allocation of packet-level forward error correction in video streaming over the internet. Journal of Electronic Imaging 16(2), 23012 (2007)
11. Claypool, M., Zhu, Y.: Using interleaving to ameliorate the effects of packet loss in a video stream. In: Proc. Of the International Workshop on Multimedia Network Systems and Applications (MNSA). Providence, Rhode Island, 508–513 (2005)

AR RAAM: A Reliable Routing Algorithim Using Ant Agents for Manets

M. Nisha, M. Ganesh Kumar, N. Hemachandar, D. Manoj Prasadh,
K.R. Ramkumar, and M. Ravichandran

Sri Venkateswara college of Engineering, Sriperumbudur – 602105
mganeshmail@gmail.com, manojprasadh@gmail.com,
hemachandhar@gmail.com

Abstract. A mobile ad hoc network (MANET) is a collection of wireless mobile hosts forming a temporary network without the aid of any centralized administration or standard support services in wide-area networks to which the hosts may normally be connected. In such an environment, it may be necessary for one mobile host to seek the aid of others in forwarding a packet to its destination, due to the limited propagation range of each mobile host's wireless transmissions. The biggest challenge in these kinds of network is to find the correct and optimal path between the communication end points, which is aggravated through the node mobility. This paper presents a comprehensive study of the impact of mobility and proposes a way to determine route stability using ant.

Keywords: MANETS, ANTS, Mobility Ratio.

1 Introduction

In ad hoc networks, routing protocols can be classified as proactive, reactive and hybrid approaches. Proactive routing protocols (e.g. DSDV [1]) maintain consistent, up-to-date routing information from each node to every other node in the network, but the maintenance of unused paths may consume a large amount of bandwidth. Reactive routing protocols (e.g. DSR [2] and AODV [3]) create routes only when necessary, thus reduce the overhead in maintaining unused path, but it may lead to a longer latency for the first packet to be transmitted. Hybrid routing protocol (e.g. ZRP [4]) uses local proactive routing and a global reactive routing, thus can achieve a higher level of efficiency. Besides obvious military applications, MANETs may be used in any environment that lacks a wireless infrastructure such as during disaster recovery operations and mountain hiking or climbing. An assured quality of connection is desirable in all these applications and has led to significant new research in providing QoS support in MANETs. The challenges in providing QoS in MANETs are widely known [5]. One of the main challenges in providing QoS in mobile ad hoc networks is the mobility of the nodes, which makes connectivity unpredictable. The movement of the nodes constantly invalidates old paths, causing the packets of the flow to wait until the routing protocol is able to get information about the new paths. This degrades the performance of the network, reducing the throughput and increasing the

L. Qi (Ed.): FCC 2009, CCIS 34, pp. 92–99, 2009.

delay. This also intuitively implies that the performance of the network will be different under different mobility scenarios of the nodes.

A. Neighborhood maintenance

Neighborhood information is very important since it provides the local topology, traffic and mobility information. To maintain the neighborhood information, every node in the network is required to periodically send out a "Hello" packet, announcing its existence and traffic information to its neighbors. Each node I will include in the Hello packet its self-traffic and computation of self. The Hello packet is sent at a default rate of once per second. Every node in the network receives the Hello packets from its neighbors and maintains a neighbors list N(I) which includes all its neighbors with their corresponding self traffic. Failure to receive any packet from a neighbor for Tlost period is taken as an indication that the link to the neighbor in question is down.

B. Route discovery

The route is discovered on-demand by propagating the route request and route reply packets between the source and the destination. We discover the route by exploration from source to destination and route registration in the reverse path.

C. Forward ants

When a source needs to send a packet to a particular node, it first checks the cache for existing routes. When no routes are known, it broadcasts Forward Request ANTS which are propagated through the network till it reaches the destination. This process can be compared to ants initially spreading out in all directions in search of food source. [6][7][8]. When a packet reaches the destination, the destination node sends a Backward ANT for every Forward Request when different Forward ANTs reach the destination through different routes; the destination sends a Backward ANT for each of them. This is to ensure that multiple paths exist between the source and the destination. Synonymously, in the case of ants, initially multiple paths exist between the nest and the food source. Slowly the best path (which for ants is the shortest path) gets strengthened through increased pheromone count.

D. Backward Ant

The route is discovered on-demand by propagating the route request and route reply packets between the source and the destination. we discovery the route by exploration from source to destination and route registration in the reverse path.

Upon arrival at the destination d, it is converted into a backward ant, which travels back to the source retracing the path. At each intermediate node i, coming from neighbor n, the ant updates the entry i T_{nd}^i which is the pheromone value indicating the estimated goodness of going from i over neighbor n to reach the destination d, in the i's pheromone table. The way the entry is updated depends on the path quality metrics used to define pheromone variables. For instance, if the pheromone is expressed using the number of hops as a measure of goodness, at each hop the backward ant increments an internal hop counter and uses the inverse of this value to locally assign the value τ_d^i which is used to update the pheromone variable T_{nd}^i [7]

$$T_{nd}^i = \gamma T_{nd}^i + (1 - \gamma)\tau_d^i \gamma \epsilon[0,1] \qquad (1)$$

E. Route Maintenance

Route Maintenance plays a very important role in MANETs as the network keeps dynamically changing and routes found good during discovery may turn to be bad due to congestion, mobility ratio, signal strength, etc. Hence when a node starts sending packets to the destination using the[7][Probabilistic Route Finding algorithm explained above, it is essential to find the goodness of a route regularly and update the pheromone counts for the different   routes at the source nodes. To accomplish this, when a destination node receives a packet, it probabilistically sends an Update message to the source which informs the source of the REM value for that route. This Update message also serves as an ACK to the source. This Update messages are sent probabilistically (say with prob of 0.1), so that they have minimum overhead and do not increase much the congestion if the route is already overloaded.

2   Proposed Algorithm

A. Neighborhood maintenance

Neighborhood information is very important since it provides the local topology, traffic and mobility information. To maintain the neighborhood information, every node in the network is required to periodically send out a ''Hello'' packet, announcing its existence and traffic information to its neighbors. Each node I will include in the Hello packet its self-traffic and computation of self. The Hello packet is sent at a rate of once per Thello. Every node in the network receives the Hello packets from its neighbors and maintains a neighbors list N(I) which includes all its neighbors with their corresponding self traffic. Failure to receive any packet from a neighbor for Tlost period is taken as an indication that the link to the neighbor in question is down. We introduce two other parameters HITS (h) and MISSES (m) which we use to calculateμ.

Table 1. Neighbor Table

Node	Traffic	Hits	Misses	Tlost	μ	N

B. Route Stability

We in this paper propose a novel idea to determine the route stability μ_p over the route P for a node say (i=1) to destination d using the Mobility Ratio μ of each node in the route P . When backward ant returns from destination to source over the path P it updates not only the pheromone value but also the sums up each node's mobility ratio . Each node's mobility ratio is maintained in its neighbor. When ant is in node (i) it has the μ value for node (i+1) . so the ant sums up μ till it reaches source node (i=1) . Route stability μ_p for a path P is given by the equation below.

$$\mu_P = \frac{\left(\sum_{i=1}^{n-1} \mu_i \right)}{n-1} \tag{2}$$

Where

$$\mu_i = \mu_i^{(i+1)d} \tag{3}$$

$\mu_i^{(i+1)d}$ is the mobility ratio of node (i+1) which is the neighbor of node (i) to reach the destination node d. Now in case we have many routes to destination this value along with pheromone value can be used to determine the best route . A route having a high value is highly stable and can be chosen as our primary path in parallel data transmission.

C. Ant Structure
We propose the following ant structure common to both forward ant and backward ant. F=1 represents the forward ant and F=0 represents the backward ant . The field Mobility Ratio μ serves to track the mobility ratio of the path P which is stored in the Dynamic Stack. The other field serves for maintaining pheromone value and other housekeeping purpose for effective ant transportation.

F	P		Ant Id
	Hop Count		Max Hop Count
Source Address			
Destination Address			
Timer/Pheromone Value			
Mobility Ratio μ			
Dynamic Stack			

Fig. 1. Ant Structure

D. Node Level Algorithm

```
for every Thello seconds
for each node n in neighbourTable
if( isHelloPacketReceived()==TRUE)
{
    set N=1
    set h=h+1
    μn=h/h+m
    tloss=0;
}
else
{
    tloss = tloss+thello
for given Threshold value Tloss
    if(tloss==Tloss)
    {
```

```
        N=0}
    }
        M++
        μn=h/h+m
}
for every Tlimit Second
for everyNode in NeighboutTable
if(N==0)
{
if(μn < μminThreshold)
    {
        Delete(N)
    }
        N=0
        M++
        μ=h/h+m
}
If (h> m) declare the Node as Reliable
Neighbor
Else if(h<m) declare the Neighbour as moving away node
Else if(h more or less equal to m) then it is a highly
mobile node.
```

The Mobility Ratio can be accumulated to test the reliability of a path Combine both Mobility Ratio and Pheromone values to select a node for data transaction.

3 Experimental Results

The performance of the proposed algorithm was evaluated through extensive simulations. The network consists of three kinds of mobile nodes. 1) Stable node 2) Unstable node 3) Random nodes. Collection of these nodes was taken in the simulation and each node was analyzed individually. Java was used to implement the MANET environment and the proposed algorithm was implemented on the network. Initially 20 neighbors was taken and then same was scaled to 100 nodes. Fig 3 shows the basic mobility ratio of the neighbor which is stable (i.e the node is approaching or stable in a position). As the time increases the mobility ratio increases indicating the stability of the node is high.

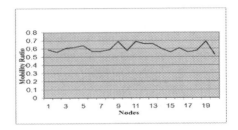

Fig. 2. Node Mobility for 20 randomized neighbors

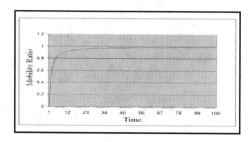

Fig. 3. Typical Stable Node

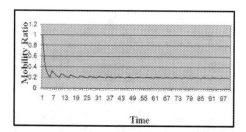

Fig. 4. A Typical Mostly Away Node

Fig 4 shows the basic mobility ratio of the neighbor which is leaving or moving out of position. As the time increases the mobility ratio decreasing indicating the dependability of the node is low. Fig 5 shows the basic mobility ratio of the neighbor which is highly stable. As the time increases the mobility ratio fluctuates in a high degree so these kind of nodes are highly non dependable. Fig 6 shows a very highly mobile node even though this case though rare is highly undependable These Two types of nodes are great threat to the functionalities of MANETs. So these kinds of nodes must be given less priority while transmitting the information. The proposed algorithm works on this issue and produces better result than the existing model. From fig2 we can infer that the mobility ratios of the neighbors are controlled and they are always in a optimum value. This makes the QoS of the network better.

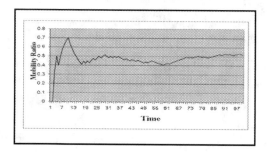

Fig. 5. A Random Nodes Mobility

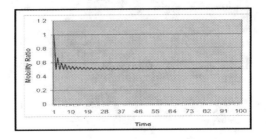

Fig. 6. A Highly Unstable Node

References

1. Perkins, C.E., Bhagwat, P.: Highly Dynamic Destination-Sequenced Distance-Vector Routing (DSDV) for Mobile Computers. Computer Communications Review, 234–244 (October 1994)
2. Johnson, D.B., Maltz, D.A.: Dynamic Source Routing in Ad Hoc Networks. In: Imielinski, T., Korth, H. (eds.) Mobile Computing, pp. 152–181. Kluwer, Dordrecht (1996)
3. Perkins, C.E., Royer, E.M.: Ad-hoc On Demand Distance Vector Routing. In: Proceedings of the 2nd IEEE Workshop on Mobile Computing Systems and Applications, New Orleans, LA, February 1999, pp. 90–100 (1999)
4. Haas, Z.J., Pearlman, M.R.: The Zone Routing Protocol(ZRP) for Ad hoc Networks, Internet draft - Mobile Ad hoc NETworking (MANET) Working Group of the Internet Engineering Task Force (IETF) (November 1997)
5. Chakrabarti, S., Mishra, A.: QoS issues in AD hoc wireless networks. IEEE Communications Magazine 39(2), 142–148 (2001)
6. Guine, M., Sorges, U., Bouazzi, I.: ARA-the ant-colony based routing algorithm for MANETs. In: Proc. of IWAHN 2002, pp. 79–85 (August 2002)
7. Baras, J.S., Mehta, H.: A Probabilistic Emergent Routing Algorithm for Mobile Ad Hoc Networks. In: Proc. of WiOpt 2003 (2003)
8. Di Caro, G., Ducatelle, F., Gambardella, L.M.: AntHocNet: An Adaptive Nature-Inspired Algorithm for Routing in Mobile Ad Hoc Networks. Tech. Rep. No. IDSIA-27-04-2004, IDSIA/USI-SUPSI (September 2004)
9. Hinchey, M.G., Sterritt, R., Rouff, C.: Swarms and Swarm Intelligence. IEEE Computer 40(4), 111–111 (2007)
10. Sim, K.M., Sun, W.H.: Ant Colony Optimization for Routing and Load-Balancing: Survey and New Directions. IEEE Trans. on Systems, Man, and Cybernetics 33(5), 560–572 (2003)
11. Di Caro, G., Dorigo, M.: AntNet: Distributed Stigmergetic Control for Communications Networks. Journal of Artificial Intelligence Research 9, 317–365 (1998)
12. Hinchey, M.G., Sterritt, R., Rouff, C.: Swarms and Swarm Intelligence. IEEE Computer 40(4), 111–111 (2007)
13. Sim, K.M., Sun, W.H.: Ant Colony Optimization for Routing and Load-Balancing: Survey and New Directions. IEEE Trans. on Systems, Man, and Cybernetics 33(5), 560–572 (2003)
14. Di Caro, G., Dorigo, M.: AntNet: Distributed Stigmergetic Control for Communications Networks. Journal of Artificial Intelligence Research 9, 317–365 (1998)

15. Matsuo, H., Mori, K.: Accelerated Ants Routing in Dynamic Networks. In: 2nd International Conf. on Software Engineering, Artificial Intelligence, Networking & Parallel/Distributed Computing, pp. 333–339 (2001)

16. Johnson, D.B., Maltz, D.A.: Dynamic Source Routing in Ad Hoc Wireless Networks. In: Imielinski, T., Korth, H. (eds.) Mobile Computing, pp. 153–181. Kluwer Academic Publishers, Norwell (1996)

17. Hong, X., Xu, K., Gerla, M.: Scalable routing protocols for mobile adhoc networks. IEEE Network 16, 11–21 (2002)

18. Jardosh, A.P., Belding-Royer, E.M., Almeroth, K.C., Suri, S.: Toward realistic mobility models for mobile ad hoc networks. In: Proc. ACM MOBICOM, San Diego, CA, September 2003, pp. 217–229 (2003)

19. Camp, T., Boleng, J., Davies, V.: A survey of Mobility Models for Ad hoc Network Research. Wireless Communications and Mobile computing: A special issue on Ad hoc network Research 2(5), 483–502 (2002)

20. Safwat, A.M., Hassanein, H.S.: Infrastructure-Based Routing in Wireless Mobile Ad Hoc Networks. Computer Communications 25(3), 210–224 (2002)

21. Liao, W.-H., Sheu, J.-P., Tseng, Y.-C.: GRID: A Fully Location-Aware Routing Protocol for Mobile Ad Hoc Networks. Telecommunication Systems 18(1-3), 37–60 (2001)

22. Amis, A.D., Prakash, R., Thai, H.P., Dung, V., Huynh, T.: Max-Min D-Cluster Formation in Wireless Ad Hoc Networks. IEEE Infocom, 32–41 (2000)

23. Toh, C.-K.: AD HOC Mobile Wireless Networks Protocols and Systems. Prentice Hall PTR, Englewood Cliffs (2002)

24. Toh, C.-K., Delwar, M., Allen, D.: Evaluating the Communication Performance of an Ad Hoc

25. Su, W., Lee, S.-J., Gerla, M.: Mobility prediction and routing in ad hoc wireless networks. Int. Journal of Network Management 11(1), 3–30 (2001)

26. Kamat, A., Prakash, R.: Effects of Link Stability and Directionality of Motion on Routing Algorithms in MANET. IEEE, Los Alamitos

Traffic Video Based Cross Road Violation Detection and Peccant Vehicle Tracking

Tao Gao, Zheng-guang Liu, and Jun Zhang

School of Electrical Engineering and Automation, Tianjin University,
Tianjin 300072, P.R. China
{gaotao09}@yahoo.cn

Abstract. For the requirement of monitoring cross road violation in intelligent traffic system, a method to recognize and track the peccant vehicle is presented. The static background is modeled by mixture Gaussian model, and the location of lane line is detected by Hough transformation, thus, coordinated series can be obtained from the monitor image. Information of vehicles can be obtained by background-frame binary discrete wavelet transforms (BDWT) method, and according to the distance between the vehicle and line, the peccant vehicle can be detected. An improved mean-shift method is used to track the peccant vehicle, and a close range camera is used to snapshoot the license plate according to the center of tracking window. Actual road tests show that the work efficiency of this method is high, and the accuracy is up to 80%; run-time of mean-shift tracking system is about 0.085s for each frame. So it has a certain practical value in the field of intelligent traffic.

Keywords: ITS; cross road violation; mixture Gaussian model; Hough transformation; mean-shift.

1 Introduction

Intelligent Transportation Systems is a hot research field today, and peccant detection is one of the key points. The main task is to extract lane lines. In recent days, with the increase in the number of vehicles, cross road violation always occurs. Vehicles driving cross roads may lead to traffic jam, and even accidents. Therefore, by cooperating with Tianjin traffic bureau, we develop a cross-road violation detection system to solve this problem. First, the static background is modeled by mixture of Gaussian (MOG) method. The position of the lane lines can be obtained by Hough transformation according to the background in-formation. And then, background-frame BDWT method is used to detect the location of the vehicle. According to the mutual location between vehicle and the line, violation can be detected. For the peccant vehicle, a improved mean-shift method is used to track it, and the license plate can be snapshot by a close range camera by determining the position of the tracking window.

L. Qi (Ed.): FCC 2009, CCIS 34, pp. 100–108, 2009.

2 Mixture of Gaussian Background Model

In Mixture of Gaussians (MoG) [1-3], each pixel location is represented by a number (or mixture) of Gaussians functions that sum together to form a probability distribution function F :

$$F(i_t = \mu) = \sum_{i=1}^{k} \omega_{i,t} \cdot \eta(\mu, \sigma) \tag{1}$$

To determine if a pixel is part of the background, we compare the input pixels to the means μ_i of their associated components. If a pixel value is close enough to a given component's mean, that component is considered a matched component. Specifically, to be a matched component, the absolute difference between the pixel and mean must be less than the component's standard deviation scaled by a factor D : $\left| i_i - \mu_{i,t-1} \right| \leq D \cdot \sigma$. The probability of observing the current pixel value is:

$$P(X_t) = \sum_{i=1}^{K} \omega_{i,t} * \eta(X_t, \mu_{i,t}, \sum_{i,t}) \cdot \tag{2}$$

Gaussian probability density function:

$$\eta(X_t, \mu, \sum) = \frac{1}{(2\pi)^{n/2} \left| \sum \right|^{1/2}} e^{-\frac{1}{2}(X_t - \mu_t)^T \sum^{-1}(X_t - \mu_t)} \cdot \tag{3}$$

Every new pixel value X_t is checked against the existing K Gaussian distributions. A match is defined as a pixel value within 2.5 standard deviations of a distribution. The parameters of the distribution which match the new observation are updated as follows:

$$\mu_t = (1 - \rho)\mu_{t-1} + \rho X_t \cdot \tag{4}$$

$$\sigma_t^2 = (1 - \rho)\sigma_{t-1}^2 + \rho(X_t - \mu_t)^T (X_t - \mu_t) \cdot \tag{5}$$

$$\rho = \alpha\eta(X_t \mid \mu_k, \sigma_k). \tag{6}$$

$$\omega_{k,t} = (1 - \alpha)\omega_{k,t-1} + \alpha(M_{k,t}) \cdot \tag{7}$$

Background Model Estimation:

1 Consider the accumulation of supporting evidence and the relatively low variance for the "background" distributions.

2 New object occludes the background object, increase in the variance of an existing distribution.

(1) The Gaussians are ordered by the value of ω / σ.

(2) The first B distributions are chosen as the background model:

$$B = \arg \min_b (\sum_{k=1}^{b} \omega_k > T) \cdot \tag{8}$$

T is a measure of the minimum portion of the data that should be accounted for by the background. Figure 1 shows the static background model by MOG.

Fig. 1. Static background image

3 Lane Line Detection Based on Hough Transformation

First, 'sobel' operator is used to extraction the edge of lane line from background image; for the binary image after edge detection, a Hough transformation is used to detect the lines, thus the coordinates of lines can be obtained. In this paper, 'Isotropic Sobel' is used to detect the level and vertical edges, that is:

$$H_1 = \begin{bmatrix} -1 & 0 & 1 \\ -2 & 0 & 2 \\ -1 & 0 & 1 \end{bmatrix} \quad H_2 = \begin{bmatrix} -1 & -2 & -1 \\ 0 & 0 & 0 \\ 1 & 2 & 1 \end{bmatrix}$$

The steps of Hough transformation [4-5] are: (1) Get the line cluster $\{(r, \theta)\}$ which passes every white pixel in the binary image, and increase the line number meanwhile.

For $\theta = \Delta\theta, 2\Delta\theta, 3\Delta\theta, ..., \pi,$
Let $\Delta\theta = \pi/30$, $r = x\cos(\theta) + y\sin(\theta)$;
content(r,θ)=content(r,θ)+1; end

---

(2) Get one line (r_{amx}, θ_{max}): $(r_{amx}, \theta_{max}) = \text{argmax} \{content (r, \theta)\}$.
(3) Check every white pixel (x, y), if it is at the line (r_{amx}, θ_{max}):

$r = x_1\cos(\theta) + y_1\sin(\theta)$;
If $(r == r_{amx})$, extract(x,y); end

Proof: (1) The line cluster which pass (x_0, y_0) is: $x_0\sin(\theta) + y_0\cos(\theta) = r$.

Prove: if (x, y) is one point of the line cluster, θ is the polar angle determined by (x_0, y_0) and (x, y), so: $-\dfrac{y - y_0}{x - x_0} = \dfrac{\sin(\theta)}{\cos(\theta)}$, that: $x\sin(\theta) + y\cos(\theta) = x_0\sin(\theta) + y_0\cos(\theta) = r$.

So The line cluster which pass (x_0, y_0) is: $x_0\sin(\theta) + y_0\cos(\theta) = r$.
(2) If (x, y) is one point of the line (r,θ), $x\sin(\theta) + y\cos(\theta)$ identifies the polar radius.
Prove: if $(x1, y1)$ is the point of line (r,θ) which is the nearest to origin, so:

$$\begin{cases} x_1 / a + y_1 / b = 1 \\ a = r / \cos(\theta) \\ b = r / \sin(\theta) \end{cases} : r = x_1\cos(\theta)+y_1\sin(\theta). \quad -\dfrac{y_2 - y_1}{x_2 - x_1} = \dfrac{\sin(\theta)}{\cos(\theta)} : x_1\sin(\theta)+y_1\cos(\theta)=$$

$x_2\sin(\theta) +y_2\cos(\theta)$. So if (x, y) is one point of the line (r,θ), $x\sin(\theta)+y\cos(\theta)$ identifies the polar radius.

Figure 2 shows the edge detection for background image, and Figure 3 shows the extraction of line points by Hough transformation.

Fig. 2. Edge detection   **Fig. 3.** Extraction line points

4   Vehicle Detection Based on Background-Frame BDWT and Cross Road Violation Detection

4.1   Background-Frame BDWT

One dimension signal $f(t)$, the binary discrete wavelet [6] transforms are as follows:

$$S_{2^j} f(t) = f(t) * \phi_{2^j}(t) \tag{9}$$

$$W_{2^j} f(t) = f(t) * \varphi_{2^j}(t) \tag{10}$$

$S_{2^j} f(t)$ is the projection of $f(t)$ in the V_j space, and $W_{2^j} f(t)$ is the projection of $f(t)$ in the W_j space. Equation (9) (10) can be rewritten as:

$$S_{2^j} f(t) = \sum_{l \in Z} S_{2^{j-1}} f(t-l) h_{j-1}(l) \cdot \tag{11}$$

$$W_{2^j} f(t) = \sum_{l \in Z} S_{2^{j-1}} f(t-l) g_{j-1}(l) \cdot \tag{12}$$

For a digital signal $d(n) = S_1 f(t)|_{t=nT} = S_1 f(n)$,

$$S_{2^j} f(n) = \sum_{l \in Z} S_{2^{j-1}} f(n-l) h_{j-1}(l) \quad j = 1, 2, \cdots \cdot \tag{13}$$

$$W_{2^j} f(n) = \sum_{l \in Z} S_{2^{j-1}} f(n-l) g_{j-1}(l) \quad j = 1, 2, \cdots \cdot \tag{14}$$

Because the coefficients of the sub-bands of the BDWT are highly correlated, and the direction and size are the same as the image, also, there is no translation in the sub-bands; we define the difference between digital signal $d_1(n)$ and $d_2(n)$ as:

$$DE = \sum_{j=J_0}^{J_1} \{ \left| S_{2^j} f_1(n) - S_{2^j} f_2(n) \right| + \left| W_{2^j} f_1(n) - W_{2^j} f_2(n) \right| \} \cdot \qquad (15)$$

The J_0 and J_1 are the starting and ending scales. For a two dimensions digital image, we perform the BDWT to the rows and then the columns. After acquiring the DE between two frames, the motion area is obtained by setting a threshold which can be obtained automatically by otsu [7] method. The noise can be removed by mathematical morphology method. One of the two frames is a background image; the other is the current frame. Figure 4 shows the vehicle detection results.

Fig. 4. Vehicle detection

4.2 Cross Road Violation Detection

According to the distance between the center of vehicle (or motion area) and lane line coordinates, the peccant vehicle can be detected. If the distance between the center of vehicle and the nearest coordinate of lane line is less than five pixels showed in figure 5, then the cross road violation occurs, we begin to track the peccant vehicle. By dong this, we can avoid the shadow influence, that the vehicle and shadow can be seen as a whole motion area, only considering the center of the motion area showed in figure 6.

Fig. 5. Sketch map of cross road violation   **Fig. 6.** Shadow crosses the road while car does not

5   Mean-Shift Tracking the Peccant Vehicle

The vehicle is represented by a rectangle region in the image. Let $\{x_i^*\}_{i=1,...n}$ be the normalized pixel locations in the region. The probability of the feature (color) of the target is modeled by its histogram with kernel [8-11]:

$$\hat{q}_u = C\sum_{i=1}^{n} k(\|x_i^*\|^2)\delta[b(x_i^*)-u], \quad u=1,...m \text{ bins} \cdot \tag{16}$$

The kernel K has a convex and monotonic decreasing kernel profile, k assigning small weights to pixels farther away from the center. The profile of kernel K is defined as a function $k:[0,\infty]\to R$, such that: $K(x)=k(\|x\|^2)$. The target candidate is modeled as:

$$\hat{p}_u(y)=C_h\sum_{i=1}^{n_h} k\left(\left\|\frac{y-x_i}{h}\right\|^2\right)\delta[b(x_i^*)-u], \quad u=1,...m \text{ bins} \cdot \tag{17}$$

The similarity function is defined as the metric distance between the candidate and the target model: $d(y)=\sqrt{1-\rho[\hat{p}(y),q]}$, Choose ρ as the Bhattacharyya coefficients: $\rho[\hat{p}(y),q]=\sum_{u=1}^{m}\sqrt{\hat{p}_u(y)q_u}$, Minimizing the distance is equivalent to maximizin ρ . Assume the target candidate histogram does not change drastically, using Taylor expansion around the values $\hat{p}_u(y_0)$ at location y_0 :

$$\rho[\hat{p}(y),q]\approx\frac{1}{2}\sum_{u=1}^{m}\sqrt{\hat{p}_u(\hat{y}_0)\hat{q}_u}+\frac{1}{2}\sum_{u=1}^{m}\hat{p}_u(y)\sqrt{\frac{\hat{q}_u}{\hat{p}_u(\hat{y}_0)}} \approx\frac{1}{2}\sum_{u=1}^{m}\sqrt{\hat{p}_u(\hat{y}_0)\hat{q}_u}+\frac{C_h}{2}\sum_{i=1}^{n_h}w_i k\left(\left\|\frac{y-x_i}{h}\right\|^2\right)\cdot$$

Where $w_i = \sum_{i=1}^{m}\sqrt{\frac{\hat{q}_u}{\hat{p}_u(\hat{y}_0)}}\delta[b(x_i)-u]$. Only need to maximize the second term, which is the density estimate with kernel profile $k(x)$ at y in the current frame, with the data being weighted by w_i . In practice, mean-shift method has some disadvantages: sometimes get stuck at local minimum, and difficult to handle abrupt motion: due to use of the kernels, the center of the target in the current frame has to be covered by the target model in the previous frame. Otherwise, the local maximum of the Bhattacharyya coefficient would not be a reliable indicator. Adopting the same distance measure, we use the Marr wavelet function kernel based mean-shift tracking method [12]:

$$y = \frac{\sum_{i=1}^{n} x_i w_i g_N\left(\left\|\frac{y_0-x_i}{h}\right\|^2\right)}{\sum_{i=1}^{n} w_i g_N\left(\left\|\frac{y_0-x_i}{h}\right\|^2\right)}\cdot \tag{18}$$

where $K_N'(x)=-g_N(x)$, and $K_N(x)=c\cdot\left(\exp\left(-\frac{1}{2}\|x\|^2\right)-0.5\exp\left(-\frac{1}{8}\|x\|^2\right)\right)$. Due to the obvious advantages of extracting characters of the tracking target, the performance of mean-shift method can be improved.

6   System Frame and Experimental Results

The monitor system frame showed in figure 7 contains two cameras and an industrial control computer. The close range camera snapshots the license plate and the remote range camera is used to detect cross road violation. Our software runs in the industrial control computer. Figure 8 shows the tracking result for paccent vehicles. The video is sampled at a resolution of 680x480 and a rate of 25 frames per second. Once the frames are loaded into memory, our algorithm averages 20 frames per second on a 2700 MHz Xeon CPU. In practice, tracking window needn't change its size according to the vehicle; as long as it is still in the region of vehicle, the close range camera can snapshoot the license plate correctly according to the center of tracking window. For multiple paccent vehicles, each vehicle can be processed with the same method of violation detection and mean-shift tracking. Figure 9 shows the run-time of improved mean-shift tracking system for video sequence (40 frames sampled) of each vehicle.

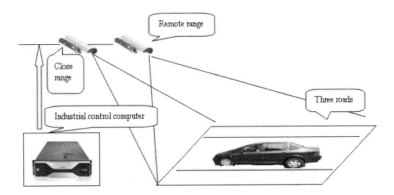

Fig. 7. Monitor system frame

Frames 379, 382, 385, 389, 392, 398, 402, and 405 are displayed

Fig. 8. Tracking results

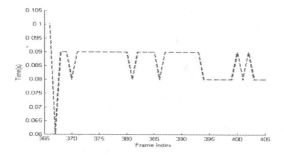

Fig. 9. Run-time of improved mean-shift tracking

7   Conclusions

This paper presents a method to recognize and track the cross road peccant vehicle. The background is modeled by mixture Gaussian model, and the location of lane line is detected by Hough transformation, thus, the coordinated series can be obtained from the monitor image. The information of vehicles can be obtained by the background-frame BDWT method, and according to the distance between the vehicle and lane line, the peccant vehicle can be detected. An improved mean-shift method is used to track the peccant vehicle. Actual road tests show that the work efficiency and accuracy of the method is high; it has a certain practical value.

Acknowledgments. The research is funded by Tianjin Traffic Bureau, China.

References

1. Stauffer, C., Grimson, W.E.L.: Learning Patterns of Activity Using Real-Time Tracking. IEEE Transactions on Pattern Analysis and Machine Intelligence 22(8), 747–757 (2000)
2. Wren, C.R., Azarbayejani, A., Darrell, T., Pentland, A.: Pfinder: Real-Time Tracking of the Human Body. IEEE Transactions on Pattern Analysis and Machine Intelligence 19(7), 780–785 (1997)
3. Power, P.W., Schoonees, J.A.: Understanding background mixture models for foreground segmentation. In: Proceedings of Image and Vision Computing, Auckland, New Zealand, pp. 267–271 (2002)
4. Jiang, Y.-h., Pi, Y.-m.: Road Detection in SAR Image Based on Hough Transformation and Genetic Algorithm. Radar Science and Technology 3(3), 156–162 (2005)
5. Wang, Q., Hu, W., Lu, Z., et al.: The Study of Hough Transformation Real Time Detect Algorithm. Computer Engineering and Design 22(3), 76–80 (2001)
6. Gao, T., Liu, Z.-g.: Moving Video Object Segmentation Based on Redundant Wavelet Transform. In: IEEE Int. Conf. on Information and Automation, Hunan, China, pp. 156–160 (2008)
7. Otsu, N.: A Threshold Selection Method from Gray-Level Histogram. IEEE Trans. SMC 9(1), 62–66 (1979)
8. Bradski, G.: Computer Vision Face Tracking for Use in a Perceptual User Interface. Intel Technology Journal 2(Q2) (1998)

 9. Collins, R.: Mean-Shift Blob Tracking Through Scale Space. In: Proc. IEEE Conf. Comp., vol. 2, pp. 234–240 (2003)
10. Comaniciu, D., Ramesh, V.: Mean Shift and Optimal Prediction for Efficient Object Tracking. In: IEEE Inter-national Conference on Image Processing, Vancouver, Canada, vol. 3, pp. 70–73 (2000)
11. Comaniciu, D., Ramesh, V., Meer, P.: Kernel-based Object Tracking. IEEE Transactions on Pattern Analysis and Machine Intelligence 25(5), 564–577 (2003)
12. Gao, T., Liu, Z.-g., Zhang, J.: BDWT based Moving Object Recognition and Mexico Wavelet Kernel Mean Shift Tracking. Journal of System Simulation 20(19), 5236–5239 (2008)

An Anomaly Detection Immune Model Inspired by the Mechanism of DC- T Cell Interaction

Junmin Zhang and Yiwen Liang

School of Computer, Wuhan University, Wuhan, Hubei 430079, China
zhangjm81@sohu.com, 119231535@qq.com

Abstract. Artificial immune systems (AISs) inspired by the biological immune system have been successfully applied to a number of problem domains including fault tolerance, data mining and computer security. The aim of the research introduces the mechanism of DC-T cell interaction in danger theory into the research of anomaly detection. In danger theory (a recently developed hypothesis in immunology), DCs (Dendritic Cells) within innate immune system are sensitive to changes in concentration of different signals derived from their tissue environment. DCs combine these signals internally to produce their own output signals in combination with related antigens. And then DCs present the "signals-antigens" to T cells in adaptive immune system. The role of T cells is to confirm and assess anomalous situations and then either respond to or tolerance the source of the effect. We extract several key features of the mechanism and map them into the anomaly detection domain, then propose a artificial immune model for anomaly detection. The paper illustrates that the novel approach shows considerable promise for future anomaly detection.

Keywords: danger theory; negative selection; dendritic cells (DCs); naïve T cells; anomaly detection.

1 Introduction

An intrusion detection system (IDS) is an automated system for the detection of computer system intrusions. The main goal of IDS is to detect unauthorized use, misuse and abuse of computer systems by both system insiders and external intruders. Traditional IDS to computer security define suspicious signatures based on known intrusions and probes [1]. One problem with the type of IDS is that slightly modified intrusions or brand-new intrusions are not detected as they are not contained within the database resulting in false negatives [2].

Anomaly detection, a technique used in IDS, offers an alternative approach, by using a defined database of "self", either in terms of machine behavior or user behavior. Data at run time is compared against the self profile and sufficient deviation causes the generation of alert [2]. Similarly, the Human Immune System (HIS) adaptively generated new immune cells so that it is able to detect previously unknown and rapidly evolving harmful antigens. So, anomaly detection is one notable application area of Artificial Immune System (AIS) inspired by HIS.

L. Qi (Ed.): FCC 2009, CCIS 34, pp. 109–116, 2009.

This paper proposes a novel aritificial immune model of anomaly detection, which is inspired by the mechanism of DC (Dendritic Cell) -T cell interaction in the Danger Theory. The Danger Theory is a hotly debated hypothesis in immunology and suggests that the human immune system can detect danger in addition to antigens in order to trigger appropriate immune responses. We carefully study the several salient features of the Danger Theory and show the possibility and advantages of adopting these features for anomaly detection, then propose the artificial immune model and describe the main components of this model.

In our algorithm, DCs in innate immune layer collect various input signals and related antigens, then present related antigens to different T cells in adaptive immune layer for the secondary detection according to the output signals.

The paper is structured as follows: section 2 contains previous AIS research on anomaly detection and brief information of the mechanism of DC-T cell interaction in the Danger Theory; section 3 presents the architecture for a novel anomaly detection immune algorithm. In section 4, the paper ends with conclusion drawn from this work and a mention of future work.

2   Related Work

2.1   Previous Work

In previous research into anomaly detection in the context of AIS, the negative selection algorithm inspired by the classical self-nonself theory forms the majority of anomaly detection research within artificial immune systems. In order to provide viable IDS, it must build a set of detectors that accurately match antigens. In its application for IDS, both network connections and detectors are modeled as strings. Detectors are randomly created and then undergo a maturation phase where they are presented with good, i. e. self, connections. If the detectors match any of these they are eliminated otherwise they become mature. These mature detectors start to monitor new connections during their lifetime. If these mature detectors match anything else, exceeding a certain threshold value, they become activated. Then, the detectors are promoted to memory detectors with an indefinite life span and minimum activation threshold. However, defining what is self is non-trivial and has a tendency to change over time, giving rise to systems with a high false positive rate [1].

In [1], Uwe Aickelin et al. firstly discussed Danger Theory in immunology on the possibility of IDS research. Greensmith *et al.* abstracted a number of properties of DCs in innate immune system of Danger Theory to propose the Dendritic Cell Algorithm for anomaly detection [3]. In the algorithm, Greensmith *et al.* categorised DC input signals into four groups (PAMPs, Safe Signals, Danger Signals and Inflammatory Cytokines). Each artificial DC combines these signals internally to produce its output signal in combination with related antigens. Different output signals (either danger or safe) determine the differentiation status of DC (either semi-mature or mature). Kim *et al* [7] continued Greensmith *et al*'s work by discussing T-cell immunity and tolerance for computer worm detection. This work presented how three different processes within the function of T-cells, namely T-cell maturation, differentiation and proliferation could be embedded within the Danger Theory-based AIS.

2.2   The Mechanism of DC-T Cell Interaction in Danger Theory

Classical immunology stipulates that an immune response is triggered when the body encounters something non-self or foreign. In order to undertake this role the immune system needs to be able to discern difference between foreign, and possibly pathogenic, invaders and non-foreign molecules. The Danger Theory [4] challenges the classical self-nonself viewpoint. The central idea in the Danger Theory is that the immune system does to respond to nonself but to danger. This theory suggests that the human immune system can detect danger in addition to antigens in order to trigger appropriate immune responses. The Danger Theory states that appropriate immune responses produced by the immune system emerge from the balance between the concentration of danger and safe signals within the tissue of a body, not by discrimination of self from nonself.

The HIS is a complex and robust system, viewed as a homeostatic protection agent. It seeks out harmful pathogens, clearing them from the body and performing maintenance and repair. It is commonly thought to work at two levels: the innate and adaptive immune system [2].

The innate immune system contains a variety of cells including macrophages and DCs amongst other. Dendritic Cells are a diverse class of cells whose main function are phagocytosis, antigen presentation, and regulation of the adaptive immune system through the production of immunoregulatory cytokines. Immature DCs collect multiple antigens and are exposed to signals, drives from dying cells in the tissue (safe or danger signals). DCs can combine these signals with bacterial signatures (PAMPs) to generate different output concentrations of costimulatory molecules, semi-mature cytokines and mature cytokines. The different types of cytokines indicate the context (either safe or dangerous) of an environment where the collected antigens exist, which lead DCs to differentiate into two types: semi-mature DCs and mature DCs. PAMPs, based on a pre-defined signature, and danger signals (released on damage to the tissue) cause an increase in mature DC cytokines. Safe signals cause an increase in semi-mature DC cytokines and have suppressive effect on both PAMPs and danger signals. Whilst immature DCs also ingest the related antigens from the extracellular milieu and then process them internally. During processing, antigens are segmented and attached to major Histocompatibility complex (MHC) molecules. Once the antigen has been ingested in the peripheral tissue, the semi-mature or mature DCs travel to the lymph nodes where they present their cell surface MHC-antigen complex with related cytokines to naïve or memory T cells, presentation of intracellular antigen in an MHCI complex stimulates cytotoxic T cells (CTLs), whereas presentation in an MHCII complex of extracellular antigen which has been ingested by the DC stimulates T helper cells (Th) [2] [5] [6].

T cells, members of the adaptive immune system, have receptors which bind to antigen presented in an MHC- antigen complex on the surface of DCs and respond to the strength of the match between receptor and antigen. Naïve T cells are T cells that have survived the negative and positive selection processes within the thymus, and have migrated to continuously circulate between the blood and lymphoid organs as they wait antigen presentation by DCs. Naïve T cells reach an activated state when the T cell receptor (TCR) on the surface of the naïve T cells successfully binds to the antigen MHC-antigen complex on the surface of the DC, and costimulatory molecules are sufficiently upregulated on the surface of the DC to reflect the potential danger. Naïve T cells that do not receive sufficient danger signals do not become activated and so the system becomes tolerant to such antigens. These activated T cells gain the ability to proliferate and their clones will begin to differentiate into either T helper cells or cytotoxic T cells. These cells will finally reach effector status when they interact with a second antigen source. Th cells can develop into either Th1 or Th2 cells. Th1 and Th2 cells have different functionality as activated Th1 cells release cytokines that activate cytotoxic T cells whilst activated Th2 cells release cytokines that activate B cells. If the DCs themselves do not express sufficient costimulatory molecules to cause CTL activation, then DCs can be induced to upregulate those signals by Th1 cells who also bind to the DC, Activated CTLs will undergo proliferation. When they receive stimulation from subsequent antigen, they will reach an effector status [6] [7].

3   An Anomaly Detection Immune Model

As described in the previous section, different mature states of DCs play varying roles in evoking tolerance or activation of T cells in the HIS. This section introduces the overall architecture and components of the AIS based on the Danger Theory. Because of the change in problem domain, these are implemented differently.

3.1   The Anomaly Detection Immune Model Overview

The overall architecture of the novel artificial immune model is developed as part of this work is presented in Figure 1. In our model, a local network can be considered as an artificial body and each host consists of the DC functional module and the T cell functional module. And the DC functional module plays the central role in the system and controls the behavior of the T cell functional module. The DC functional module interacts with input data (various signals and related antigens). It gathers and

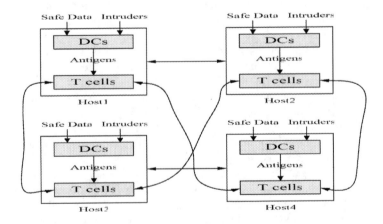

Fig. 1. Overview architecture of the anomaly detection immune model

evaluates the input data and then presents the related antigens to the T cell functional module for the further detection according to the danger degree of evaluation results. This results in a pairing between signal evidence and antigen suspects, leading to information which will state not only if an anomaly is detected, but in addition the culprit responsible for the anomaly. Naïve T cells in T cell functional module are activated or tolerance for different antigens and then perform response or not. And when a host can not completely ascertain an invasion, it will seek the help of other peer hosts (For example, worms usually infect a number of peer hosts in the network). In the following text, we will provide more detailed descriptions of the interaction of the DCs and T cells.

3.2 DC Functional Module

The module consists of three sub-modules: antigens collector, signals extractor and signals evaluation, see Figure 2. The aim of antigens collector is to collect and transform safe data or intruders into antigens which are forward to the T cell functional module for tolerance or activated. The aim of signals extractor is to collect various behavior signals of system and network caused by safe data or intruders. And the signals evaluation is responsible for evaluating various input signals that are collected by signals extractor, then generates a corresponding output signal which controls the T cells tolerance or activated for the related antigens.

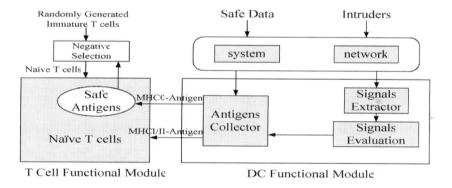

Fig. 2. The interaction mechanism of the DC functional module and the T cell functional module

Signals collector. In computer security, anomaly detection includes the detection of worms, viruses, network exploits, and distributed denial of service. These intrusions usually cause a series of system infection symptoms. Well known infection symptoms include excessive CPU load and memory usage at the host level, bandwidth saturation at the network level, and abnormal rate of connection requests etc. Signals are mapped a reflection of the victim system and network and represent the infected symptoms of system and network. Each signal has itself parameter, such as C-the rate of CPU load, M-the change rate of memory usage, L-the connection number of the local host, etc. The method of converting behavioral information into signals can be seen [8] [9].

Antigens collector. The signals collected by the signals extractor are a reflection of the status of the attacked system. Therefore, antigens are potential culprits responsible for any observed changes in the status of the system. For example, in distributed denial of service a large number of semi-connections which cause the changes in status of the system can be defined as antigens. In our representation, an antigen is compressed to a single n-bit binary string: $Ag=g_1g_2...g_n$.

Signals evaluation. Each parameter has itself weight. Such as C, M, L, ...,their weights are respectively w_C, w_M, w_L, ... signals evaluation combines these input signals to generate an output signal cav:

$$cav = Signal_C w_C + Signal_M w_M + Signal_L w_L + ...$$

We can set two thresholds for the output signal: low danger threshold value a and high danger threshold b. The degree of output signals can be defined as the following:

If $cav<a$, the output signal is safe signal; if $a \le cav < b$, the output signal is low danger signal; if $cav \ge b$, the output signal is high danger signal.

The output signal decides the category of the related antigen, which finally effects T cells tolerance or activation for the related antigen.

Antigens classification and presentation. According to the different degree of output signals related with specific antigens, we can classify these antigens into three categories: MHC0-antigens, MHCI-antigens and MHCII-antigens. If the output signal related with an antigen is safe signal, the antigen belongs to MHC0-antigens (safe antigens) and is present to existing T cell for tolerance (via negative selection); if the output signal is danger signal (either low danger signal or high danger signal), the related antigen belong to MHCI/II antigen (low danger antigen or high danger antigen) and is presented to naïve T cells for further detection.

3.3   T Cell Functional Module

The module has two processes: naïve cells generation process, and naïve cells detection and activation, see Figure 2. It consists of the training phase and the detection phase.

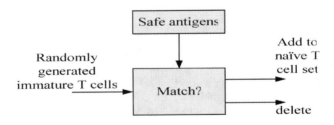

Fig. 3. The process of negative selection

Naïve cells generation. In the training phase, all MHC0-antigens (safe antigens) presented by the DC functional module in a safe environment forms a safe antigen set. They represent the normal data of the protected system. Randomly generated immature T cells (a series of n-bit binary strings) are negatively selected with these safe antigens. When a MHC0- antigen is presented, all existing T cells are negatively selected with the new antigen: If a match occurs, the immature T cell is deleted; else the immature T cell is reserved and becomes a naive T cell, see Figure 3. These newly generated naïve T cells are tolerance for the safe antigen set. These naïve T cells play a dual role in the system: For the local host they are CTLs, and for other hosts they perform the role of Th cells. If the number of safe antigens reaches to a constant n_1, the system shifts to the detection phase.

Naïve T cell detection and activation. In the phase, if a MHC0- antigen is presented, it is used to negatively select only newly create immature T cells, but not those naïve T cells that have already passed the negative selection, in which all naïve T cells in the T cell functional module is tolerance for the MHC0-antigen. At the same time, the oldest MHC0-antigen is deleted from the safe antigen set. This aging and continuous updating provides the current version of "dynamic safe antigens". When an antigen presented to naïve T cells is MHCI/II- antigen and matches with a naïve T cell, the naïve T cell is activated and the system makes a different response. If the presented antigen is MHCII-antigen (high danger antigen), indicating that the DC detects a severe attack, the naïve T cell (CTL) in the local host directly starts a strong response to that antigen. If the presented antigen is MHCI-antigen (low danger antigen), the naive T cell in the local host does not directly have a response to that antigen and needs the help of the same type of naïve T cells in other peer hosts. These naïve T cells in other peer hosts play the function of Th cells for the local host. If the number of the same activated naïve T cells in other peer hosts exceeds the threshold n_2, the naïve T cell in local host has a response to that antigen.

4 Conclusion

This paper introduces the mechanism of DC-T cell interaction in danger theory into the research of anomaly detection and then proposes a novel anomaly detection immune approach that responds appropriately according to the danger degree of output signals. The illustrated system absorbs several key features of the mechanism. According to the theoretical analysis for the model, our system has the following advantages but need to verify: 1) The DC functional module has a pre-processing function and classifies the related antigens into three categories according the output signals; 2) The system can complete a dual detection: DCs combining uniquely multiple signals with the correlated antigen for primary detection and presenting the antigen for to T cells for secondary detection; 3) for a uncertain attack, the other peer hosts assist the local host to complete the detection, which can decrease false detection rate. We believe that these above advantages can decrease false detection rate of the system

As for future work, in the following several months we will develop an experimental system to verify that our model performs better than other approaches.

And the definition of danger signals and the process of catching danger signals should be studied more. Other features of the mechanism also have good prospect in future artificial immune models, such as the clone of T cells and memory T cells. Additionally, we would like to collaborate with researchers who are interested in our research.

References

1. Aickelin, U., Bentley, P., Cayzer, S., Kim, J., McLeod, J.: Danger theory: The link between AIS and IDS. In: Timmis, J., Bentley, P.J., Hart, E. (eds.) ICARIS 2003. LNCS, vol. 2787, pp. 147–155. Springer, Heidelberg (2003)
2. Greensmith, J., Aickelin, U., Tedesco, G.: Information Fusion for Anomaly Detection with the Dendritic Cell Algorithm (01-06-2009), http://www.dangertheory.com/
3. Greensmith, J., Aickelin, U., Cayzer, S.: Introducing Dendritic Cells as a Novel Immune-Inspired Algorithm for Intrusion Detection. In: Jacob, C., Pilat, M.L., Bentley, P.J., Timmis, J.I. (eds.) ICARIS 2005. LNCS, vol. 3627, pp. 153–167. Springer, Heidelberg (2005)
4. Aickelin, U., Cayzer, S.: The Danger Theory and Its Application to AIS. In: 1st International Conference on AIS, pp. 141–148 (2002)
5. Greensmith, J., Aickelin, U.: Dendritic Cells for Real-Time Anomaly Detection. In: The Workshop on Artificial Immune Systems and Immune System Modelling (AISB 2006), Bristol, UK, pp. 7–8 (2006)
6. Twycross, J.: Integrated Innate and Adaptive Artificial Immune Systems Applied to Process Anomaly Detection. PhD thesis, University Of Nottingham (2007)
7. Kim, J., Wilson, W., Aickelin, U., McLeod, J.: Cooperative Automated Worm Response and Detection Immune Algorithm (CARDINAL) inspired by T-cell Immunity and Tolerance. In: The 3rd Int. Conf. on AIS (ICARIS 2005), pp. 168–181 (2005)
8. Zhang, J., Liang, Y.: A Novel Intrusion Detection Model Based on Danger Theory. In: The IEEE Pacific-Asia Workshop on Computational Intelligence and Industrial Application (PACIIA 2008), Wuhan, China, pp. 867–871 (2008)
9. Zhang, J., Liang, Y.: A Double Layers Detection for DoS Based on the Danger Theory. In: 2009 International Conference on Computer Modeling and Simulation (ICCMS), Macau, China (accepted, 2009)

Design and Realization of Encoding Module for UHF RFID Based on FPGA

Chao Li and Yu-lin Zhang

School of Information science and Engineering
University of Jinan, 106 Jiwei Road, 250022 Jinan, P.R. China
wslc-007@163.com

Abstract. Radio Frequency Identification (RFID) is an identification technique such as the barcode or magnetic strip technology. And it is a new automatic identification technique, which widely used in many aspects such as transportation systems, military and other fields. Physical data coding module is an important part for RFID systems. ISO18000-6C provides a new air communication interface protocol of RFID systems. ISO18000-6C is after 18000-6A, B and modifies and extends A, B's content. ISO 18000-6C greatly improves the key technologies such as the physical data encoding, modulating type, anti-collision arithmetic and so on. This paper realizes data encode based on the ISO18000-6C standard and validates with FPGA.

Keywords: RFID; ISO18000-6C; Data Encoding; FPGA.

1 Introduction

Radio Frequency Identification (RFID) is an identification technique such as the barcode or magnetic strip technology [1]. Compared to other identification technique, RFID system has many advantages: firstly, it can identify object in long distance; secondly, it can store large amounts of data; last but not least, it can work in the wet, dry, and other surroundings. It is nowadays already used in many applications such as automated library systems, public transport, and security, product tracking or logistics, and has not yet exploited its potential to full extent. RFID systems operate in different frequency bands, from very low frequencies (around 130 kHz) over high frequencies (HF) range at 13.56MHz up to ultra high frequencies (UHF, 868 - 950 MHz).

The RFID system includes three parts: one reader or interrogator, antenna and tag. Nowadays, the research on RFID systems has focused on the frequency of 125 KHz and high frequency at 13.56 MHz. But at a higher frequency such as the microwave band, which is few people to research [2][3].

ISO18000-6C standard is the latest international standard for UHF RFID, it provides the mode of encode and data exchange between electronic tags and reader in RFID systems, and also includes the mode of modulation and demodulation. This paper using FPGA realizes data encode for UHF RFID systems based on ISO18000-6C standard.

L. Qi (Ed.): FCC 2009, CCIS 34, pp. 117–121, 2009.

2   ISO18000-6C Standard

ISO18000-6 standard is jointly developed by ISO (International Organization for Standardization) and IEC (International Electro technical Commission), which is the latest air communication interface protocol for UHF RFID systems. ISO18000-6 standard includes TYPE A and TYPE B communication types, and on this basis to expand TYPE C (ISO18000-6C). EPC global organizations Class-1 GEN-2 RFID specification is adopted in ISO18000-6C standard, which is promoted as a common standard all over the world [4]. In ISO18000-6C standard, it provides physical communication interface between reader and tags. The communication mode from reader to tag is shown in Figure 1.

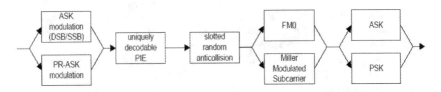

Fig. 1. Type C Interrogator Architecture

From the Figure 1 we can see that an interrogator communicates with one or more tags by modulating an RF carrier using DSB-ASK, SSB-ASK, or PR-ASK with uniquely decodable PIE encoding. And ASK or PAK modulation and FM0 or Miller coding method are adopted when tags send message to interrogator. Protocol architecture suitable for UHF RFID interrogator is proposed [5]. This paper focused on the design of coding circuit.

3   The Principle and Realization of PIE Coding

3.1   The Principle of Digital Communication

Compared to analog communication systems, digital communication systems have more advantages. Digital communication systems have good performance in error detection, anti-interference ability, security and integration. And it is convenient for digital communication system to process and store information.

The basic structure of digital communication is shown in Figure 2, the information from the source is encoded by digital signal coding circuit, and then transmitted through the channel. We can check easily whether the information, which received in the terminal, is right or wrong. The quality of data transmission sharply improved with coding circuit.

Fig. 2. The Basic Structure of Digital Communication

3.2 PIE Coding Principle

The meaning of PIE is Pulse Interval Encoding, which denotes information through the definition of pulse width between the different falling edges. Data 0 and data 1 are distinguished through the different length of pulse interval. An interrogator (TYPE C) communicates with one or more tags by modulating an RF carrier using ASK, or PR-ASK with uniquely decodable PIE encoding. So the reader link shall use PIE, shown in Figure 3. Tari is the reference time interval for interrogator-to tag signalling, and is the duration of a data-0. High values represent transmitted CW; low values represent attenuated CW.

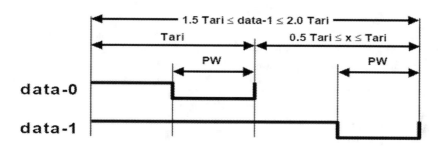

Fig. 3. PIE Symbols

The information of an interrogator (TYPE C) communicates with tags contain four parts: SOF (START OF FRAME), EOF (END OF FRAME), 0 and 1. The relationship between the PIE encoding and the time period of "Tri"is shown in Figure 4.

Symbols	Tri	1	2	3	4
0	1				
1	2				
SOF	3				
EOF	4				

Fig. 4. PIE waveform

3.3 The Realization of PIE Encoding Circuit

The design for UHF RFID reader chip includes many modules, for example modulation and demodulation circuit, encoding and decoding circuit, and so on. This paper focuses on the design of coding circuit. The basic rule of PIE coding is summarized through the Figure4, and for RF systems, NRZ (non-return-to-zero) coding is used generally. The waveform for above four symbols is indicated use NRZ encoding as shown in table 1.

Table 1. PIE Encoding corresponds to NRZ Encoding

PIE coding	NRZ coding
0	01
1	0111
SOF	01011111
EOF	01111111

Based on FPGA , this text uses the embedded designing method to design high speed real time encoding circuit. We use Verilog hardware description language to design this circuit, and run program in ISE. Some codes as following:

```
For(i=0;i<N;i++)
  if ( clk rising )
    begin
      PIE_out [M] <=1'b0;
      PIE_out [M+1] <=1'b1;
      if(data_in[i]==1'b1)
      begin
    PIE_out [M+2] and PIE_out [M+3] <=1'b1;
    end
      ...........
    end
```

4 The Effect of Design

After complete the program, we should check out the functions of this circuit right or wrong using simulation equipment such as Modelsim. Some codes of the testbench for Modelsim as following:

```
PIE_top PIE    (.clk(clk),
                .reset(reset),
                  .data_in(data_in),
                  .data_out(data_out))
    initial
      begin
        data_in    <=8'b01100101;
        reset    <=1'b0;
        clk    <=0;
        #40  reset <=1'b1;
        #400 reset <=1'b0;
      End
```

The final simulation effect as shown in Figure 5

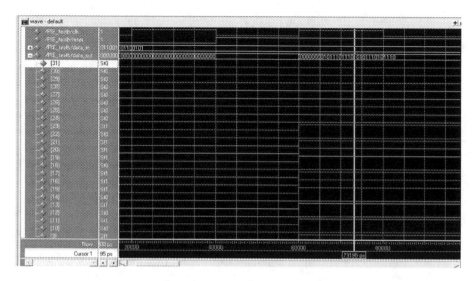

Fig. 5. The Final Simulation Result

5 Conclusions

With the wide application of Radio Frequency Identification (RFID) and the latest air communication interface protocol for UHF RFID systems proposed, the encoding and decoding method have applied in this field.

In this paper, an effective method for UHF RFID systems encoding is proposed. the circuit is designed in that way, and achieves a satisfying effect by experimental verification. This design provides a common model for encoding circuit of UHF RFID system based on ISO18000-6C standard.

References

1. Kipnis, I., Chiu, S., Loyer, M., et al.: A 900MHz UHF RFID reader transceiver IC. IEEE Int Solid-State Circuits Conf. Dig. Tech. Papers, 214 (2007)
2. Shen, Y.-c.: Modularized design in communication protocols of RFID system. Journal of Communications 22(2), 54–58 (2001)
3. Li, K.-r.: The Design of Practical Read-write System of the Untouched IC Card. Journal of Chongqing University of Posts and Telecommunications 6, 141–143 (2001)
4. ISO/IEC FDIS 18000-6:2003(E). Information technology automatic identification and data capture techniques-Radio frequency identification for item management-Part 6:Parameters for air interface communications at 860MHz-960MHz
5. Rao, K.V.S.: An overview of backscattered radio frequency identification system (RFID). In: Proc. Asia Pacific Microw. Conf., vol. 3, pp. 746–749 (November- December 1999)

FPGA-Based CMOS Image Acquisition System

Chao Li, Yu-lin Zhang, and Zhao-na Zheng

School of Information science and Engineering, University of Jinan,
Jinan, 250022, P.R. China
wslc-007@163.com

Abstract. This paper provides a plan about the high-speed acquisition and real-time process of image data based on FPGA (Field Programmable Gate Array). This design manages to acquire digital image data and store them into SDRAM with FPGA chips which belongs to Cyclone's series of Altera Company, and sends them to VGA display in the end after the real-time process of image data using FPGA. This design is distinguished from traditional image acquisition system, and provides a universal solution that implements image acquisition with logic controlling based on FPGA. The system designed by above-mentioned way achieves a satisfying effect by experimental verification.

Keywords: Image Acquisition; Real-time; FPGA.

1 Introduction

With the rapid development of image processing technology, image acquisition and processing systems are applied in all aspects increasingly [1]. In the current market of image sensors, CMOS sensor has more and more favor of consumers owing to its low prices. In the current applications, the majority of image acquisition and processing systems use DSP to control image sensors and collect image data, which is transmitted to PC through the USB interface. And these systems read image data with software, which will waste instruction cycles undoubtedly. Therefore, these image acquisition systems cannot meet real-time data acquired in high-speed [2].

For real-time image acquisition systems, which need high performance requirement because of a large amount of image data processed [3]. So, special hardware or technology of parallel processing is particularly important, and FPGA chips have natural advantages for real-time image processing system because of their specific units on the logical structure [4]. Therefore, in order to collect a mass of image data in real-time, this paper provides a design is that high-speed image acquisition system based on FPGA, which is realized with the OV9620 CMOS image sensor.

2 The Structure Performance and Working Principium of CMOS Image Sensor

The system use OV9620 color digital CMOS image sensor of Omni Vision company, The OV9620 (color) are high-performance 1.3 mega-pixel for digital still image and video

L. Qi (Ed.): FCC 2009, CCIS 34, pp. 122–127, 2009.
© Springer-Verlag Berlin Heidelberg 2009

camera products. The resolution for the OV9620 is 1280 x 1024(SXGA) pixels and 640 x 480(VGA) pixels, which can up to 30 frames per second (fps), and with some features such as high sensitivity, wide dynamic range, anti-blooming. All the parameters of images such as exposure, gain, white balance, frame rate, the output image data format, image timing signal polarity, window size and location, etc, can be set up through the SCCB interface, and take effect immediately [5].

The key parameters of OV9620 as following: Image Area is 6.66 mm×5.32 mm; Pixel Size is 5.2µm×5.2µm; resolution is 1280 x 1024 pixels (SXGA) and 640 x 480 pixels (VGA); Dynamic Range is 60dB; Scan Mode is Progressive. OV9620 embedded within a 10-bit A / D converter, which can simultaneously output 10 bit video streaming D [9...0]. In the output of digital video streaming, while CMOS senor also providing simultaneous pixel clock (PCLK), and the horizontal reference signal (HREF) and frame synchronization signal (VSYNC), facilitates the external circuit to read image data [6].

3   The Structure of System Design

Diagram of the structure of this system as shown in Figure 1, as shown of the figure 1, the CMOS image sensor responsible for image acquisition, and FPGA is used to control CMOS image sensor, SDRAM is used to store image data. When the system runs, firstly, CMOS mode is initialized by FPGA through the SCCB bus, and then through the FPGA to control CMOS image acquisition, and then the collected CMOS sensor data transit into RGB format and storage to SDRAM. Finally, the image data are sent to the VGA display when one frame of image data are acquired.

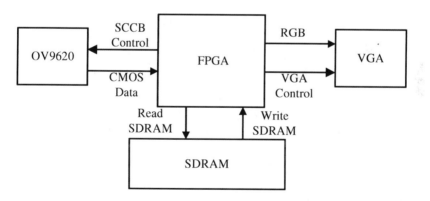

Fig. 1. Basic Diagram of System's structure

4   Operating Principle and Implementation of System Modules

4.1   Implementation of CMOS Image Acquisition

The OV9620 CAMERA CHIP offers 10-bit RGB raw data output. The default output sequence for the odd lines of output will be: RGRG... RG. The even lines of output will be: GBGB... GB. CMOS image sensor collects image data by FPGA.

Once power on, the system first initializes CMOS image senor chip, and to determine its mode of operation. These parameters are controlled by corresponding value of the register within OV9620, FPGA controls the SCCB bus to configure these parameters. If system configuration is correct and the work mode is assured, the CMOS image senor begins to work. Figure 2 and figure 3 are pixel output timing drawing and frame output timing drawing respectively in VGA mode. In the figures, the VSYNC is vertical synchronization signal, the HREF is horizontal reference signal, PCLK is the pixel output synchronization signal. From figure 2 can be seen that CMOS image senor begins to collect valid data when the HREF signal is high, and the arrival of PCLK falling edge shows that valid data is generated, the system transmits one datum when one PCLK falling edge arrives. In the period of HREF is high, the system transmits 640 data in all. From figure 3 can be seen that HREF will appear 480 times high during the VSYNC is low. And one frame image that resolution is 640 × 480 is collected completely when the next VSYNC signals rising edge arrives.

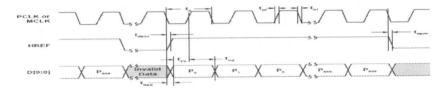

Fig. 2. Pixel output timing

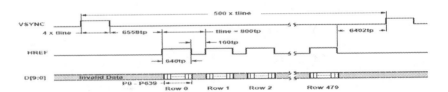

Fig. 3. Frame output timing

In the programming, this design uses two conditions to control VSYNC and HREF signals. First when VSYNC is low, the design is enter a cycle, and then begin to collect image data if HREF is high. The part code of this module is following:

```
If (mCMOS_VS is low) && (mCMOS_HS is high)
Begin to work:
  if (X_Cont<N)
  begin
    mCMOS_DATA <=iDATA;
    X_Cont <= X_Cont+1'b1;
  end
else
  begin
    X_Cont <= 0;
      if (Y_Cont <M)
```

```
        Y_Cont <= Y_Cont + 1'b1;
        else
        Y_Cont <= 0 ;
    end
```

4.2   The Module of VGA

With the rapid development of computer display technology, computer industry has developed many kinds of display interface protocol, from the original MDA interface protocol to the mainstream VGA (video graphics array) interface protocol at present. in the framework of VGA interface, which is divided into different display mode according to the resolution and refresh rate: VGA(640×480), XGA (800×600) and VGA(1024 ×768).

The timing of VGA include the horizontal timing and the vertical timing, which have parameters following: The horizontal (vertical) synchronization pulses; the interval between the end of horizontal (vertical) synchronization pulses and the beginning of display area(Back porch); display interval; the interval between the end of display area and the beginning of horizontal (vertical) synchronization pulses (Front porch).

The function of VGA display module is to be processed image data signal displayed on the monitor. VGA timing parameters is required by look-up table after the display mode is determined. The resolution is 640 × 480, field frequency is 60HZ, which parameters are shown in Table 1.

Table 1. VGA timing parameter

Format	Pixel Clock (MHZ)	Horizontal (in Pixels)				Vertical (in Pixels)			
		Active Video	Front Porch	Sync Pulse	Back Porch	Active Video	Front Porch	Sync Pulse	Back Porch
640×480 60HZ	25	640	16	96	48	480	11	2	31

Digital signals of images should be in accordance with the VGA timing signals in line as the format requested, and adding to some synchronization control signals. In this design, the synchronization signal is especially important, the reason is that if the synchronization signal is not correct, there will be some problems, such as display is divided into two part at a time and the image distortion.

5   The Results of This Design

The final effect picture is shown in Figure 4. As a real-time acquisition system, the system has strict requirements in processing speed. In the current market, the majority of image acquisition and processing systems use DSP to control image sensors and collect image data, which is transmitted to PC through the USB interface. And these systems read image data with software, which will waste instruction cycles undoubtedly. Therefore, these image acquisition systems cannot meet real-time data acquired in high-speed.

Fig. 4. The final effect

This image acquisition system is based on the FPGA, which has the following advantages compared to other image acquisition systems. First of all, it can improve system speed and system flexibility and adaptability; Secondly, it can improve sharply the performance of the system because of use FIFO to data buffer in FPGA; last but not least, it is fully implemented in hardware description language to control the image data collection and storage and also send the image to the VGA display in the end, therefore which makes external hardware circuit is simple and reduce the complexity in hardware design.

6   Conclusions

As the price of FPGA chips is cheaper, and the real-time data acquisition for image system was designed based on FPGA has satisfying performance. This method is fitted to some cases which call for acquired in high speed and cost-effective.

The system is designed in that way, and achieves a satisfying effect by experimental verification. This design provides a common model for the real-time data acquisition for image system.

References

1. Lei, S.-M., Sun, M.-T.: An entropy coding system for digital HDTV applications. IEEE Transactions on Circuits and Systems for Video Technology 1(1), 147–155 (1991)
2. Murat Tekalp, A.: Digital Video Processing. Tsinghua University Press, Beijing (1998)

3. Akermatt III, A.: Pyramidal Techniques for Multi-sensor Fusion SPIE: Sensor or Fusion V, vol. 1828, pp. 124–131 (1992)
4. Shui-ming, C.: The Application of FPGA on Real-time Image Pretreatment Algorithm. Electronic Technology of Shanxi Province (05) (2007)
5. Omni Vision Technologies, Inc. OV9620 Data Sheet (Version 2.5). September 15 (2003)
6. Gokhale, M.: Building and Using a Highly Parallel Programmable Logic Array. IEEE Computer, 81–89 (January)

Parallel Implementation of A5/2 Algorithm

Longmei Nan, Zibin Dai, Wei Li, and Xueying Zhang

Insititute of Electronic Technology, The Information Engieering University,
Zhengzhou 450004, China
nanlongmei@yahoo.com.cn

Abstract. A high-speed parallel implementation method of A5/2 algorithm is proposed by improving the conventional architecture in this paper. The operating parallel design of A5/2 algorithm is exploited in initialization, clock controlling stream generation, clock controlled stream generation and key stream generation to enhance the operating speed and the throughput rate of key stream with no increasing of complication in circuit and no decline of the clock frequency nearly. As to the different high-speed methods, this paper performs detailed comparison and analysis. The design has been realized using Altera's FPGA. Synthesis, placement and routing of this parallel design have accomplished on 0.18μm CMOS process. The result proves the critical throughput rate can achieve 1.06Gbps.

Keywords: A5/2, compute in advance, LFSR, parallel level.

1 Introduction

Stream cipher [1] has been widely used due to its simple realization, high speed in encryption or decryption and the characteristic of small error propagation in cipher transmission. A5/2 [2] algorithm is just a typical application of Stream cipher. As one kind of A5 [3] algorithm, A5/2 algorithm is used in many countries in order to ensure privacy of conversations on GSM [4] mobile phones. So it is important to enhance the throughput rate to protect information of the subscribers and avoid fraud in the mobile communication.

In previous work, there are two main methods to implement A5/2 algorithm, one obeys the basic architecture of A5/2 algorithm and the other adds parallel processing cells to the basic architecture. Limited by its own characteristic of A5/2 algorithm, the operating speed and the throughput rate of the former means is both low, as referred in Ref [5], the throughput rate is only 1.45bit/clock. The operating speed and the throughput rate of the later means is higher than that of the former one, however, for the data correlation coming from the updating of LFSRs, the exploitation of its parallel level is limited, the delay from computing updating data is also becoming greater, and this results in great decline of the clock frequency, as referred in Ref [6].

In this paper, a high-speed parallel implementation method of A5/2 algorithm is proposed. First, obeying the principle of A5/2 algorithm, the architecture is improved by computing updating data in advance. Further, the parallel level is exploited and

L. Qi (Ed.): FCC 2009, CCIS 34, pp. 128–135, 2009.

enhanced, including initialization parallel design, clock controlling stream generating parallel design, clock controlled stream generating parallel design and key stream generating parallel design. The max parallel level can reach four, and this greatly increases the operating speed and the key stream throughput rate without decline of the clock frequency nearly.

2 The Introduction of A5/2 Algorithm

A5/2 algorithm is a kind of stream cipher based on line feedback shift registers. The secret key size of it is 64bit, and the IV size of it is specified to be 22bit frame number. As is shown in Fig 1, A5/2 algorithm is built from four LFSRs of lengths 19,22,23,17 bits denoted by R1, R2, R3 and R4 respectively. Each register is updated by its own primitive feedback polynomial as is shown in Ref [5]. Clocking of R1, R2 and R3 is controlled by R4 which is regularly clocked in each clock cycle. Majority of the bits R_4^3, R_4^7 and R_4^{10} is calculated and a binary result according to majority rule is obtained. If the result is the same as R_4^3, then R2 is clocked, if the result if the same as R_4^7, then R3 is clocked and if the result is the same as R_4^{10}, then R1 is clocked. After the clocking of R1, R2 and R3, R4 are clocked, the output bit is generated.

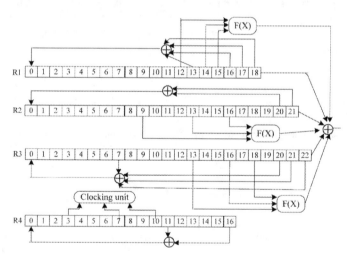

Fig. 1. The A5/2 stream cipher

The process flow of A5/2 algorithm can be described as follows [7]. The initialization of the registers loads the bits of secret key and the bits of the frame number, followed by setting R_1^{14}, R_2^{15}, R_3^{17} and R_4^9 to "1", then 100 output bits. After the initialization, 228 bits of output stream are computed. The former 114 bits are used to encrypt data from the center to the mobile phone, and the latter 114 bits are used to encrypt data from the mobile phone to the other center.

3   The Parallel Realization of A5/2 Algorithm

By researching on A5/2 algorithms, clocking of R1, R2 and R3 is controlled by R4 and R4 is regularly clocked in each clock cycle, so the clock controlling stream generation and the clock controlled stream generation can be designed separately. Furthermore, the last four bits of the four shift registers are all not used in the feedback functions or in the key stream generating functions. This allows the speed to be easily multiplied by up to 4 through computing updating feedback data in parallel in advance [8]. Naturally, each of the shift registers needs to be implemented such that each of the steps is shifted n bits instead of one bit when the speed is increased by a factor n. The number of clocking used in the key initialization becomes 86/n. Besides, in the key generation phase, the cipher outputs n bits/clock key stream. Of course, some necessary hardware should be set up. It is quite feasible to increase the key throughput by this way.

Combining the two ideas having been told in above paragraph, the modified algorithm structure can be reached. As is shown in Fig. 2, the whole modified structure includes four function blocks mainly. The parallel updating feedback function block is designed to initialize each LFSR with secret key and frame number, also to compute and update each LFSR in key generating process. The clock controlling stream generation block is designed to generate the controlling stream of each controlled LFSR. The clock controlled stream generation block is designed to generate each tap stream in parallel under the master of controlling stream. The parallel key stream generation block is designed to generate key stream with the parallel taps having been gained from clock controlled stream generation block.

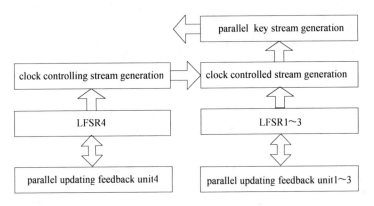

Fig. 2. The modified algorithm structure of A5/2 algorithm

In the following chapters, each of the parallel function blocks will be designed in detail with the factor n equaling to 4.

3.1   The Parallel Realization of the Initialization

Four LFSR in A5/2 algorithm have different primitive feedback polynomial, yet their principium and the initial process is the same, so the similar realization method can be adopt to initialize each of the LFSRs. Illustrating with R4, the parallel realization of initialization is given in Fig 3.

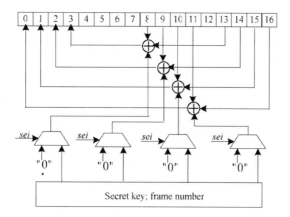

Fig. 3. The parallel realization of initialization

Firstly, it is mentioned above that the last four bits of the four shift registers are all not used in the feedback functions or in the key stream generating functions, so each of them can be used to store the output of each parallel updating feedback function in advance. Secondly, 4 multiplexers are added, selecting initial key(secret key and frame number) or "0", to dominate R4 working at initialization or key stream generating process. If the controlling node sel is "1", multiplexers select initial key and R4 works at initialization, otherwise multiplexers select "0" and R4 works at key stream generating process. After that R4 is shifted to right by 4bit under the master of a clock, by repeating this step, parallel updating 4bits/clock of R4 can be achieved. The other LFSRs can be initialized by this same method.

3.2   The Parallel Realization of Clock Controlling Stream Generation

It has been analyzed above that clock controlling stream generation and clock controlled stream generation can be designed separately. Clock controlling stream generation is just shown in Fig 4. Four clocking units which will be told soon are appended to the structure of initialization, by the same way as the multiplexers: beginning with each of the taps R_4^3 , R_4^7 and R_4^{10} , 4 bits data are extracted to left

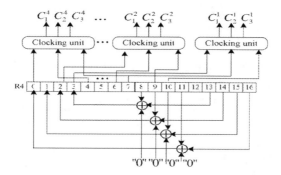

Fig. 4. The parallel realization of clock controlling stream generation

continuously which are denoted by $R_4^3[4:1]$, $R_4^7[4:1]$ and $R_4^{10}[4:1]$, $R_4^{10}(4:1)$ respectively. Then they are sent to each of the corresponding clocking units one by one, as inputs of clocking units. After that, the controlling streams for R1, R2 and R3 denoted as $C_1[4:1]$, $C_2[4:1]$ and $C_3[4:1]$ respectively are gained. It should be pointed that at this phase the initialization has finished and the controlling node sel should be set to "0". Each of the clocking units has the same function and can be realized by the same non line Boolean function with three inputs three outputs. The following expressions and Fig 5 just indicate how to generate one bit of each clocking stream.

$$C_1(i) = 1 + R_4^{10}(i) + R_4^{10}(i)R_4^3(i) + R_4^{10}(i)R_4^7(i) + R_4^3(i)R_4^7(i) \tag{1}$$

$$C_2(i) = 1 + R_4^3(i) + R_4^{10}(i)R_4^3(i) + R_4^3(i)R_4^7(i) + R_4^{10}(i)R_4^7(i) \tag{2}$$

$$C_3(i) = 1 + R_4^7(i) + R_4^{10}(i)R_4^7(i) + R_4^7(i)R_4^3(i) + R_4^{10}(i)R_4^3(i) \tag{3}$$

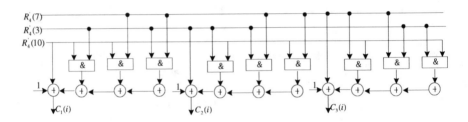

Fig. 5. The realization of each clocking unit

Adopting the realization of clock controlling stream generation analyzed above, parallel 4bits controlling stream for each dominated LFSRs can be achieved in one clock. This is very essential to exploit the parallelity of the A5/2 algorithms.

3.3 The Parallel Realization of Clock Controlled Stream Generation

The domination from each controlling stream mentioned above, to the activity of each controlled LFSRs, is the same as it to the value of each tap stream used to calculate the final key stream. Here is an example. we use controlling stream $C_1[4:1]$ to dominate $a[4:1]$ in order to gain the correct value of the tap stream $Y[4:1]$. Supposing parallel extracting the tap R_1^{12}, then $a[4:1]$ denotes the states from R_1^{12} to R_1^9. By analyzing $Y(4)$ equals to $a(4)$, no matter what vale of $C_1(4)$ is; $Y(3)$ equals to $a(4)\overline{C_1(4)} + a(3)C_1(4)$. By the same way, the vale of $Y(2)$ and $Y(1)$ can be reached, and all possible vales of $Y(1)$ are shown in Fig 6, if $C_1(4) + C_1(3) + C_1(2)$ equals to "0", $Y(1)$ equals to $a(4)$; if it equals to "1", $Y(1)$ equals to $a(3)$; if it equals to "2", $Y(1)$ equals to $a(2)$; if it equals to "3", $Y(1)$ equals to $a(1)$.

$C_1(4)$	$C_1(3)$	$C_1(2)$	$C_1(1)$	$\overrightarrow{Y_1}$
0	0	0	×	a_4
One "1"			×	a_3
Two "1"			×	a_2
Three "1"			×	a_1

Fig. 6. The possible vales of Y1

It is obvious that the generation of clock controlled stream $Y[4:1]$ dominated by controlling stream $C_1[4:1]$ is just like the selection from $a(4:1)$ by controlling stream to each state of $Y[4:1]$ . .So we design the realization shown in Fig 7 to finish the task.

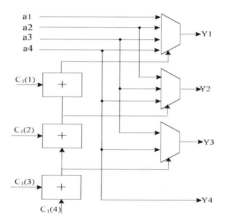

Fig. 7. The parallel realization of clock controlled stream generation

The value of $Y(4)$ can be gained straightly. Others can be selected from each multiplexer under the control of its selecting node which is configured by the code of each value of the cumulater. By this means, the parallel 4bits controlled stream of each enlisting tap can be achieved in one clock.

3.4 The Parallel Realization of Key Stream Generation

Through the three processes mentioned above, parallel 4bits of each correlative tap have been gained, and used as inputs to generate the key stream in parallel, so 4 key stream generation units are designed to support the parallel level of 4. By predigesting, the key stream generating function can be described as follow:

$$Z = R_1^{18} \oplus R_2^{21} \oplus R_3^{22} \oplus (R_1^2 R_1^{15}) \oplus R_1^{15} \oplus (R_1^{15} R_1^{14}) \oplus R_1^{12} \oplus (R_1^{12} R_1^{14})$$
$$\oplus (R_2^9 R_2^{13}) \oplus R_2^9 \oplus (R_2^9 R_2^{16}) \oplus R_2^{13} \oplus (R_2^{13} R_2^{16})$$

$$(4)$$

Each of the key stream generation units can be realization as the same method as clocking units, and parallel 4bits key stream can be achieved in one clock.

4 Analysis and Comparison of Performance

4.1 Analysis of Performance

The prototype has been accomplished RTL description using Verilog language, followed by the synthesis using QuartusII 6.0, and has been verified successfully based on Altera's Cyclone EP1C12Q240C8. The performance is shown in Table 1.

Table 1. The performance of parallel A5/2 algorithm based on the FPGA

Factor	Maximum Frequency (MHz)	Logic Elements (LEs)	Throughput rate(Mbit/s)
n=1	180	430	180
n=2	173	510	346
n=3	170	560	540
n=4	167	590	660

Furthermore, the design has been synthesized under 0.18μm CMOS process using Synopsys' Design Complier to evaluate performance more accurately. Synthesis, placement and routing of the prototype based on architecture have accomplished. The performance results of the prototype have been shown in Table 2.

Table 2. The performance of Grain algorithm based on ASIC

Factor	Maximum Frequency (MHz)	Area (μm^2)	Throughput rate(Mbit/s)
n=1	285	149673	285
n=2	280	170713	554
n=3	275	180713	809
n=4	268	197876	1060

From Table1, it can be seen clearly that being verified by FPGA , the max Maximum Frequency is 180MHz, the max Logic Elements used is 660, and they all change smally, yet the Throughput rate enhances greatly and can reach 660Mbit/s. From Table2, it can be reached that being verified by ASIC, the max maximum frequency is 285MHz, the max area is 197876 um^2, and they also changes smally, however the throughput rate can enhance to1060Mbit/s.

4.2 Comparison of Performance

Based on the performance parameters, no matter being verified by FPGA or by ASIC, it can be known easily that with the increasing of factor n, the area of circuit is getting a litter larger, yet the key stream which generates in each clock cycle is increasing obviously, and the maximum frequency hardly descends, the throughput rate is improved visibly. This is due to no increasing of complication between updating data by the means proposed in this paper, and this is just the main merit different from other methods, such as Ref[6]. In Ref[6] the data correlation coming from the updating of LFSRs limits the exploitation of its parallel level, increases the delay from computing updating data, and decreases the maximum clock frequency seriously, yet this is improved by the means proposed in this paper commendably.

5 Conclusion

As a word, this paper proposes a high-speed parallel architecture by computing updating data in advance, and exploits the operating parallel on it. Under the parallel realization of initialization, clock controlling stream generation, clock controlled stream generation and key stream generation, the paper makes the detailed comparison and analysis to the other high-speed realization. Furthermore, Synthesis, placement and routing of parallel design have accomplished on 0.18μm CMOS process. Compared with conventional designs, the result proved architecture has an obvious advantage in the speed and throughput-to-area ratio.

References

1. Qibin, L., Jian, Z.: Status Quo and Development of stream Cipher. Information and Electronic Engineering 4(1) (February 2006)
2. Biham, E., Dunkelman, O.: Cryptanalysis of the A5/1 GSM Stream Cipher. In: Roy, B., Okamoto, E. (eds.) INDOCRYPT 2000. LNCS, vol. 1977, pp. 43–51. Springer, Heidelberg (2000)
3. Golić, J.D.: Cryptanalysis of Alleged A5 Stream Cipher. In: Fumy, W. (ed.) EUROCRYPT 1997. LNCS, vol. 1233, pp. 239–255. Springer, Heidelberg (1997)
4. Lo, C.C., Chen, Y.J.: Stream ciphers for GSM Network. Computer Communications 24(11), 1090–1096 (2001)
5. Erguler, I., Anarim, E.: A Modified Stream Genrator for the GSM Encryption Algorithms A5/1 and A5/2. ECRYPT Stream Cipher Project Report (2005), http://www.ecrypt.eu.org/stream
6. Wei, L., Zibin, D.: Research and Implementation of A High-speed Reconfigurable A5 algorithm. Computational Intelligence and Industrial Application, 93–97 (2008)
7. Galanis, M., Kitsos, P., Kostopoulos, G.: Comparison of the Hardware Implementation of Stream Ciphers. The International Arab Journal of Information Technology 2(4) (October 2005)
8. Hell, M., Johansson, T., Meier, W.: A Stream Cipher Proposal: Grain-128. ECRYPT Stream Cipher Project Report (2005), http://www.ecrypt.eu.org/stream

The Study of Model for Portfolio Investment Based on Ant Colony Algorithm

Wang Ting[1] and Yang Xia[2]

Department of Economic Management, North China Electric
Power University, Baoding, Hebei 071003, Hebei, China
yx869@163.com

Abstract. The risk and benefits are consided synthesizely in portforio invest-ment based on the Markowitz portfolio theory. A multi-objective programming model of portforio investment is established and studied the model solution with the ant group algorithm, then obtained a better result compared to using the Lingo model. Unified the ant group algorithm and the modern computer's formidable operational capability, making the investor to be more convenient in the actual operation.

Keywords: multi-objective programming, portfolio investment, ant colony al-gorithm, Lingo1.

1 Introduction

China's stock market is full of vigor and vitality, and also full of confusion and risk. Speeding up the research step in the field of financial and investment will provide certain theoretical support for the development of capital market and investors to improve the investment activities,so it is imperative to explore operational mechanism which adapts to Chinese socialist market economy.for a long time, the investor's decision-making depends on the experiences in the practice and has not risen to the theory altitude. Since the 1950s Markowitz founded the modern portfolio theory, many scholars underwent the difficult research work to carry on and have enriched and developed this theory,so they obtained many effective methods in solving many problems of the portfolio, but how to make the portfolio model become optimization decision-making model is an urgent problem that needs to be solved.

In recent years, with the development of artificial intelligence, applied the intelli-gent optimization method in the investment profolio question has become the broader research area. This paper used the continuous optimization ant algorithm to solve the optimal solution problem of the portfolio model, the experimental result has indicated that this model is accuracy and validity.

2 Multi Objective Decision-Making Model of Portfolio Investment

Supposed invest n kinds securities, the kind of i securities's returns rate is $r_i (i = 1,2,\cdots,n)$. Due to r_i receives the influence of stock market's various factors,

L. Qi (Ed.): FCC 2009, CCIS 34, pp. 136–141, 2009.
© Springer-Verlag Berlin Heidelberg 2009

thus r_i could be regarded as a random variability. $R_i = E(r_i)$ is the mean of r_i, $\sigma_i^2 = E(r_i - R_i)^2$ is the variance of r_i, x_i indicates t he proportion of portfolio investment which i security invests in($\sum_{i=1}^n x_i = 1$).Then the portfolio investment's expectation returns ratio and the variance respectively are:

$$R = \sum_{i=1}^n x_i R_i, \sigma^2 = \sum_{i=1}^n \sum_{i=1}^n x_i x_j \sigma_{ij} \tag{1}$$

Here $\sigma_{ij} = E(r_i - R_i)(r_j - R_j)$ is the covariance of i-securities and j-securities then multi-objective programming model of portfolio investment can be reveived:

$$\max R = \sum_{i=1}^n x_i R_i$$

$$\min \sigma^2 = \sum_{i=1i=1}^n \sum^n x_i x_j \sigma_{ij} \tag{2}$$

$$s.t \begin{cases} \sum_{i=1}^n x_i = 1 \\ x_i \geq 0 \quad i = 1,2,\ldots,n \end{cases}$$

$x_i \geq 0$ expressed that our country does not permit short selling.

$X = (x_1, x_2, \ldots, x_n)^T, R = (R_1, R_2, \ldots, R_n)^T, C = (\sigma_{ij})_{n \times n}$

C is symmetric positive definite matrices,R is covariance matrix , $E = (1,1,\ldots,1)^T$ and (2) expresses the matrix: max R=$R^T X$

$$\max R = R^T X$$
$$\min \sigma^2 = X^T C X$$
$$s.t \begin{cases} E^T X = 1 \\ X \geq 0 \end{cases} \tag{3}$$

Namely: $\min F(x) = \left\{ \left[f_1(x), f_2(x) \right]^T \mid \sum_{i=1}^n x_i = 1 \right\}$

$$f_1(x) = -R^T X, f_2(x) = X^T C X \tag{4}$$

Hence constructed a multi-objective decision making model to be able to optimize the income and the risk simultaneously. The solution of multi-objectives optimize emerges one after another incessantly, but transforming the multi-objective questions as the simple target question is the basic philosophy, with the aim that using a maturer simple-target optimize method to obtain optimal solution. Each kind of solution may divide into two kinds approximately: One kind aims at optimizing one component of the multi-objective functions, but takes other components become the constraints, or constructs a sequence simple target to optimize; Another kind make the multi-objective function

$$\min F(\sigma^2,-R) = \mu\sigma^2 - (1-\mu)R$$
$$s.t \begin{cases} E^T X = 1 \\ X \geq 0 \end{cases} \tag{5}$$

Aversion coefficient μ's scope is $0 \leq \mu \leq 1$. The great number showed that the investor cannot accept the risk, when $\mu = 1$ the investors can completely avoid risks.

3   Ant Colony Algorithm

To determine the fitness function: In this paper, the constraints will join the objective function as the the penalty factorization, the fitness function will be:

$$\min F(\sigma^2,-R) = \mu\sigma^2 - (1-\mu)R + M\left|E^T X - 1\right| \tag{6}$$

In order to achieve the ant colony algorithm's search process, the structure of the transition probability criteria are as follows: Supposed there are m groups artificial ant, each group has n artificial ants, starts to put the stochastically division region of the solution space $[0,1]$'s $l \times n$ in certain positions randomly, each regional ant's condition transition probability is:

$$p_{ij} = \begin{cases} (\tau_j)^\alpha (\eta_{ij})^\beta, \eta_{ij} < 0 \\ 0, \quad\quad 其他 \end{cases} \quad i,j=1,2,..,l \tag{7}$$

Therefore used the group ant's unceasingly moves in $l \times n$ division regional in $[0,1]$, as well as in some region's part random searching carries on, ant k's shift and tsearch's rule in the region i is:

$$\begin{cases} \arg\max_j \{ p_{ij} \}, \text{Shift region j to conduct random search } i,j=1,2,...,l \\ \text{else,} \quad\quad \text{Conduct random search} \end{cases} \tag{8}$$

The renewal equation of the egion j's information element is:

$$\tau_j(t+1) = \rho\tau_j(t) + \sum_{k=1}^{m} \Delta\tau_j^k, \quad j=1,2,...,l$$
$$\Delta\tau_j^k = \begin{cases} QL_j^k, L_j^k > 0 \\ 0, \quad L_j^k \leq 0 \end{cases} \quad j=1,2,...,l \tag{9}$$

In the formula, $\Delta\tau_j^k$ reflected the ant k's increasing attract intensity in this circulation in the region j's partial search; L_j^k expressed the objective function's change quantity of this circulation ant k's partial search in the region j, the definition is:

$$L_j^k = f(x_{j0}^k) - f(x_j^k) \tag{10}$$

$$x_{ij} = x_{i0} + \frac{1}{l}(j - 1 + \gamma_j^k) \tag{11}$$

$$x_{ij0} = x_{i0} + \frac{1}{l}(j - 1 + \gamma_{j0}^k) \tag{12}$$

$$i = 1, 2, \ldots, n \quad j = 1, 2 \ldots, l$$

Among them γ_j^k, γ_{j0}^k are the random number which obey the uniform distribution in $[0, 1/l]$ and the random number which express the ant k's partial search in this circulation in the region j,

$X_j^k = [x_{1j}^k, x_{2j}^k, \ldots, x_{nj}^k]$ and $X_{j0}^k = [x_{1j0}^k, x_{2j0}^k, \ldots, x_{nj0}^k]$ are the search point 's position vector of the n Uygur space.

4 Computation Example

This article gave a combination about two kinds of securities to confirm this model, each securities' returns ratio vector was: $R = (0.151, 0.137)$. The two securities' returns ratio shown in Table 1.

Table 1. Securities returns

Economic conditions	Possible returns ratio		Probability
	Securities 1	Securities 2	
1	-0.188	0.188	0.2
2	0.26	-0.248	0.1
3	0.221	0.238	0.4
4	0.246	0.27	0.2
5	0.253	-0.246	0.1
Mean	0.151	0.137	-

In the experiment various algorithms parameter's value respectively is: Ant's Information density $Q = 1$ which releases in various region's search, the various region's attraction intensity durable coeffi cient $\rho = 0.7$ the attraction intensity heuristic factor $\alpha = 1$ the expectation heuristic factor $\beta = 1.5$, the operation stop condition is the difference between optium value which the ant algorithm achieved and the corresponding theory optimum value of optimized question namely: $\delta = 0.001$; The district number of function solution space $l = 10$, and the number of ants group is $m = 9$. In this paper, based on different risk preferences, separately obtained different combinations when $\mu = 0.3$, $\mu = 0.4$, $\mu = 0.5$, $\mu = 0.6$, $\mu = 0.7$, $\mu = 0.8$.

Table 2. Two model's income portfolio in different risk preference

risk preferences	Algorithm				
	Securities 1	Securities 2	σ^2	R	Objective Function Value
0.3	0.834	0.1659	0.023	0.149	-0.1009
0.4	0.754	0.2458	0.0187	0.1479	-0.085
0.5	0.706	0.2938	0.017	0.1472	-0.0693
0.6	0.674	0.3257	0.0163	0.1468	-0.0538
0.7	0.651	0.3486	0.016	0.1465	-0.0348
0.8	0.634	0.3657	0.0158	0.1462	-0.0229
risk preferences	Lingo				
	Securities 1	Securities 2	σ^2	R	Objective Function Value
0.3	0.723	0.277	0.0175	0.1474	-0.0977
0.4	0.683	0.3172	0.0165	0.1469	-0.0814
0.5	0.659	0.3414	0.016	0.1464	-0.0651
0.6	0.643	0.3575	0.0159	0.1463	-0.0489
0.7	0.631	0.369	0.0158	0.1462	-0.0327
0.8	0.622	0.3776	0.0157	0.1461	-0.0166

The above result showed that under each kind of risk condition, the objective function value obtained by this article's algorithm is smaller than the objective function value obtained by lingo, which indicated that the algorithm in solving the multi-objective programming question is better than lingo.

5 Conclusion

According to the present securities-investment market's situation of China(do not allow short-selling secure-Ties), proposed a objective model of the securities investment combination optimization under conditions of the nonnegative investment ratio, and designed ant group algorithm to solve this model's continual optimazation. Through the example of computer simulation, we can see that this algorithm is effective in solving the multi-objective programmings and in optimizing portfolio investment's application. Unified the ant group algorithm and the modern computer's formidable operational capability, making the investor to be more convenient in the actual operation.

References

1. Zhengchun, L.: The Multi-factor Portfolio Investment Decision-making Model Based onGenetic Algorithm. Mathematics practice and understanding 34(6), 32–37 (2004)
2. Hanjun, J., Hongfeng, W.: The simulation analysis of portfolio optimization problem based on genetic algorithm. Central of China Normal university journal 38(4), 37–39 (2004)
3. Xia, L., Hongxia, L., Kejun, W.: Portfolio investment model research based on grain of sub-group algorithm, vol. 16, pp. 49–51 (2006)

4. Qingfang, J.: The decision-making model of securities investment risk preferences and expectations of the effectiveness, auditing and economic study 21(5), 77–81 (2006)
5. Foster, I., Kesselman, C., Nick, J., Tuecke, S.: The Physiology of the Grid: an Open Grid Services Architecture for Distributed Systems Integration. Technical report, Global Grid Forum (2002)
6. Bencan, G., Layuan, L.: Efficient ant colony Algorithm Based on RightPheromone Updating and Mutation. Computer Engineer and Applications 44(1), 45–47 (2008)

Design of Embedded Network Interface Controller Based on ARM9 and ARMLinux

Shaoke Chen and Shaojun Jiang

Key Laboratory of Intelligent Manufacture Technology of Ministry of Education,
Shantou University, Shantou, Guangdong 515063, China
skchen@stu.edu.cn

Abstract. With the development of industrial Ethernet technology, Ethernet has infiltrated into the control layer and equipment layer of control system network. However, a large number of industrial site equipment is not equipped with network interfaces, and they perform communication through serial ports, so they fail to be connected to Ethernet directly. With the development of technology, 32-bit microprocessor has become the mainstream of embedded market application. In the article, the 32-bit microprocessor S3C2410 is chosen to be the embedded interface controller developed as main chip to realize the conversion between serial port data and Ethernet data. Without changing the original equipment, network interface is added so that the conventional serial port equipment can be connected to the Internet through standard TCP/IP protocol.

Keywords: ARM9; ARMLinux; serial port; Ethernet; Embedded.

1 Introduction

As the LAN technology with the widest application currently, Ethernet has enjoyed more and more application in industrial automation and the process control field. The conventional control system adopts Ethernet in the information layer mostly, and adopts different site buses or other dedicated networks in the control layer or equipment layer. At present, with the development of industrial Ethernet technology, Ethernet has infiltrated into the control layer and equipment layer. The most typical application form of an Ethernet-based control network is Ethernet+ TCP/IP, and its bottom layer is Ethernet. The network layer and transmission layer adopt the internationally recognized standard TCP/IP. However, for a large number of industrial site equipment, such as NC machines, robots, PLC, instruments and sensors etc, the most common communication mode is RS-232/485/422 serial interface as they don't have network interfaces, so that they fail to be connected to Ethernet directly. Therefore, how to alter the original serial port equipment at the lowest cost to connect them to the Internet through TCP/IP protocol is a problem faced by many enterprises.

With the development of semiconductor industry and IC technology, the embedded system with microcontroller/microprocessor as the hardware core has enjoyed rapid development, and has been widely used in wireless communication, network equipment and industrial control etc. In this article, embedded network interface controller

L. Qi (Ed.): FCC 2009, CCIS 34, pp. 142–149, 2009.

developed based on ARM9 and ARMLinux are chosen to realize the mutual conversion between serial port data and Ethernet data, through which the conventional serial port equipment are equipped with network interfaces. [1]

2   Operating Principle of Embedded Network Interface Controller

The embedded network interface controller chooses DM9000E chip as the Ethernet controller to complete data exchange with the Ethernet at upper layer. The 32-bit microprocessor S3C2410 and embedded Linux are used for protocol realization and data processing, and then the processed data are passed down to the equipment terminal at bottom layer. The data received at the equipment terminal go through data processing and protocol realization, and then are transmitted to the Internet through DM900E. Flow chart of function realization is shown in the Fig. 1.

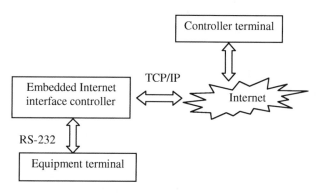

Fig. 1. Flow chart of function realization

2.1   Hardware Platform of Embedded Network Interface Controller

The entire connection diagram for the hardware platform of embedded network interface controller is shown in the Fig. 2. The system chooses the 32-bit microprocessor S3C2410 based on ARM9 kernel ARM9TDMI as the main control chip. The processor S3C2410 is the one based on ARM Company's ARM920T processor core by Samsung Company, and it can run at 203MHz at highest speed. The FLASH memory for the system chooses 28F128 of INTEL company, and the SDRAM chip chooses the memory system with two HY57V561620 consisting of 32-bit.

The chip for Ethernet controller chooses DM9000 which is a fully integrated, single and fast one at low cost and with universal processor interface. It is 10/100M self-adapting and has 4K double-byte static access memory. It features low power consumption and high processing performance, and supports allowance of 3.3V to 5V. DM9000 provides an MII interface which connects to HPNA device or other transceiver that supports MII interface, and it also supports 8-bit, 16-bit and 32-bit interface to access to internal memory by different processors. It fully supports IEEE 802.3u specification and IEEE 802.3x full-duplex flow control. The network isolating transformer HR601627 from HanRun Electronic Co., Ltd. must be used for connection between DM9000 and RJ45 interfaces. The transformer has the functions of signal transmission, impedance matching, waveform repair, clutter rejection and isolation of high voltage as well as protection of system safety.

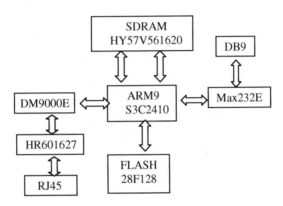

Fig. 2. Frame diagram for the hardware of embedded network interface controller

2.2 Selection of Embedded Operating System

At present, there are many popular embedded operating system products on market, and here the embedded Linux is chosen according the actual condition. The reasons are as follows:

1. Linux can be applied in multiple types of hardware platforms. It has been transplanted to multiple types of hardware platforms, which is attracting to R&D projects with limited expense and time. The prototype can be developed on a standard platform, and then transplanted to specific hardware, which speeds up the software and hardware development process.
2. The source code is free, which is the most attracting point. Undoubtedly, this will save a lot of development expense.
3. Linux has excellent network support. The micro-kernel provides network support directly, and Linux needs no outside hang TCP/IP protocol package like other operating systems since it is developed on the basis of network.

In the design of the system, the network card driver and TCP/IP protocol is the key of realization. By choosing, the protocol stack has been embedded so that TCP/IP protocol can be realized. The embedded Linux system supports multiple types of network cards, such as various 10M, 100M and 1000M Ethernet network cards, Token Ring and Wireless LAN etc. For DM9000 and its NE2000-compatible Ethernet controller, the embedded Linux has provided good support. During transplanting, it is only necessary to modify the source code and configure corresponding module in order to realize support to network.

3 Realizing Conversion between Ethernet Data and Serial Port Data

The interface controller developed in the article mainly completes two functions, i.e. sending the data received by serial port to Ethernet through network card, and sending the data received by network card to the other serial port end through serial port. The working mode can be chosen as the mode of server or client end. The data transmission protocol can choose TCP (Transmission Control Protocol) mode or UDP (User Datagram Protocol) mode [2]. TCP and UDP are two types of transmission protocols for Ethernet data. TCP is connection-based protocol, and reliable connection must be established with the other party before receiving and sending data formally. While UDP is non-connection-oriented data direct transmission protocol, so it needs no answer and confirmation by the other party.

3.1 The Development Environment and Network Programming of Application Programs

The development and implementation of embedded system program should be done on two different platforms PC and ARM, so cross compiling and connection is necessary. Connect the host machine and target board with serial port and Ethernet, and program development is compiled in RedHat9.0 Linux operating system. After debugging passes, add the program developed by myself to recompile armlinux kernel, and harden the compiled binary file into ROM of the development board, so that it can run automatically after start-up [3].

The TCP/IP process module is realized by using SOCKET programming. SOCKET was an interface program developed on UNIX system for TCP/IP network communication in the beginning. Later, it was transplanted to DOS and Windows operating system successfully, and became the most universal API function for network development on Internet. SOCKET which is used for network development has two types, namely Stream Sockets, Datagram Sockets and Raw Sockets. Stream Sockets corresponds with TCP protocol, while Datagram Sockets corresponds with UDP protocol. Raw Sockets is mainly used for protocol development and some bottom layer operation [4].

3.2 Software Design

The system adopts the working mode of TCP Server, and waits the client end to request connection to realize the data transmission function. The flow chart of the program is shown in Fig. 3. First, open the serial port. Opening of the serial port under Linux is operated through standard file opening function. The program code is as follows:

```
int fd;
   fd=open("/dev/ttyS0",O_RDWR);
   if(fd=-1) {perror("error alert!");}
```

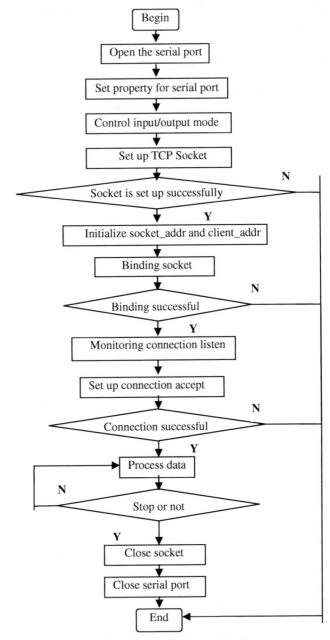

Fig. 3. Flow chart of function realization

Then set the baud rate, check bit and stop bit of serial port. Socket must be created first in order to receive and send data with network card. The program code is as follows:

```
int sock_fd;
sock_fd=socket(AF_INET,SOCK_STREAM,0)
 if(sock_fd==-1)
{
perror("socket");
exit(1);
}
```

Then set the property, and wait connection of the client end. Once connection is established, data receiving and sending can be realized.

Data processing is a critical link in the entire program. The link realizes mutual exchange between network data and serial port data. Network data can be converted to parallel data or data with other types of interfaces according to actual needs. Here, interactive processing of network data and serial port data is divided into two parts. One part is network data being converted to serial port data, and another part is serial port data being sent to network. The flow chart is shown in Fig. 4 and Fig. 5. The embedded network interface controller receives the data sent by bottom layer device through serial port, and stores the data in the buffer area. Then the controller completes data packing by packing them into TCP/IP data package from up to bottom layer by layer, and sends them to Ethernet through the Ethernet controller DM9000.

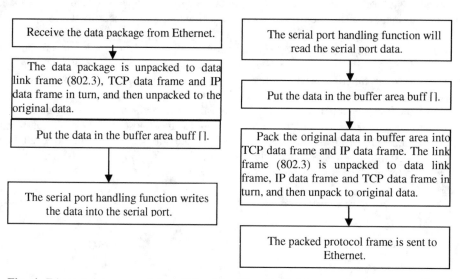

Fig. 4. Ethernet data are sent through serial port

Fig. 5. Serial port data are sent through network card

Call the Select () function in the data processing program [5]. The function not only solves the condition of blocking, but also makes full use of the system resources. Select () function allows the user to hang the process itself, and enables the system to monitor any activity of the required group of file descriptors at the same time. If it is confirmed that activity occurs on any monitored file descriptor, Select () will return to direct the information prepared by the file descriptor. Thus, random change can be chosen for the process without CPU expense on input test done by the process. The prototype of Select () function is as follows:

```
int select(int numfds,fd_set *readfds,fd_set
*writeset,fd_set *exceptset,const struct timeval
*timeout);
```

Return: number of the prepared file descriptor (can be 0), -1 indicates error.
The definition of timeval structure is as follows:

```
Struct timeval{
        long tv_sec;
        long tv_usec;
}
```

4 Application Examples of Embedded Network Interface Controller

At present, embedded network interface controller has enjoyed initial application in numerical control machining center which only has RS-232 serial port interface. It is hoped that these NC machining centers can be fully utilized during implementation of network manufacturing. However, problem exists in network connection, especially data acquired by serial port failing to realize seamless integration with upper layer management software. With the embedded interface controller developed in the article, it is convenient to connect the NC machining center to the Internet to realize network manufacturing.

First, develop the transmission software of NC program with Winsock under VC++ development environment. Then connect the NC machining center to the LAN hub through the embedded network interface controller. Set the IP address of the controller as 192.1683.2.222 and the monitoring port as 6555. Choose the client end on the transmission software to set the server name and port number. Press the connection button to establish connection with the controller, and NC program can be sent. The transmission interface is shown in the fig. 6.

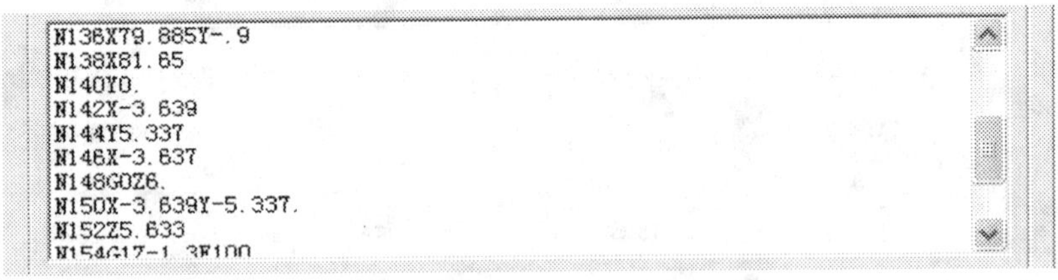

```
N136X79.885Y-.9
N138X81.65
N140Y0.
N142X-3.639
N144Y5.337
N146X-3.637
N148G0Z6.
N150X-3.639Y-5.337.
N152Z5.633
N154G17-1.3F100
```

Fig. 6. Transmission interface

With this mode, any computer on LAN can transmit NC program to NC machining center through the embedded network interface controller, or all serial port devices can be connected to LAN to realize remote control. This makes information integration more convenient, laying a foundation for better realization of network manufacturing and remote control.

5 Summary

This article develops an embedded network interface controller which can realize conversion between Ethernet data and serial port data based on ARM9 and Armlinux successfully. With the developed embedded network interface, the bottom layer device can have network interface for access to industrial Ethernet without changing the original structure. Its control software is redesigned on the new network control system platform, and the advanced programming language VC++ is used for development to realize the NC program transmission module and network monitoring module. Test and debugging is also conducted on the machining center. The result proves the feasibility of the new system.

References

1. Bertoluzzo, M., Buja, G., Vitturi, S.: Ethernet networks for factory automation. In: Proceedings of the 2002 IEEE International Symposium on, Industrial Electronics. ISIE2, pp. 175–180 (2002)
2. Yiming, A., Eisaka, T.: Industrial hard real-time communication protocol over switched Ethernet. WSEAS Transactions on Computers 5, 844–851 (2006)
3. Xiao-jin, C., Xiang-dong, H.: Control system of wastewater treatment based on industrial Ethernet. In: 2006 First IEEE Conference on Industrial Electronics and Applications, IEEE Cat. No. 06EX1215C, pp. 886–889 (2006)
4. Polsonetti, C.: Industrial Ethernet value proposition. International Journal of Computer Applications in Technology 4, 175–181 (2006)
5. Ai-guo, W., Jin, L., Wen, J.: The developing status of industrial Ethernet. Information and Control 10(466), 458–461 (2003)

The Design of Body Welding Line Base on the Virtual Manufacturing and Assembling Environment

Xiaoping Xiong and Quandong Jin

School of Electromachanical Automobile Engineering,
Yantai University, Yantai, China
xxp2001@163.com, kimqd2000@tom.com

Abstract. The intensive market competition requires the automobile industry to spend much less time develop cars of high quality at lower price. So we promote the design of body welding line base on the virtual manufacturing & assembling environment technology. In order to provide more information to designers or researchers in the phase of product development and design. Then optimize the design process through simulate assembly performance and process ability. This paper introduces the virtual design in the body welding line , discusses the feature and key technique of designation in the Virtual Manufacturing & Assembling environment , points out the virtual design is the direction of body welding line in our country.

Keywords: Body welding line, Virtual Design, Modeling Simulation.

1 Introduction

Car-Body manufacturing is a large systematic engineering in automobile manufacturing industry. With the development of worldwide Automobile industry, people more and more pursue personalized profile of the body, this drives the body design and manufacture to more varieties and less batch. It's helpful to meet the diversification of demands and reduce the stock, but it will go against reducing cost and shortening delivery time. The intensive market competition requires the automobile industry to spend much less time develop cars of high quality at lower price. So we must consider technical innovation.

The automobile industry in China is in a rapidly developing stage. The demand of body welding line is huge. It's not enough to just introduce and assimilate foreign advanced techniques. We have to develop body welding line by ourselves which is suitable for China, which mostly lies in doing our best to improve the manufacturing standard while efficiently combining design and manufacture capacity.

So, we promote the design of body welding line base on the virtual manufacturing & assembling environment technology. In order to provide more information to designers or researchers in the phase of product development and design. Then optimize the design process through simulate assembly performance and processability[1]. It's a revolution for traditional technique and has great advantage and potential in reducing cost, shortening time and improving quality, It becomes the key to win in market competition.

L. Qi (Ed.): FCC 2009, CCIS 34, pp. 150–156, 2009.
© Springer-Verlag Berlin Heidelberg 2009

2 The Virtual Design System in Body Welding Line and Key Technology of Design

Body welding line is a combination of automation equipments which welds body stamping parts into body in white. It includes under body line, side frame line, door line, hood line, trunk lid line, roof line etc. welding subassembly and assembly line (main line). According to the cycle time, the level of automation and mode of production the assembly and subassembly line are divided into several work stations, every station includes welding jig, welding equipment, transform system, control system, auxiliary equipment and so on[2]. In the process of body parts welding, locating and clamping with the jig, by using suspended spot welding machines fitted with all kinds of special welding tong and welding torch, even install robots. Automation is realized upon various forms of controlling and conveying equipments, which demands highly on the manufacturing of welding equipment[3]. In order to reduce the rate of failure, labor intensity and cost, we introduce virtual manufacturing and assembly technology.

Virtual design bases on virtual reality technology. It makes use of information technology, simulation technology and computer technology to complete the reality information and manufacture, assembly process simulation, in order to find out the problems in manufacture and assembly process, and then we can take valid preventive measure before practical production. Through shortening the manufacturing cycle, costs are reduced and competitiveness is increased[4]. This technology has gone into practical phase in some fields abroad, but domestically, the research of virtual system is still in development in each field.

We consider computer, internet and 3D-CAD/CAM software of UG as basic support, using data base, artificial intelligence, and rich design experience. Then establish all kinds of standard parts and typical model database orienting body welding line form the virtual design system of body welding line. See as figure 1.

Before welding line trial production, we determine the general process scheme depending on this system, generate the product model, then put them into virtual environment to simulate loading, clamping, welding, unloading and transporting. through computer data analysis and optimize the result, so the modeling and simulation technology cross the whole design process, it's key technology of welding line virtual design.

2.1 Welding Line Process Modeling

Using group technology principle, establish all kinds of equipments database and design open structure, with the accumulation of experience, we supply and perfect the database that is beneficial for designer to share the data and information resource, then realize concurrent design better.

1)Establish all kinds of body welding line technologic scheme related to cycle time, the level of automation and mode of production, generate scheme layout depending on certain condition or restriction.

2)Establish original body converted and analysis data base, automatically generate section drawings for body parts in directions.

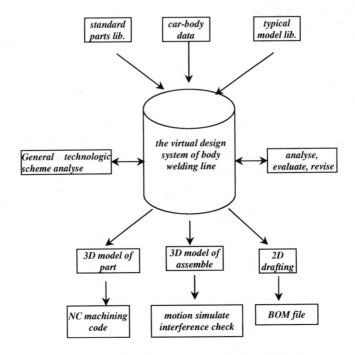

Fig. 1. The virtual design system of body welding line

3)Apply the sketch design and dimension parameters drive function based on features, establish 3D standard parts database and typical model database based on actual example, being convenient for using and revising.

4)Establish 2D drafting symbol and document database. After structural optimization design, it automatically generates 2D engineering drawing of assembly and part, it can be dynamically modified upon the change of 3D model. At the same time generate the list of making part, standard part and purchased part.

2.2 Welding Line Process Simulation

The layout of welding equipment display on the screen by modeling, through simulating the process of assembly dynamically, to check the whole welding line for assembly and static interference, then determine the best structure and space control.

After virtual assembly of equipment, determine welding points, the angle of welding gun and the robot position by the software according to the certain rules of operation which can simulate process of motion and analyses performance, check dynamic interference resistance between components.

To ensure the accuracy for the shape and dimension of the locating surface which contact with body part, the most components in the welding line were manufactured by NC machining or wire cutting. Compiling processing technologic specification to realize the computer aided programming of the work pieces in NC machine tools, the generating of the cutter location file and the NC instructions. And the manufacturing process can be simulated dynamically.

2.3 Welding Line Process Design

The key technique of body welding line virtual design are the existing design and manufacturing resources which can be used effectively in the whole design process of new welding line. The design procedure includes three stages:

The Stage of Scheme Design
According to the requirements of uers, design and modeling the general scheme of the welding line. Finally find the design scheme and principle that can meet the needs of users.

The Stage of Preliminary Design
In the stage, general structure of Welding line contains structural layout, major shape of the parts and assemble relations are made sure. This course is a key stage from the theory to practical shape and structure, and determine the amount, structure, material, and important required precision, and is very significant for the manufacturability, assembly and the usage of design resources on design and manufacturing. In this stage of design, assembling ability and manufacturability index must be analyzed and estimated. The assembling ability index which includes the number and the type of parts, the degree of standardization as well as the manufacturability index which includes the time of manufacture, cost and the machinability are decided by the structure of blue print. If time and cost can meet the requirement of users, more detailed of design is needed, otherwise, new design plan is required.

The Stage of Detailed Design
Design detailed assembly drawing and part drawing for the identified principle scheme, and covert into practical 2D engineering drawings.

3 Examples of Designed Operation

Using this system, we designed the welding lines for SL-1 car model of Shanghai Maple. The 3D assembling model as figure 2 showed is the welding station of car engine room. Compared with previous traditional 2D Design, the period of design seems to slightly increased. But due to virtual assembling and manufacturing during the process of design, the time put in practical manufacturing, assembling and setting was significantly shorter than before. Especially, for this reason, the interference phenomenon caused by the equipments during site installation and trial operation was decreased significantly. And the workload of modification on design and production was greatly reduced at the same time repair rate was decreased. Based on these conditions, the aim of shortening the development period and reducing the development cost was realized.

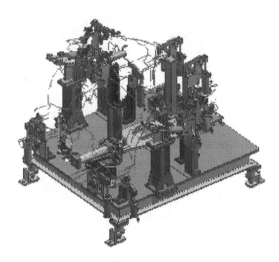

Fig. 2. The welding station of car engine room

4   The Design Feature of Body Welding Line Base on the Virtual Manufacturing and Assembling Environment

Product design is the predecessor of virtual manufacturing and it not only determines manufacturing cost, quality and periods of product, but also is the important foundation and prerequisite to organize and implement virtual manufacturing. The design of body welding line base on the virtual manufacturing & assembling environment shows the following features:

4.1   Effective Utilization of the Existing Designs and Resources Is the Core of Welding Line Design Base on the Virtual Manufacturing and Assembling Environment

Due to a great variety of the type of automobile product, the jigs and welding guns used in the welding process are not identical according to different model. That makes the design workload enormous. To improve this condition, the existing structures components and typical welding line should be specified, standardized and serialized to build the standard parts database and typical model database which face to body welding line. Utmost utilization of the existing design resources in the database during the process of welding line design of new vehicle model not only can reduce a large amount of work for product preparation such as part design, drafting, process design and manufacturing etc., shorten the producing prepare period, but also can control the diversity of tooling equipment and reduce the product cost because of decreased sorts of new part. At the same time, to adopt component product verified by production practice can improve the reliability and agility of design.

4.2 Full Utilization of the Advanced Computer Technique Is the Means of Welding Line Design Base on the Virtual Manufacturing and Assembling Environment

The CAD data of automobile body is data synthesis which includes shape parameters of visible part in the bodywork surface and structure parameters base on body inside. And it is the foundation of body welding line design. Designers exchange data stream through internet to realize the knowledge sharing of designing process. Using computer modeling and simulation, the working conditions of welding jig and welding gun, interference checking between them and the adjustment method for interference avoided can be simulated dynamically in the virtual manufacturing & assembling environment. And the working status and the process of manufacturing and assembling, the whole process of transform, clamping and welding of bodywork on the production line and working condition of the whole line can also be simulated dynamically.

4.3 Flexible Design Is the Trend of Development of Welding Line Design Base on the Virtual Manufacturing and Assembling Environment

Flexible bodywork welding and assembling system can produce multiple vehicle types on a production line. It has the advantages of simple and quick model replacing, short period of exploitation, less repeatable cost and higher efficiency. It adapts the trend of small-batch and multi-variety production. The flexible bodywork welding and assembling system couples with the computer simulation technology can confirm the layout of welding clamp on the CAD drawing, the position of solder joints and the angle of welding torch. So they can ensure the most adaptive interval to achieve maximum productivity.

4.4 Combination Design Is the Model of Welding Line Design Base on the Virtual Manufacturing and Assembling Environment

The welding line is general term of all working stations used to form body-in-white. It is constitute of assembly line and many subassembly lines. And every assembly line or subassembly line is made up of many independent welding stations of car parts. Transfer equipment such as auto feed machine, robot etc. can be used to implement the loading and discharge as well as transferring of components between every two lines and every two working stations in order to assurance the continue of the work in lines. Owing to the enormous workload of the whole welding line design, it will be done by the cooperation of different persons even cross regional according to the working status and performance. That is coordinated mutually through internet, which involves problem of resource sharing and cooperation in design etc.

4.5 The Optimal Selection of Outsourced Manufacturing Enterprise Should Be Considered Simultaneously in the Course of Welding Line Design

The design Scheme of welding line determines the component of the outsourced manufacturing enterprise. At the same time the design and manufacturing capability of the outer-cooperated manufacturing enterprise also influence the quality, cost and period of the final welding line design scheme. Therefore both sides should be considered simultaneously so as to obtain the optimized welding line design scheme and the optimal syndicate.

5 Conclusion

Virtual technique is a modern advanced manufacturing technology. It is the most challenging subject in product design for the time being. A product can be predefined and analyzed from its properties, manufacturability and assembly with the implementation of this technology before it is created in the real world. Thus production can be carried forward in a more effective and economic way to shorten product development time, lower cost, optimize product design quality and improve efficiency. It overcomes the limitations of traditional company and the incompleteness during the course of design and manufacture, reduces the repeated input of resources, reduces the product preparation cycle of, raises the flexibility and agility of the course from designing to manufacturing, and strengthens the competitive capacity of enterprise. But it is fairly hard to realize the virtual environment of the full functions in term of cost. It is recommended to adopt simple equipments instead of the complex equipments in the virtual environments to realize the advantage of software simulation.

References

1. Sheng, B.Y.: The Design method of car body welding jig in virtual manufacturing System. Journal of Wuhan Automotive Polytechnic University (March 1998)
2. Wang, Y.-x., He, K.-j., Ding, H.-m.: A Study on CAD/CAM System of car Body Welding Production Line. Automobile Technology & Material (July 2002)
3. Cai, W., Hu, S.J., Yuan, J.X.: A variational method of robust fixture configuration design for 3D workpieces. Journal of Manufacturing Science and Engineering 119(11), 593–602 (1997)
4. Yuan, Z.W., Jian, L.W., Cheng, H.Q., Ming, L.Z.: The Method of The Knowledge base on Universal Jig Expert System When Select Jig Module Machine Tool and Auto Manufact. Technology (January 1994)
5. Bo, M.Q., Zheng, H.K.: Basic Research and Exploitation of New CAD System about Jointing-Assembly Clamb on Car Protion. Mechatronics (June 2005)
6. Zhou, Z.-q., Luo, L.-j., Lin, Z.-q.: Development of welding fixture designing database for covering component of automobile. Journal of Machine Design (October 2002)

Modeling Economic Spatial Contact among Cities with the Intensity and Structure Model of Urban Flow

Yaobin Liu and Xiao Cai

Research Center of the central China Economic Development,
Nanchang University, Nanchang P.R. China
Liuyaobin2003@163.com

Abstract. The paper employs the intensity model to analyze the spatial contact among cities that attribute to process of urban agglomeration, and builds a structure model to reveal the causality running urban agglomeration system. The study shows that Jiangxi province in China is still in the embryo of urban agglomeration at present, which is in the low degree of formation and development and hasn't had the high density urban clusters with close correlation. And the economic spatial contact among cities is not powerful. Therefore, each city should make better use of its advantages to improve their overall ability, meanwhile enhance their comprehensive service capacity and strengthen the contact quantity of the outward functions. All of this is to provide the dynamics for the formation and development of urban agglomeration.

Keywords: urban agglomeration; urban flow; spatial contact; intensity model; structure model.

1 Introduction

Although many scholars pay more attention to the urban clusters in the developed areas of western countries, the modern researches have been extended to the developing areas including Africa and Asia countries. Mechanism and pattern of urban agglomeration are still a focus and topic in urban planning field. Here, for example, Naude and Krugell analyzed the spatial development of urban agglomeration in South Africa, and thought that the size of the primate city might be relatively too large [1]. Kanemoto et al. took Tokyo metropolitan as an example, and analyzed the rational size of Tokyo as the primate city[2]. Qin et al. analyzed formation mechanism and spatial pattern of urban agglomeration in central Jilin of China [3].

Most modern scholars of urban development acknowledge that transnational processes are having an increasingly important influence on the evolution of urban agglomeration. An early observation was the recognition of an emerging system of world cities, a kind of urban elite which is shaped in part by the new international division of labor [4]. These urban agglomerations are also thought to be controlling and coordinating global finance, producer and business services [5]. The view of world cities as the "key nodes" of the international urban system is a widely held one, underpinned in particular by rapid advances in the development of information technology and telecommunications. However, because the

L. Qi (Ed.): FCC 2009, CCIS 34, pp. 157–163, 2009.
© Springer-Verlag Berlin Heidelberg 2009

surrounding metropolitan area has experienced profound changes of spatial organization, with suburbanization bringing the most radical reorganization of metropolitan space[6], the growing role of suburbanization in metropolitan development is not unique as other major cities in post-communist countries follow a similar path [7][8]. Suburbanization should thus be considered as one of the crucial topics in the study of urban agglomeration in post communist cities. Regulating planning is a critical task in urban agglomeration development. It shapes our urban agglomeration form and its future development direction[9]. Consequently, a variety of explanations attribute to urban agglomerations at present.

As an opening system, the primary dynamics of urban development is to provide products and services for the outside regions [10]. The spatial contact of urban economic is the creation of geographical division of labor, and also is the inherent requirement and necessary condition of urban economic development. The higher intensity of economic contact between cities is the primitive power of regional development and evolvement as well as the basic condition of forming urban compact area or urban agglomeration [11]. Consequently, studying the spatial contact of urban economic is first and foremost for analyzing the economic of urban agglomeration. For this, based on the intensity model of urban flow, the paper analyzes the intensity of urban economic by taking Jiangxi province as a case, and studies the direction by the structure model. All of this is to provide strategic basis for nurturing the competitive capacity of urban agglomeration in Jiangxi province.

2 Database and Methodology

2.1 Database

Jiangxi province of China is defined to include 11 perfecture-level cities. Provincial boundaries as administrative units play an important role while preparing local and regional development plans. Therefore, the areas outside the provincial boundary were excluded in the study. It represents about 1.8% of the surface of the P.R. of China and 3.5% of its population. In Jiangxi province, agricultural production dominates its economy. The share of agriculture in GDP was 17.93% in 2006, i.e. 5.32% higher than the average level of the whole country. Its GDP per capita in 2006 was equal to 9440.62 Yuan (US$8.19), i.e. 67.24% of the national average[12]. As a result, agriculture in Jiangxi province plays the primary role in all the economic activities and most cities only take an inward function. However, urban agglomerations are not fully developed in Jiangxi province. Therefore, to strengthen the development of other industries and to enhance the urban spatial contact is the important method for the formation and evolvement of urban agglomeration in Jiangxi province.

2.2 Methodology

Intensity model. The intensity of urban flow is the influencing quantity produced by urban outward function (cluster and radiation) in the urban contact, and is one of the quantified guidelines reflecting the contact among cities. It is defined as[13]:

$$F = E \times N \tag{1}$$

Where F is the intensity of urban flow; E is the quantity produced by urban outward function; N is the urban function efficiency which is the practical influence produced by per outward function quantity.

According to the direction among cities in different areas, urban functions are divided into urban outward function and urban inward function. The former is the economic activity produced in the outward contact among cities, and the latter is the economic activity produced in the inward contact. Urban flow indicates the economic activities produced in the outward contact among cities, so these activities constitute the outward functions of cities. In practical operations, considering the presentation and the flexibility of special indexes operated, the number of residents employed is taken as the measurement index of urban functions. As a result, the quantity E produced by the urban outward functions mainly depends on the location entropy of the employees engaging in certain departments. The location entropy Lq of the employees in the jth department of the ith city is defined as:

$$Lq_{ij} = \frac{G_{ij}/G_i}{G_j/G}(i = 1,2,\cdots,n; j = 1,2,\cdots,m) \tag{2}$$

Where G_{ij}, G_i, G_j, G denotes the number of employees in the jth department in the ith city, the total number of employees in the ith city, the number of employees in the jth department in the whole province and the number of employees in the whole province respectively. If $Lq_{ij}<1$, the jth department in the ith city doesn't exist outward functions, i.e. $E_{ij}=0$. If $Lq_{ij}>1$, the jth department in the ith city has outward functions. Because the proportion of employees of the jth department in the ith city is greater than that of the whole province, the jth department in the ith city is the specialized department in the whole province, and is able to provide services for the outside function. Accordingly, the quantity of outward function E of the jth department in the ith city is greater than the average level of the whole province. It is defined as:

$$E_{ij} = G_{ij} - G_i(G_j/G) = G_{ij} - G_{ij}/Lq_{ij} \tag{3}$$

The quantity E_i of all outward functions of the overall departments in the ith city is:

$$E_i = \sum_{j=1}^{m} E_{ij} \tag{4}$$

If the function efficiency in the ith city is expressed as per GDP of employee, the equation can be defined as:

$$N_i = Y_i/G_i \tag{5}$$

Where Y_i denotes GDP in the ith city; N_i denotes the function efficiency in the ith city. Therefore, the intensity of urban flow can be expressed as:

$$F_i = N_i \times E_i = (Y_i/G_i) \times E_i = Y_i \times (E_i/G_i) = Y_i \times K_i \tag{6}$$

Where F is the intensity of urban flow in the ith city; K_i is the percentage of the quantity of outward functions in the ith city, which can be called as the tendency degree, reflecting the outward degree of all the quantity of functions in the ith city.

Structure Model. The intensity of urban flow for all the cities has structural differences. To reveal the structural differences, the paper introduces the structure decomposition formula. The structural intensity refers to the ratio relationship between factors of the intensity of urban flow. From the formula $F_i = Y_i \times K_i$, we can conclude the two factors for the intensity of urban flow, i.e. urban comprehensive strength and the tendency degree of urban flow. The comparative ratio relationship between the two factors influences the intensity of urban flow directly. The decomposition formula defines as:

$$\begin{cases} Y'_i = \dfrac{Y_i}{\max Y_i} \\ K'_i = \dfrac{K_i}{\max K_i} \end{cases} \tag{7}$$

Where Y'_i and K'_i are the standardized values of Y_i and K_i respectively; $\max Y_i$ and $\max K_i$ denotes the maximum values of Y_i and K_i respectively.

3   Result and Analysis

3.1   Intensity and Direction

Taking 14 main outward service departments of the 11perfecture cities in Jiangxi province and analyzing the intensity of urban flow, we calculate the location entropy for the outward departments in these prefecture cities. The results reveal that only the location entropy of most outward service functions in Nanchang which is the provincial capital city is greater than 1. However, most of them are less than 1. It shows the central status of Nanchang in urban system of Jiangxi province and indicates the cluster and radiation capacities of all cities in Jiangxi province are weaker comparatively, as well as these cities are in the early developing stage of urban agglomeration. The gaps of location entropy for primary departments in these cities are not evident, which shows the distribution of each industry is even.

Calculating the quantity E of the outward functions of the jth department in the ith city ($Lq_{ij}>1$, $E_{ij}>0$ or $Lq_{ij}<1$, $E_{ij}=0$). The quantity E of outward functions of the provincial capital city and in regional central cities such as Xinyu, Jian, Yichun, Ganzhou and Jiujiang is 4.14, 4.83, 0.87, 0.78, 0.73 and 0.71 respectively, which indicates the prominent status of the six cities in Jiangxi province. The quantity E of outward functions in other five cities, is no more than 0.7, which indicates the radiation capacity of these cities is weaker.

To calculate the tendency degree of urban flow K_i and the intensity of urban flow F_i, the result are showed as Fig.1. As Fig.1 can be seem that Nanchang as the regional central city plays the role in radiating and promoting and Xinyu becomes the regional central city in the western of Jiangxi province because of the advantages in iron and steel industry, whole sale and retail industry, accommodation catering industry as well as residential service. The cities of Jian, Shangrao, Ganzhou and Jiujiang with middle urban flow are the subcenters of regional contact. Jiujiang city is the radiation center in the northern of Jinxing province because of the position as a door and the geographical advantage in adjacency to Yangtze river; Ganzhou. Jian becomes the subcenter of city cluster in the southern of Jiangxi province because it radiates and promotes the whole southern of Jiangxi.

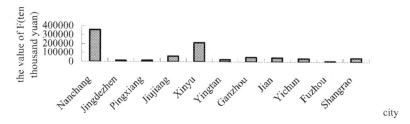

Fig. 1. The intensity of urban flow for 11 prefecture cities in Jiangxi province

3.2 Structure Difference

The Y_i and K_i of the 11 prefecture cities in Jiangxi province can be processed with the formula normalization technique employed, and the comparative values of Y_i' and K_i' can be seem from Fig. 2. The structural urban flow reveals that: (1) the diversion of the economic strength and outward service functions occurs in Nanchang and Xinyu are the highest. As for Nanchang, the most powerful city in economic strength but with middle level of comprehensive service capacity, there exists $Y_i' > K_i'$, which indicates that the intensity of urban flow from Nanchang mainly depends on its comprehensive economic strength. However. Xinyu with a weaker economic strength but with powerful service capability, there exists $Y_i' < K_i'$, which indicates that the intensity of urban flow from Xinyu preeminently depends on the advantageous industries development. (2) in the four cities with middle urban flow such as Jian, Shangrao, Ganzhou and Jiujiang, there are more powerful cities in economic strength ,such as Jiujiang and Ganzhou ,but with less powerful outward service capacity and there exists $Y_i' > K_i'$. Meanwhile, there are also weaker cities in economic strength such as Shangrao and Jian but with more powerful outward service capacity. As a result, there exists the relationships $Y_i' > K_i'$ or $Y_i' < K_i'$ coincidently. (3) in the five cities with low urban flow such as Jingdezhen, Pingxiang, Yingtan, Fuzhou and Shangrao, there are more powerful cities in economic strength(Jingdezhen, Pingxiang and shangrao) and there are also weaker cities in economic strength (Yingtan and Fuzhou), in which their common characters are $Y_i' > K_i'$ and their outward service capacities are comparatively not powerful.

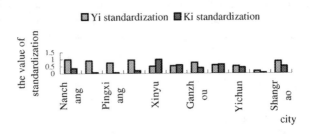

Fig. 2. The structural urban flow of 11 prefecture cities in Jiangxi province

4 Discussion and Conclusion

Urban flow is the presentation of urban spatial contact. By the technique of intensity of urban flow, we make the quantitative evaluation of economic spatial contact. This paper explores the quantitative analysis and the horizontal comparison with the urban spatial contact. The study shows that Jiangxi province is still in the embryo of urban agglomeration at present, which is in the low degree of formation and development and hasn't had the high density urban clusters with close correlation. And the economic spatial contact among cities is not powerful. Therefore, each city should make better use of their own advantages to improve their overall strength, meanwhile enhance their comprehensive service capacities and strengthen the contact quantity of the outward functions. All this is to provide the dynamics for the formation and development of urban agglomeration. In addition, when the quantity of outward function is calculated, the paper doesn't consider the weight of indicators and the relative importance of each indicator to urban spatial contact, which are left for further study.

Acknowledgement

This research was supported by funding from Provincial Education Department of Jiangxi (No. GJJ08014) and National Social Science Foundation of China (NSSC) (No.07CJL031).

References

1. Naude, W.A., Krugell, W.F.: Are South Africa's Cities Too Small? J. Cities 20(3), 175–180 (2003)
2. Kanemoto, Y., Kitagawa, T., Saito, H., et al.: Estimating Urban Agglomeration Economies for Japanese Metropolitan Areas: Is Tokyo Too Large? Graduate School of Economics, University of Tokyo (2005)

3. Qin, G., Zhang, P.Y., Jiao, B.: Formation Mechanism and Spatial Pattern of Urban Agglomeration in Central Jilin of China. J. Chinese Geographical Science 16(2), 154–159 (2006)
4. Hall, P.: The World Cities, 3rd edn. Weidenfeld and Nicolson, London (1984)
5. Thrift, N.: Globalization, Regulation, Urbanization: The Case of The Netherlands. J. Urban Studies 31, 365–380 (1986)
6. Sykora, L.: Changes in The Internal Spatial Structure of Post-Communist Prague. J. Geographical Journal 49(1), 79–89 (1999)
7. Leetmaa, K., Tammaru, T.: Suburbanization in Countries in Transition: Destinations of Suburbanize in The Tallinn Metropolitan Area. J. Geographical Annaler: Series B, Human Geography 89(2), 127–146 (2007)
8. Tammaru, T.: Suburbanization, Employment Change, and Commuting in the Tallinn Metropolitan Area. J. Environment and Planning A 37(9), 1669–1687 (2005)
9. Tang, B.S., Choy, L.H.T.: Modeling Planning Control Decisions: A Logistic Regression Analysis on Office Development Applications in Urban Kowloon, Hong Kong. J. Cities 17(3), 219–225 (2000)
10. Zhou, Y.X.: Urban Geography. The Commercial Press (1995)
11. Jing, J.J.: The Functional Connection and Structural Improving of The Shandong Peninsula Urban Agglomeration. J. Economic Geography 26(3), 469–472 (2006)
12. State Statistical Bureau.: China Statistical Yearbook. Beijing, China (2003)
13. Du, J., Sun, X.H., Gao, Z.Q., et al.: Research on The Intensity of the Urban Flow of Shandong Peninsula City Groups. Journal of Shandong Normal University (Natural Science) 21(4), 91–93 (2003)

Development of USB Device Driver in WinCE.Net

Ping Wang and Na Zhang

Dept. electronic information engineering, Nanchang University,
Nanchang, China
nddzwp@163.com, zhangna7261@163.com

Abstract. This paper describes USB host software architecture and basic knowledge of stream interface driver in the embedded operating system Windows CE.Net. After explaining the essential functions which should be involved in stream interface drivers, it mainly analyses USB device driver load and unload process associated with the flowchart diagram of the load process.

Keywords: WinCE.Net; USB; Stream Interface Driver.

1 Introduction

Windows CE.Net, Microsoft's operating system targeted toward embedded devices, is an open, scalable, 32-bit operating system (OS) that integrates reliable, real time capabilities with advanced Windows technologies. And it is a system that supports Universal Serial Bus (USB)2.0.

USB is a communication protocol that describes fast serial data transfer between a single USB host and numerous USB peripherals [1]. As more and more productions of USB-capable devices appear, development of USB device driver plays a more significant role in Embedded Development.

This paper is intended to explain the development of USB device drivers in WinCE.Net.

2 USB Host Software Architecture in WinCE.Net

USB Host Software in WinCE.Net can be divided into three sections (listed in here from the highest level to lowest) [1]:

- Client Software
- Universal Serial Bus Driver (USBD)
- Host Controller Driver (HCD)

Client software lies highest. It consists of application programs and USB device drivers for specific USB peripherals attached to WinCE.Net. A USB device driver is a software module that manages the operation of a virtual or physical device, a protocol, or a service. USBD and HCD modules are collectively referred as USB System Software. Configuration of devices and other such details are implemented by these two modules. The USBD manages all the hardware in the host controller system and

L. Qi (Ed.): FCC 2009, CCIS 34, pp. 164–170, 2009.

what communicates directly with USB peripherals is it. In USB device drivers, USBD interface functions are called to ask USBD to communicate with the specific USB peripherals. And the USBD provides a basic and generic interface to HCD. The HCD drives the Host Controller by manipulating programmable hardware registers inside the Host Controller. And all transactions on the bus originate from the host side; the peripherals perform only as slaves in this master-slave environment.

The flow of the three levels' operation explained above is typically:

(1). A USB device driver initiates transfers by using USBDI APIs to issue requests to the USBD module.

(2). The USBD module divides requests into individual transactions based on its knowledge of the bus and characteristics of the USB devices connected to the bus.

(3). The HCD module schedules these transactions over the bus.

(4). The host controller hardware actually performs or completes the transactions.

Hierarchy is important in USB host software. The lower level is for physical USB peripherals, such as USB-Disks, and USB device drivers which lie higher are presented as special files which can be accessed by applications in the operating system. The two levels together make the USB peripherals well-balanced. Development of USB device driver this paper researches is based on the higher client software level.

3 Development of USB Device Driver in WinCE.Net

Windows CE.Net is a modular and scalable operating system that supports a variety of devices. There are two driver models based on WinCE.Net which are native driver model and stream interface driver model [2]. The native driver model is used for development of built-in device drivers in WinCE.Net. And the stream interface driver model is mostly used for most of the USB peripherals, like the printer, because the stream interface is better suited for those devices. This paper is based on the stream interface driver model.

Creating a string interface driver includes the following:

(1). Writing a DLL that exposes specific functions
(2). Building the device driver
(3). Configuring the registry

Building the device driver is writing the required entrypoints for USB Device Driver, and the work of configuring the registry is implemented in one of these entrypoints.

Both Platform Builder and EVC++ can be used to develop USB device drivers. All that need to do are creating a Windows CE DLL project, exporting the proper entrypoints and writing the code.

3.1 Required Entrypoints for USB Device Driver

Stream interface driver in WinCE.Net is implemented as dynamic-link library (.dll file). All USB device drivers must expose entrypoints in their DLL. These entrypoints will allow them to configure and set up the devices attached to the system, and they also allow them to set up the registry.

Required entrypoints for USB device drivers are USBDeviceAttach function, US-BInstallDriver function and USBUnInstallDriver function [3].

USBDeviceAttach Function. Fig. 1 shows the functional control flowchart diagram of USBDeviceAttach.

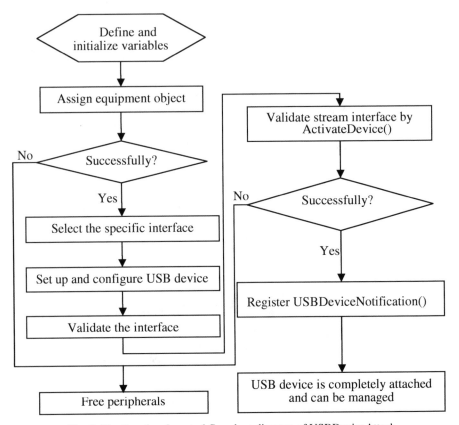

Fig. 1. The functional control flowchart diagram of USBDeviceAttach

When the USB device for some USB device driver is attached to USB bus and HCD detects the device existing, this entrypoint is called by USBD model. The main responsibilities of this function are setting up the USB devices, getting information and configuring them. When implemented, it calls function ActivateDevice to validate the stream interface so that an application can access the USB device by file API. It creates a subkey for the USB device driver under HKEY_LOCAL_MACHINE\Drivers\Active and specifies an index which specifies the numeric portion of the driver name in the file system .

At last, it calls function RegisterNotificationRoutine to register device call-back function USBDeviceNotification.

USBInstallDriver Function. USB driver module calls this function when an unrecognized device is attached to USB bus. And this function gives the driver a chance to create its registry keys by writing device information (such as Product ID) under

HKEY_LOCAL_MACHINE\Drivers\USB\ClientDrivers. USBInstallDriver should create the keys indirectly by calling RegisterClientSettings and RegisterClientDriverID functions loaded from USBD.dll, rather than invoking the registry APIs.

USBUninstallDriver Function. When deregistering a USB device driver from the platform WinCE.Net, this function is called. Its main responsibility is to delete all the registry keys which are created by function USBInstallDriver in the USB device driver.

3.2 Stream Interface Driver

Stream interface drivers follow a unique file naming convention, which is composed of a three-letter prefix, a digit which is also named as index that identifies a specific device when multiple instances are available, and a colon [4].

When the stream interface driver is implemented, the three-letter prefix should be designated. The three-letter prefix can be any combination of three uppercase letters, although a common prefix may be used, if the driver is the same class of device as other drivers. For example, drivers for serial devices, such as modems, could use the common prefix COM, even though other drivers might already be using that prefix. The driver can distinguish itself from other drivers by using a different index which is specified in the entrypoint USBDeviceAttach by function ActivateDevice. Valid names of stream interface drivers are COM1:, COM2:, BCR1:, and so on.

In contrast to the native drivers, stream interface drivers all share a common interface composed of 10 entrypoints.

The related driver is loaded at detection time of the USB device. When loading drivers, it will look for stream interface functions in the related driver. So in stream interface drivers it should expose stream interface functions, regardless of the type of device controlled by the driver.

For a given driver, each stream interface function must start with the driver's prefix which is the three-letter prefix shown as "xxx". The driver's prefix is namely the prefix value in its registry key.   Stream interface functions include XXX_Init, XXX_Deinit, XXX_Open, XXX_Close, XXX_Read, XXX_Write, and so on. In Table 1 it shows when these functions will be called.

When loading the DLL which is indicated by the DLL value, it creates a subkey for the driver under HKEY_LOCAL_MACHINE\Drivers\Active. So when initializing an application, Device Manager calls XXX_Init by function ActiveDeviceEx() and passes the path to the driver's Active key with the dwContext parameter to XXX_Init. Using the path it gets in return, the XXX_Init routine should call RegOpenKeyEx to get a handle for this key, and then call RegQueryValueEx to look for the key value which contains a string corresponding to the registry key. After that applications can access USB peripheral by file API because stream interface driver presents the peripheral as a special file, which can be opened, read, written, closed, and so on.

File API include CreateFile, DeviceIoControl, ReadFile, WriteFile, CloseHandle and SetFilePointer [5].

Table 1. Stream interface functions

Function	Called When
XXX_Init	The driver is loaded
XXX_Deinit	The driver is unloaded
XXX_Open	An application opens the driver
XXX_Close	An application closes the driver
XXX_Read	An application reads device-dependent data
XXX_Write	An application writes device-dependent data
XXX_IOControl	An application issues a driver-dependent command
XXX_PowerUp	Power is turned on (restored)
XXX_PowerDown	Power is turned off (suspend mode)

The following shows about how an application accesses USB device driver by file API through CreatFile as an example:

The form of calling CreateFile in an application is:

hS=CreateFile(TEXT("COM1:"),GENERIC_READ,0,NULL, OPEN_EXSITING, 0, NULL).

After an application calls CreateFile, the DLL handles the API Call and switches to device.exe which calls XXX_Open. Then CreateFile returns the return value of XXX_Open which is a handle to the device. The handle can be used to read or write device-dependent data.

And when an application closes the driver, XXX_Close is called. If an application wants to read or write device-dependent data, XXX_Read or XXX_Write will be called.

3.3 USB Device Driver Load Process

USBD module is responsible for loading the matched USB device driver when a USB device is attached. And the method in which the driver is attached is dependent on registry settings [6].

The flowchart diagram of USB Device Driver load process is shown in Fig. 2.

After USBD receives attaching notification from HCD, it gets descriptor and tries to find a driver from registry. USBD locates the correct driver by using a set of registry keys, which track both the drivers and devices. The registry keys are stored as subkeys of the HKEY_LOCAL_MACHINE\Drivers\USB\LoadClients key. USBD uses the HKEY_LOCAL_MACHINE\Drivers\LoadClients portion of the registry to identify the matched USB device driver for an attached device. If it does find a matched driver in the registry, it will try to load it and call the entrypoint USBDeviceAttach. The entrypoint passes in a USB_HANDLE and a set of function pointers which enable the device driver to make other USBD calls. Using the function pointers, the driver can retrieve various USB descriptors to validate the stream interface and retrieve parameters. If USBD does not find a matched driver in registry, it queries the user for the name of the device driver DLL and then searches for it. If searched successfully, the DLL will be loaded. It firstly calls function USBInstallDriver to create an active key for the driver and configure the registry. If that is done successfully, the DLL will be released. And then the USBD module calls entrypoint USBDeviceAttach. The USB device driver load process is over after the entrypoint successfully called. Then applications can access the USB device driver by file API.

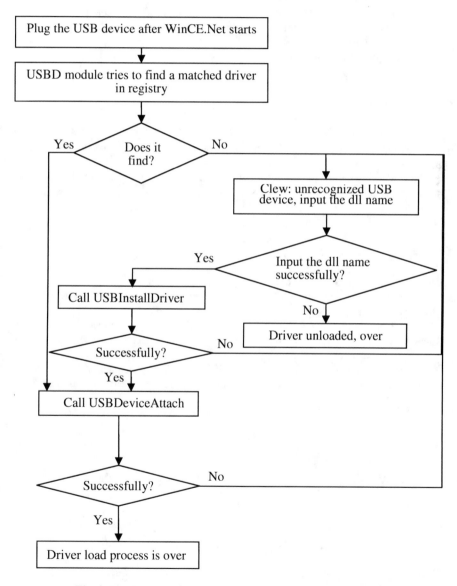

Fig. 2. The flowchart diagram of USB Device Driver load process

3.4 USB Device Driver Unload Process

When loading a device driver, it calls function RegisterNotificationRoutine to register the device call-back function USBDeviceNotification in USBDeviceAttach. And when removing the USB peripherals which have been attached to the system, it will call the device call-back function USBDeviceNotification. Parameter provided by call-back function is a context that has a reference to the device driver instance which can be used to translate commands to free peripherals. Then function USBUninstallDriver will be called to delete all the registry keys which are created by USBInstallDriver. The work of deleting registry keys is done by functions which are loaded by USBUninstallDriver from USBD.dll.

4 Conclusion

This paper mainly analyses the development of stream interface drivers of USB in WinCE.Net. And it explains the responsibilities and called order of essential functions which should be involved in the USB device driver.

The innovation of this paper is that it has analyzed how an application accesses USB peripherals and explained USB device driver load and unload process. In additional, it has presented the flowchart of USB device driver load process.

References

1. Universal Serial Bus Specification, http://www.usb.org
2. Microsoft Corporation: Microsoft Windows CE Device Driver Kit. Hope Electronic Press, Beijing (1999) (in Chinese)
3. Hongyang, N., Yang, L., Wentong, Y.: Development of The Client Driver of USB Bu. The Embedded System WinCE.Net. Microcomputer Applications. 27, 238–240 (2006) (in Chinese)
4. Stream Interface Driver Strategy in the WinCE.Net, WinCE.Net Help Online
5. Muench, C.: Windows Powered Solutions for the Developer. Pearson Education Press, America (2000)
6. USB Driver Registry Settings, http://msdn.microsoft.com/library

Time-Varying Weighting Techniques for Airborne Bistatic Radar Clutter Suppression

Duan Rui, Wang Xuegang, and Chen Zhuming

Electronic Engineering College, University of Electronic Science and Technology of China
610054 Chengdu, Sichuan, China
rui_duan@126.com

Abstract. In this paper, a new nonlinearly time-varying weighting (NTVW) technique is proposed to mitigate the nonstationarity of bistatic clutter. The nonlinear factors contained in the range-varying characteristics of angle-Doppler frequency are taken into accounted by the method, and can effectively suppressing the bistatic clutter returns reflected from the far, middle and near distance scenarios. Moreover, the NTVW is a data-dependent method and can adaptively compensate the range nonstationarity of bistatic clutter without the prior knowledge of the moving platforms and the environment. The simulation results manifest that the NTVW has superior clutter rejection performance compared with the linear time-varying weighting and the traditional bistatic the space-time adaptive process (STAP) without any compensation strategies in the scenarios of different bistatic range.

Keywords: airborne bistatic radar, clutter suppression, STAP, TVW, nonstationarity.

1 Introduction

Airborne bistatic radar is a desirable surveillance system in military applications for its reliable survivability and the excellent stealth target detection performance [1]. However, unlike its monostatic counterpart, bistatic clutter generally appears range nonstationary, which not only depends on the arrangement of antenna array but also is determined by the geometry of both the bistatic transceiver platforms and the range bin of interesting. Thus, the traditional space-time adaptive processing (STAP) techniques have to be modified to adapt themselves to the bistatic clutter environment [2] and [3].

To mitigate the impact of nonstationary behavior on clutter cancellation, three approaches one might consider include localizing processing STAP method [4], deterministically modifying the data to account for the known bistatic geometry [5], and time-varying the adaptive filter response [3] and [6]. However, two specific problems associate with the two former approaches: i) conventional weights (i.e. $w = R^{-1}v$) are almost stale; ii) the conventional weights will have the adaptive nulls broaden because the location of the bistatic clutter is changing rapidly within the time and the region required to train the weights. To enhance the performance of bistatic STAP under nonstationary environment, in this paper the time-varying weighting (TVW) techniques, is discussed to overcome above two issues.

L. Qi (Ed.): FCC 2009, CCIS 34, pp. 171–178, 2009.
© Springer-Verlag Berlin Heidelberg 2009

The rest paper is organized as follows: section two shows the nonstationarity of bistatic clutter and the conventional STAP performance; section three reviews the classical TVW method at first, and then a new method - the nonlinearly time-varying weighting (NTVW) technique is proposed for suppressing bistatic nonstationary clutter; section four gives the simulation results for proposed methods; finally, the conclusion is summarized in section five.

2 STAP and Bistatic Clutter

2.1 Bistatic STAP

To maximize the probability of detection for a fixed false alarm (in the presence of Gaussian disturbance), the STAP output signal-to-interference-plus-noise ratio (SINR) must be maximized as possible. Thus, the SINR improvement factor ($IF=SINR_{out}/SINR_{in}$) of STAP processor is used as the metric. The adaptive weights of STAP are computed by the estimated clutter covariance matrix $\hat{R}_k$ which is trained according to the RMB rule [7], and which is defined as

$$\hat{R}_k = \frac{1}{L}\sum_{\substack{m=1 \\ m\neq k}}^{L} x_m x_m^H \tag{1}$$

where the $x_k \in C^{NM\times1}$ is the space-time snapshot for the specified bistatic range sum and the $\{x_m\}_{m=1;m\neq k}^{m=L}$ is known as secondary data or training data set containing L realizations [8], M is spatial receiving channel and N is coherent processing pulses. If all x_m are jointly Gaussian, independent and identically distributed (IID), the (1) is a maximum likelihood estimate of real clutter covariance matrix R_k [7] and

$$E[\hat{R}_k] = \frac{1}{L}\sum_{\substack{m=1 \\ m\neq k}}^{L} E[x_m x_m^H] = \frac{1}{L}\sum_{\substack{m=1 \\ m\neq k}}^{L} R_m = R_k \tag{2}$$

where $R_m = R_k \forall m$ and $m \neq k$. Since the training data are nonstationary (non-IID) in the case of bistatic configurations, the adaptive filter converges to a response representative of the average behavior of the secondary data set, rather than a response best suited to the particular range bin of interest. Therefore, the adaptive weights of bistatic STAP will have broad nulls, making it difficult to interrogate signals close to the position of the interference.

2.2 Nonstationary Bistatic Clutter

The airborne bistatic geometry leads to nonstationary clutter and complicate the STAP implementation. To display the nonstationarity of bistatic clutter in angle and Doppler, it is necessary to briefly examine the angle-Doppler characteristics of bistatic ground clutter and its influence on bistatic STAP performance.

Basic bistatic geometry is depicted in Fig. 1. The receiver is at point R_X at height H_R above the $X - Y$ ground plane, and the transmitter is at the point T_X at height H_T. The receiver moves in δ_R direction at speed v_R and the transmitter moves in δ_T direction at speed v_T. A transmitter pulse hits the ground at a stationary point P after passing the transmit slant range R_{TS} and the reflected pulse is collected by the receiver after passing the receiver slant range R_{RS}. The sum of two slant ranges represents the bistatic range sum R_{sum}, and the set of points having same range sums forms a group of range ellipsoids. The angle φ_R and φ_T are azimuth angles of the scattering point P measured with respect to the bistatic baseline, and the angle θ_R and θ_T are elevation angles denoted by the angles between the slant range and the ground surface. The angle ψ_R and ψ_T are cone angles measured with the clutter scattering point to the moving direction of radar platforms. In this paper R. Klemm's bistatic clutter model [2] is used for establishing the space-time clutter model.

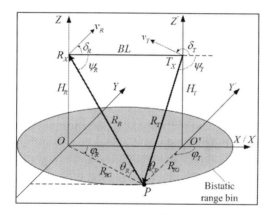

Fig. 1. Bistatic radar geometry

The bistatic Doppler frequency of an elemental ground scatter P is [2]

$$f_{d.P}(\varphi_R,\theta_R) = \frac{v_T T}{\lambda}\cos\psi_T + \frac{v_R T}{\lambda}\cos\psi_R \qquad (3)$$

where λ is the wavelength of the radar operation frequency, and $\cos\psi_T = \cos(\varphi_T - \delta_T)\cos\theta_T$ and $\cos\psi_R = \cos(\varphi_R - \delta_R)\cos\theta_R$. Also, the spatial receive frequency of P at the mth phase center is fallowed as

$$f_{s.P}(\varphi_R,\theta_R) = (d/\lambda)\cos\psi_R \qquad (4)$$

where d is channel interval.

Therefore, the relationship between Doppler and spatial frequency is more complex and higher geometry-dependent in bistatic scenarios [3]. Resorting to numerical evaluation for different bistatic geometrical configurations and bistatic range sum, the range nonstationarity of bistatic clutter in angle and Doppler can be understood. The example bistatic scenario is described in Table 1.

Table 1. Parameters for the bistatic example

Parameter	Value
Operational RF Frequency	2.4 GHz
PRF	2 KHz
Compressed Pulse	0.33 us
Antenna Configuration	Sidelooking, ULA
Transmit Weighting	40 dB Taylor
Receiver Channels, M	8
Pulses, N	16
Receiver Position (X_R, Y_R, Z_R)	(0,0,3), Unit: km
Transmitter Position (X_T, Y_T, Z_T)	(10,0,3), Unit: km
Bistatic Baseline, BL	10 km
Receiver Velocity v_R, Direction δ_R	60m/s, 0° (X-axis Referenced)
Transmitter Velocity v_T, Direction δ_T	60m/s, 45° (X-axis Referenced)
Transmitting Beam Direction	Broadside

Fig.2 (a) shows the angle-Doppler traces of bistatic range sum bins in region of 15km to 75km in the bistatic scenarios given by Table 1. In the figure the bold black line represents the trajectory of clutter spectrum center for each range bin. The figure clearly indicates that the range-dependency of clutter persists over all bistatic range, and that with the decreasing range sum for the example, this variation trend is much more significant.

Fig.2 (b) further shows the nonlinear variation of angle and Doppler frequency with respect to range. Consider the detected bistatic range bin is located at 25km , which is the center of 500 training range bins. Clearly, the significant nonlinearity appears in near range field.

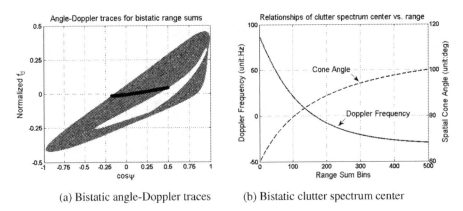

(a) Bistatic angle-Doppler traces   (b) Bistatic clutter spectrum center

Fig. 2. The nonstationarity of bistatic clutter

Fig.3 shows the processor IFs for the range sums of 16.5km and 50km , respectively. The ideal IF curves are computed by $10MN$ IID snapshots at target range bins. As anticipated, the conventional STAP SINR IF is greatly broadened due to clutter

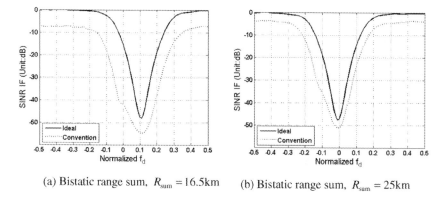

(a) Bistatic range sum, $R_{sum} = 16.5\text{km}$ (b) Bistatic range sum, $R_{sum} = 25\text{km}$

Fig. 3. SINR IF for conventional STAP algorithm

nonstationary. Moreover, for the high degree of nonstationarity for near ranges, the wide of IF curve null is significantly increased, which makes it difficult to interrogate signals close to the position of the interference.

3 Time-Varying Weighting Techniques

In this section, the classical TVW technique and its limits on bistatic clutter suppression are briefly examined at first, and then the nonlinear TVW is proposed by us to ameliorate bistatic nonstationarity.

3.1 Derivative-Based Updating Algorithm (DBU)

DBU algorithm was firstly proposed for solving the clutter suppression issues in the case of rapidly moving phased array or non-uniform linear array by M.A. Zatman [6]. Subsequently, W.L. Melvin and B. Himed, etc, introduced DBU into bistatic clutter cancellation and got depressed results for not far bistatic range. The adaptive weights w_r of classical DBU are composed of two parts: one is the fixed weight w_0, and the other is the multiplication of range r and the first-order derivative of w_r, and is

$$w_r = w_0 + r\,\dot{w}_0 \tag{5}$$

where $w_0 = w(k)$ is the fixed weight for detected range bin k, $\dot{w}_0 = \dot{w}(k)$ is the first-order weight derivative for range bin k, and r is indexed by the number from $-K$ to K if $L = 2K + 1$. When $r = k$, to exclude the detected bin from the training set, r is equal to 0.

Therefore, the DBU algorithm considers the adaptive weights w_r as a variable linearly varying with range r. But since the bistatic clutter contains complicately nonlinear behavior induced by bistatic geometry, the DBU algorithms can not provide adequately adaptability for severely nonstationary clutter. Thus, the DBU performance is substantially degraded in the near or middle range because the linearity assumption of expression (5) does not exist.

3.2 Nonlinearly Time-Varying Weighting Algorithm (NTVW)

Based on the DBU method, the NTVW algorithm is naturally formulated for bistatic clutter suppression by introducing the second-order derivative of adaptive weights into (5). The actual implementation is based on a Taylor series expansion of the weight vector $w_{r,\mathrm{NTVW}}$ and the terms in r^3 and higher are to be ignored. Then for the kth range bin, the weight vector of NTVW is given by

$$w_r(r) = w_0 + r\,\dot{w}_0 + \frac{r^2}{2}\ddot{w}_0 \tag{6}$$

The STAP out based on NTVW is

$$y_{\mathrm{NTVW}}(r) = w_r^{\mathrm{H}} X_r = \begin{bmatrix} w_0 \\ \dot{w}_0 \\ \ddot{w}_0 \end{bmatrix}^{\mathrm{H}} X_r \tag{7}$$

where X_r is the extended space-time snapshot and is $[x_r \; rx_r \; r^2x_r]^{\mathrm{T}}$. The extended clutter covariance matrix for NTVW can be estimate from L snapshots of data

$$\hat{R}_{r,\mathrm{NTVW}} = \frac{1}{L}\sum_{\substack{r=-K \\ r\neq k}}^{r=K} \begin{bmatrix} x_r \\ \xi_1 r x_r \\ \xi_2 r^2 x_r \end{bmatrix} \begin{bmatrix} x_r \\ \xi_1 r x_r \\ \xi_2 r^2 x_r \end{bmatrix}^{\mathrm{H}} = \frac{1}{L}\sum_{\substack{r=-K \\ r\neq k}}^{r=K} \begin{bmatrix} R_r & \xi_1 r R_r & \xi_2 r^2 R_r/2 \\ \xi_1 r R_r & \xi_1^2 r^2 R_r & \xi_1\xi_2 r^3 R_r/2 \\ \xi_2 r^2 R_r/2 & \xi_1\xi_2 r^3 R_r/2 & \xi_2^2 r^4 R_r/4 \end{bmatrix} \tag{8}$$

where ξ_1 and ξ_2 are the specified constants for avoiding the ill-condition of $\hat{R}_{\mathrm{NTVW}}$.

M. Zatman suggested that the scaling terms ξ_1 and ξ_2 in (8) can be set so that when the data only contains white noise, the expected extended covariance matrix in (8) is an identity [6]. Employing this method, the obtained ξ_1 and ξ_2 is

$$\begin{cases} \xi_1 = \sqrt{\dfrac{12}{(2K+1)^2 - 1}} \\ \xi_2 = \sqrt{\dfrac{2(2K+1)}{K(6K^4 + 15K^3 + 10K^2 - 1)}} \end{cases} \tag{9}$$

Therefore, the estimated weight vector for NTVW is given by

$$\hat{w}_{r,\mathrm{NTVW}} = \hat{\alpha}\hat{R}_{r,\mathrm{NTVW}}^{-1} s_{\mathrm{NTVW}} \tag{10}$$

where s_{NTVW} is the extended steering vector and $s_{\mathrm{NTVW}} = [s\,0\,0]^{\mathrm{T}}$ due to $r = 0$ for the kth range bin. The s and 0 are the vectors of $MN \times 1$ dimension, and s is the expected space-time steering vector for the interesting range bin.

Both the DBU and the NTVW approaches described above can track the time changing clutter traces within the training data set. Due to having more effective weighting strategy for drastically nonstationary clutter environment, the NTVW behaves better on bistatic clutter cancellation over full range. But the enhanced performance is at the expense of increasing the computational costs and enlarging the size of training data set. Therefore, it is highly recommended to combine the TVW techniques with other reduced-dimension STAP algorithms in realization [3].

4   Simulation Results

The example bistatic scenario given in section 2 was used to study the performance of DBU, NTVW and conventional STAP algorithms. The bistatic range sum bins located at 16.5km, 20km, 25km and 50km are selected as the target range sum bins of interesting, which represent the near range ($BL \leq R_{sum} \leq 2BL$), the middle range ($2BL \leq R_{sum} \leq 5BL$) and the far range ($R_{sum} \geq 5BL$) in simulations, respectively. To provide enough training snapshot data and evaluate the individual algorithm under the same nonstationary clutter conditions, the training snapshot data is collected from the region of 12.5km , and the detected bin is at the center of training region.

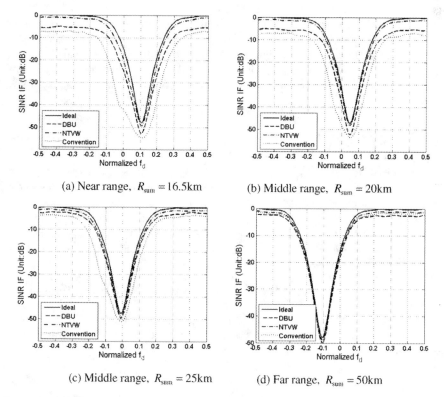

(a) Near range, $R_{sum} = 16.5$km   (b) Middle range, $R_{sum} = 20$km

(c) Middle range, $R_{sum} = 25$km   (d) Far range, $R_{sum} = 50$km

Fig. 4. SINR IF comparison of DBU, NTVW and Conventional STAP algorithms for bistatic range sum bins at 16.5km, 20km, 25km and 50km

Fig.4 contrasts the TVW method versus the conventional STAP approach and the ideal case for the near, middle and far ranges. From this figure we see that all algorithms exhibit favorable performance in far region of less nonstationarity, the NTVW method has best clutter suppression performance and the narrowest nulls for all four ranges, the DBU approach dose track the clutter adequately at far range, but appears to suffer significant loss at near and middle range, and the conventional STAP algorithm behaves worst at near and middle range which employs the fixed weights without any compensation for clutter nonstationarity.

5 Summary

In this paper the time-varying weighting techniques is studied for solving the problem nonstationary bistatic clutter suppression. We show that bistatic geometry leads to severe clutter nonstationarity and that the obviously nonlinear variations can be seen at nearer range. The clutter nonstationarity broadens the nulls of adaptive filter and degrades STAP detection performance. To enhance STAP performance, the DBU and NTVW approaches are investigated to mitigate the clutter nonstationarity. For dissatisfactory performance of DBU method in near region, the proposed NTVW algorithm affords the potential to track the nonlinear angle-Doppler changes of bistatic clutter over range and improves the STAP performance in near and middle range. As more computational costs and larger training data size required by NTVW and DBU, the combination of TVW and reduced-dimension STAP is highly recommended. The further work is being carrying out by us to reduce the computational burden of NTVW method.

References

1. Willis, N.J.: Bistatic Radar. Technology Service Corporation, Sliver Spring (1995)
2. Klemm, R.: Comparison between monostatic and bistatic antenna configurations for STAP. IEEE Trans. AES. 36(2), 596–608 (2000)
3. Melvin, W.L., Callahan, M.J., Wicks, M.C.: Bistatic STAP: application to airborne radar. In: 1998 IEEE Radar Conference, pp. 135–140. IEEE press, Los Alamitos (1998)
4. Wang, H., Cai, L.: On adaptive spatial-temporal processing for airborne surveillance radar systems. IEEE Trans. AES. 30(3), 660–670 (1994)
5. Himed, B., Zhang, Y.H., Hajjari, A.: STAP with angle-Doppler Compensation for bistatic airborne radars. In: 2002 IEEE Radar Conference, pp. 22–25. IEEE Computer Society Press, Los Alamitos (2002)
6. Zatman, M.A.: Circular array STAP. IEEE Trans. AES. 36(2), 510–517 (2000)
7. Reed, I.S., Mallett, J.D., Brennan, L.E.: Rapid convergence rate in adaptive arrays. IEEE Trans. AES. 10(6), 853–863 (1974)

Factor Analysis of Competencies of Software Project Managers in China

Xiaotao Li[1,2], Xuejun Wang[1], and Zhiliang Zhang[1]

[1] School of Economics & Management, Wuhan University, 430072, Wuhan, China
[2] School of Economics & Management, Wuhan Polytechnic University,
430023, Wuhan, China
{Xiaotao Li,xiaotaowhu}@163.com

Abstract. This paper presents a competency model for software project managers in China. Based on the results of previous research on competencies for general managers and following the procedure of competency modeling, the study conducts an empirical study of more than 20 managers in software industry in Shenzhen and Guangzhou, China by interview and questionnaire. A competency model for software project managers is established by factor analysis. Eight categories of competencies are identified through the research which are: 1) professional skills; 2) personal abilities; 3) logic thinking; 4)management ability; 5)working willingness; 6) Efficiency orientation;7) Quality orientation ; 8) Self-confidence and innovation.

Keywords: software industry, project manager, competency, factor analysis.

1 Introduction

Competitive international market of software industry calls for cutting-edge technology and innovative and creative managers, and the monopoly in traditional software market is being challenged, and traditional business model has to be changed. Project management pattern has gained momentum in many software enterprises in order to adapt to the diversity and variability of international software market. As a result, considerable risk is shifted to the project managers, which sets higher requirements for abilities of project manager. In such a condition, the human resources departments in software enterprises are seeking to establish new criteria for selection and cultivation of project mangers, and competency and abilities of excellent project managers have.

Competencies are behaviors that include the knowledge, skills, and attributes required for successful performance. By competencies individual attitude, values and self-image, motivation and other potential attributes can be distinguished between superior and average workers in a task(or organization , culture).

Competency model refers to a group of competencies required in a particular job. They refer to the knowledge, skills, and actions needed to promote organizational success. Generally speaking, professional competency model consists of three layers: type of competencies, corresponding definitions and typical behaviors, that is, the competency model for a specific profession includes the names of several types of

L. Qi (Ed.): FCC 2009, CCIS 34, pp. 179–186, 2009.

competencies needed at the given position for organizational success, their respective definitions and the typical behaviors of each competency.

Of literature referred to, most of them come up with competency models for managers in general, while few deal with competency models for project managers in software industry in particular.

Sharlett Gillard and James Price (2005) published The Competencies of Effective Project Managers : A Conceptual Analysis, in which they analyze conceptually the competencies of project managers, identifying 5 clusters of competencies: Goal and Action Management, Leadership, Directing Subordinates, Focus On Others, Results-Oriented Project Manager Profile. The five clusters include the following competencies: deductive and analytical thinking, effective work, initiative, self-confidence, oral presentation, building consensus, team cooperation, directing subordinates, use of authority, stamina and adaptability.

Spencer et. al(1993) developed a comparatively complete interview procedure and coding method to set up competency model. Behavior Event Interview (BEI), a qualitative data-collecting method, is widely acknowledged as a method for construction of competency model. By which, superior and average managers are interviewed and are required to describe in detail most effective and ineffective work states. After the interview is transcribed, codified and analyzed, the key competencies will be identified between superior and average performance of managers.

This method involves four steps. Step One: Establishment of performance criteria; Step Two: Selection of criteria samples, that is meeting–the-standard group and failing-to-meet-the-standard group; Step Three: data collecting about competencies, BEI being the most widely used method; Step Four: data analysis and establishment of competency model; Step Five: Validation the competency model.

Chen(2006), based on the results of Sharlett Gillard and James Price' study and in combination with China's practical conditions, put forward a competency model for Chinese project managers, extracting 10 factors: personal effectiveness, professional skills, physiological and psychological qualities, leadership, interpersonal communication ability, team spirit, learning ability, achievement orientation, staff development ability, consumer awareness.

With the view to the particularity of software industry, the purpos of the study is to explore the competencies of mangers in software industry in China based on the practical characteristics of China's software industry.

2   Research

Subjects: full-time managers of software enterprises in Shenzhen and Guangzhou, China.

Instruments
Interview, questionnaire

Procedure
Normally, a software enterprise is to gain the four objectives: achievements of software development team, leaders' satisfaction, satisfaction of team members and satisfaction of consumers.

Through enterprise assessment and recommendation, the authors found 8 enterprises which had met the four objectives in Tianhe Software Development Park, Guangzhou and Shenzhen Software Development Park, which are state software industry bases, of whom 7 male and 3 female. Those interviewees were asked to describe 3 work events which they believed satisfactory, and 3 unsatisfactory events. The descriptions include the time, place and causes of the event, persons involved, what happened in the event, how to deal with it, his role, task and ideas, decisions in the event, difficulties encountered and solutions, the results, their feeling after the event, and those qualities not fully displayed for which they felt regrets.

The transcript of the interview, after editing, was codified on the basis of Competency Dictionary complied by Spencer et. al. and the results of the research by Sharlett Gillard. Then, based on the codified results, 30 items of competency were determined. They are

Competencies	Attributes of competencies
1. Achievement Orientation	In pursuit of excellence, continuous challenge of own achievements, care for promotion, power, position, optimal use of resources, attainment of goal
2. Concern for order, quality, accuracy	A potential drive to reduce uncertainties in the environment to ensure work is on the right track
3. Proactive	Make full use of information and conditions available, and try to understand and solve the problem actively before required to
4. Information Seeking	Potential curiosity, and a desire to have more understanding of events and persons concerned
5. Interpersonal understanding	Ready to help others, good listener, sensitive to other's feeling
6. Customer Relationship	Care about the demands of customers, effective communications with customers and maintenance of good cooperative relationship
7. Team Leadership	Effective issue of directives and orders, assignment of tasks, management and incentive, sincere care for subordinates, effective leader towards goals
8. Use of Socialized Power	Good at winning cooperation by cultivating common interests, and team discussion to develop team, establish alliance, and settle conflicts or disputes
9. Developing others	Direct and cultivate subordinates, provide support, encouragement and help for their self-improvement and development
10. Use of Unilateral Power	Influencing others and winning support by using personal authority, positional authority or policy-making and procedure

11. Diagnostic Use of Concepts	Inductive and analytical thinking, interpret event or its context with a concept or a framework, differentiate relevant information concerned and irrelevant information so as not to miss the goal of the project
12. Professional Knowledge and skills	Good mastery of knowledge and skills in the specific field, competent operation of all the tools in the specific industry
13. Rapid Learning	Learn and master knowledge and skills in the relevant field in a short period,
14. Efficiency Orientation	Self-motivated, establishment of challenging and attainable project objectives and completion date, efficiency of team work, attainment of project goal
15. Self-Confidence	Know what one is doing, one's belief reveals itself in one's idea and ability, optimistic, resolute in decision–making and suggestion- making
16. Self-Control	Control one's emotion and mood, keep cool and calm in unfavorable condition
17. Flexibility	Adaptive to different conditions, able to get along with different persons or teams and work efficiently
18. Good health	In good shape and energetic
19. Stamina and Adaptability	Energetic and able to work for a long time and effectively, adapt to changes actively and smartly
20. Oral Presentations	Clear and persuading speech with signs, verbal and non-verbal acts, and gestures
21. Awareness of Purview	Clear understanding of the boundary and scope of one's authority in one's work
22. Business Negotiation	Professional negotiation with customers on contract and its implementation, ensuring interests of both parties
23. Risk Identity and Control	Predict and determine the effects of risks on the project, and take measures to avoid the risk
24. Project Time Management	If project deviates from the plan, take measures to bring it to right track, ensure completion of the project on schedule
25. Empowerment	Empower team members with their corresponding rights, enabling them to make decisions on their work
26. Communication	Regularly communicate with team members, contractor, customers, and high-level managerial staff, listening to their ideas carefully and disseminating correct information, discovering and solving potential problems in time to ensure the smooth operation of the project
27. Decision-making	Sound judgment and action when confronted with

	multi-schemes or complicated problems
28. Creative	Care about the latest developments, often come up with creative ideas and take initiatives
29. Responsible	Responsible for the project success, customers, team members, and people concerned, Taking the responsibility for problems to occurring
30. Problem solving	Quickly come up with solutions which are simple, appropriate and of low-risk when problems appear

A questionnaire of competencies was made out with the 30 determined competencies. The questionnaire, using a five-point Likert scale, was designed to investigate managers' attitudes towards the importance of the 30 competencies.

In order to ensure the representativeness of the samples, those who answered the questionnaire must have 3-year working experience with 2-year as manager. The questionnaire was administrated by directly distributing the questionnaire sheet. The authors visited Software Development Park in Shenzhen and Guangzhou, and found 24 managers who met the requirements. 24 questionnaire sheets were distributed and collected, 20 were valid. The valid response rate is 83%.

3   Data Analysis and Results

SPSS11.0 was used to process the data obtained through the questionnaire. The questionnaire was intended to investigate the managers' assessment of competencies, and the statistical method was principal component analysis. Before principal component analysis, the feasibility was tested. Table 1 shows the test result.

Table 1. KMO and Barlett's Test

KMO and Bartlett's Test

Kaiser-Meyer-Olkin Measure of Sampling Adequacy.		.607
Bartlett's Test of Sphericity	Approx. Chi-Square	817.294
	df	465
	Sig.	.000

The results show that KMO measure of sampling adequacy is 0.607, partial correlation is comparatively weak. And Bartlett's test of Sphericity shows that the significance is less than .001, so the null hypothesis is rejected. Both tests indicate principal factor analysis can be carried out.

With the varimax and taking factor loadings larger than 0.50, we obtained 8 factors. The cumulative rate reached 84.786%, which is larger than 70%. Therefore, the 8 factors extracted were valid.

After rotation, we obtained the component transformation matrix.

With the loadings less than 0.50 eliminated, the rotated component matrix was obtained.

Table 2. Total Variance Explained

Total Variance Explained

Component	Initial Eigenvalues			Extraction Sums of Squared Loadings			Rotation Sums of Squared Loadings		
	Total	% of Variance	Cumulative %	Total	% of Variance	Cumulative %	Total	% of Variance	Cumulative %
1	9.343	31.142	31.142	9.343	31.142	31.142	5.623	18.742	18.742
2	4.577	15.257	46.398	4.577	15.257	46.398	4.836	16.118	34.860
3	2.847	9.490	55.889	2.847	9.490	55.889	3.233	10.775	45.635
4	2.435	8.117	64.006	2.435	8.117	64.006	2.957	9.855	55.490
5	2.159	7.195	71.201	2.159	7.195	71.201	2.612	8.705	64.196
6	1.683	5.609	76.810	1.683	5.609	76.810	2.263	7.545	71.741
7	1.319	4.398	81.209	1.319	4.398	81.209	2.194	7.313	79.054
8	1.073	3.578	84.786	1.073	3.578	84.786	1.720	5.732	84.786
9	.880	2.933	87.719						
10	.796	2.653	90.372						
11	.709	2.364	92.736						
12	.482	1.606	94.341						
13	.441	1.471	95.813						
14	.409	1.362	97.175						
15	.340	1.134	98.309						
16	.232	.774	99.083						
17	.148	.492	99.576						
18	.068	.227	99.802						
19	.059	.198	100.00						
20	.000	4.04E-15	100.00						
21	.000	1.65E-15	100.00						
22	.000	5.05E-16	100.00						
23	.000	2.44E-16	100.00						
24	.000	9.49E-17	100.00						
25	.000	-1.5E-16	100.00						
26	.000	-6.1E-16	100.00						
27	.000	-9.5E-16	100.00						
28	.000	-1.3E-15	100.00						
29	.000	-1.7E-15	100.00						
30	.000	-2.1E-15	100.00						

Extraction Method: Principal Component Analysis.

Table 3. Component transformation matrix

Component Transformation Matrix

Component	1	2	3	4	5	6	7	8
1	.645	.412	.365	.356	.304	.102	.185	.133
2	-.526	.775	.162	-.035	-.200	.013	.007	.236
3	-.151	-.303	.684	-.070	-.326	.196	.502	-.125
4	-.132	-.203	.015	.598	-.218	.562	-.398	.248
5	-.122	.072	-.081	-.405	.502	.732	.070	-.129
6	-.108	.164	-.453	.458	-.107	.104	.510	-.514
7	-.471	-.233	.107	.341	.645	-.274	.207	.249
8	.138	-.103	-.386	-.138	-.184	.118	.498	.712

Extraction Method: Principal Component Analysis.
Rotation Method: Varimax with Kaiser Normalization.

Table 4. Rotated component matrix

Rotated Component Matrix

	Component							
	1	2	3	4	5	6	7	8
1								
2							.918	
3					.721			
4	.540							
5			.536					
6	.803							
7	.748							
8	.797							
9				.773				
10							.549	
11			.522	.523				
12	.885							
13	.631							
14						.715		
15								.567
16								
17			.745					
18		.880						
19				.743				
20		.932						
21			.819					
22						.825		
23	.780							
24	.795							
25				.817				
26		.776						
27			.510					
28								.760
29					.891			
30		.888						

Extraction Method: Principal Component Analysis.
Rotation Method: Varimax with Kaiser Normalization.
a. Rotation converged in 11 iterations.

Note: In the Rotated Component Matrix Table, the numbers in the first column stand for the 30 items of competency.

4 Conclusion

In the study, 30 competencies were identified through literature review and Critical Event Interview. The results of the questionnaire confirmed that those competencies are significant for the software enterprise managers. By principal component analysis, the structure of competencies model was explored and obtained, that is the competency model for software project managers is made up of the following 8 factors:

Factor One Professional skills: information-seeking, customer relationship, team leadership, team cooperation, professional knowledge, rapid learning, risk control, time management.

Factor Two Personal Abilities: physical fitness, oral expression, communication, problem-solving.

Factor Three Logic thinking: interpersonal observation, deductive and analytical thinking, flexibility, awareness of purview, decision-making.

Factor Four Management ability: develop others, empowerment.

Factor Five Work willingness: initiative, responsibility.

Factor Six   Efficiency orientation: high efficiency, business negotiation.

Factor Seven Quality orientation: care about quality, use of authority.

Factor Eight Self-confidence and innovation: self-confident, innovative.

The majorities of the factors extracted tally with what we had expected in the study. But the competencies in each factor reveal an uneven distribution. Factor One had nine competencies whereas Factor Five, Six, Seven and Eight have only two respectively.

The study mainly focused on the demands from the four objectives the software enterprises strive to achieve for the performance of the managers, but failed to study other factors that also affect the performance of the managers, such as working years, enterprise size, manager's education background, and personality. All this needs further study in the future.

References

1. Byham, W.C., Moyer, R.P.: Using competencies to build a successful organization, Development Dimensions International. Inc. (1996)
2. Chen, C.-Y.: An Examination of the Competencies Needed by Sport Managers in Taiwan, University of Idaho (2004)
3. Oshins, M.L.: Identifying A Competency Model For Hotel Managers. Boston University (2002)
4. Sandberg, J.: Understanding Human Competence at Work: An Interpretative Approach. Academy of Management Journal 43(1) (February 2000)
5. Gillard, S., Price, J.: The Competencies of Effective Project Managers: A Conceptual Analysis. International Journal of Management 22(1) (2005)
6. Spencer, L.M., Spencer, S.M.: Competence at work: Models for superior performance, pp. 222–226. John Wiley & Sons, New York (1993)
7. Peng, B.: Competency model an its application in selection of managers. Wuhan University (2004)
8. Chen, J.: A Study of Construction of Competency Model for Project Managers. Wuhan University (2006)
9. Mansfield, R.S.: Building Competency Models: Approaches for HR Professionals. Human Resource Management, 35(l) (1996)

Radio Propagation Characteristics for Short Range Body-Centric Wireless Communications

Wei Fu and Jianguo Ma

School of Electronic Engineering
University of Electronic Science and Technology of China
610054, Chengdu, China
fwwwcn@gmail.com, jgma@uestc.edu.cn

Abstract. The shadow fading in body-centric wireless propagation environments was studied. The statistical model with the linear fitting to the measured data was proposed. The results show that the radio waves are diffracted around the body. The conventional path gain model is suitable for body-centric propagation environments when taking account of the attenuation around human body calculated in this study.

Keywords: body-centric, short range, propagation, shadow fading.

1 Introduction

Body-centric wireless communications systems (BWCS) are expected to emerge in the near future with the rapid evolution of wireless technologies. It will play a key role in the development of fourth generation (4G) mobile communications and personal area networks (PANs) [1-2].

In conventional wireless communications systems, between the terminals, variation in the channel is due to the interference between multiple rays scattered from the local environment, such as buildings in the outdoor case, and walls or furniture in the indoor case [3]. For short-range communication, it is possible to arrange the radio link between the transmitter and receiver to be a clear line-of-sight (LOS) path, the blockage from fixed objects in the signal path can then be eliminated, and the blockage considered only is from human body [4].

In this paper, we discuss the radio propagation model suitable to the body-centric wireless channel over frequency band 2.4 GHz. The statistical model is proposed taking account of the effects of the shadowing with human body. The linear curve fitting to the measured data is evaluated. Furthermore, the shadowing effect of human body was calculated. The results shown the conventional path gain model can be used to the link budget only when taking account of the propagation loss of the human body. The results also show that the radio waves are diffracted around the body in the gigahertz frequency range, and there are no significant power absorption observed by the human body.

L. Qi (Ed.): FCC 2009, CCIS 34, pp. 187–192, 2009.

2   Radio Propagation with the Presence of Human Body

For short-range communication, it is possible to arrange the radio link between the transmitter and receiver to be a clear line-of-sight (LOS) path, so that the power transfer ratio is given by Frii's transmission formula to evaluate signal between transmitter and receiver in short-range communication [5]

$$P_r = P_t G_t G_r \left(\frac{\lambda}{4\pi d}\right)^2 \tag{1}$$

Where d is the separation between transmitter and receiver antennas, λ is the wavelength. G_t and G_r are the antenna gain of the transmitting and receiving antennas, respectively.

The Frii's formula (1) is for free space, when communication in multipath environments, however, the formula will lead to the extra errors. Ray tracing (RT) techniques are widely used to the site-specific prediction of radio channel characteristics in this case. It can be used to accurately determine received signal strength where the wavelength is small relative to propagation environment feature size. The multi-ray model is typical used

$$P_r = P_t \left(\frac{\lambda}{4\pi}\right)^2 \left| \frac{G_d}{l_d} + R_{f1} \frac{G_{f1} e^{-j\Phi_{f1}}}{l_{f1}} + R_{f2} \frac{G_{f2} e^{-j\Phi_{f2}}}{l_{f2}} + \ldots\ldots + R_{fn} \frac{G_{fn} e^{-j\Phi_{fn}}}{l_{fn}} \right|^2 \tag{2}$$

where for each reflection path, the phase difference $\Phi_x = 2\pi(l_x - l_d)/\lambda$, R_{fx} is the reflection coefficient. G_x is the product of the transmit and receive antenna gains corresponding to the xth ray and l_x is the path length of xth ray. The number of the ray is between 2 and 10. However, this site-specific propagation model is based on precise information of the propagation environment, which is difficult sometime to acquire, especially the presence of human body.

The statistical model, which based on the measurements, is applicable to the short-range radio prediction model. The effects of the human body can be regarded as the shadowing fading

$$PL(d)[dB] = \overline{PL}(d)[dB] + X_\sigma[dB] \tag{3}$$

Where $\overline{PL}$ (dB) is the average path loss and X_σ is the shadowing fading. The average path loss as given by

$$\overline{PL}(d)[dB] = PL_0 + 10n \log_{10}\left(d/d_0\right) \tag{4}$$

where d_0, λ and d denote the reference distance, wavelength and distance, respectively. The PL exponent n based measured ranges form 1.97-10 for non-line-of-sight (NLOS), in various different indoor environments. In the presence of human movement, measurement results [6] show that the obstruction by human can be significant and range from 18-36 dB.

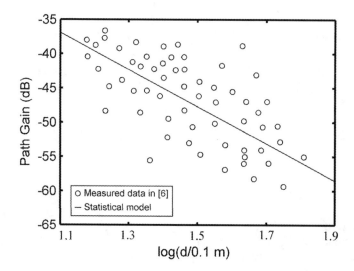

Fig. 1. The measured data in [6] and the fitting model at 2.45 GHz. The equation of the straight line is P[dB] = -32.5log(d/0.1m)+0.75.

The measured data at 2.45 GHz with presence of the human body and the linear fitting model are illustrated in Fig. 1. It gives an estimate of the signal attenuation with the distance, even though shadowing of the human body. It can be seen that the path loss exponent equals 3.25. The variation caused by the human body is large, and the conventional statistical model can only express the mean path gain.

3 Shadowing Effect of Human Body

When human body block the LOS path, the transmitted signals can arrive at the receiver by propagation through the body and diffraction around the body in addition to the reflections form nearby scatters in the radio environment [7]. The transmission attenuation between two devices blocked by the human body will be addressed in this section.

Signals in the gigahertz frequency range attenuate with distance traveled through the human body due to absorption by human tissues and energy is removed form the wave and converted to heat. The electrical field strength of a wave in human body, which an approximation of the body as a homogenous lossy dielectric is to be used, can be described as a function of the propagation distance by

$$E = E_0 \exp\left[j(\omega t - kd) \right] \cdot \exp(-\alpha s) \tag{5}$$

where s is the propagation distance, E_0 is the field amplitude, k is the wavenumber and e^{-as} depicts the attenuation factor, in which the constant α is the attenuation constant given as the real part of the propagation constant $\gamma = \alpha + j\beta$. In this case, the relative dielectric constant should be treated as a complex quantity, so that $\varepsilon_r = \varepsilon_r' - j\varepsilon_r''$, where $\varepsilon_r'' = \sigma/\omega\varepsilon_0$ and the wavelength changes

$$\lambda = \lambda_0 \Big/ \text{Re}\left[\sqrt{\varepsilon_r' - j\frac{\sigma}{\omega\varepsilon_0}}\right]$$

(6)

where Re[.] denote real part, $\lambda_0 \approx 12\,\text{cm}$ for $f = 2.45$ GHz. Thus, the attenuation factor can be expressed as

$$e^{-\alpha s} = \exp\left(-\omega s\sqrt{\frac{\mu\varepsilon_r'\varepsilon_0}{2}\left[\sqrt{1+\left(\frac{\sigma}{\omega\varepsilon_r'\varepsilon_0}\right)^2}-1\right]}\right)$$

(7)

where $\varepsilon_0 = 10^{-9}/36\pi$ (Fm^{-1}), $\mu_0 = 4\pi \cdot 10^{-7}$ (Hm^{-1}), and the relative dielectric constant and conductivity selected in [8] are very similar to the tissue of human body. The result of the transmission attenuation form (7) is shown in figure. 2. We can find that the attenuation factor is almost equal to zero when the propagation distance is approximate to 20 cm, so very little signal propagation takes place through the body in the gigahertz frequency range.

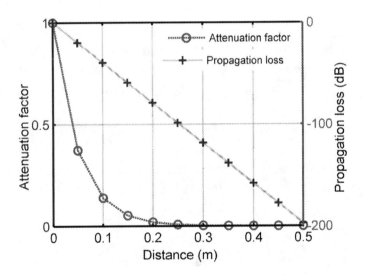

Fig. 2. The calculated propagation loss through human body at 2.45 GHz

Then, a measurement has been conducted to investigate the influence of diffraction around the body. The transceivers were separated by a distance of 5 m and one person moved alone the LOS path at a distance of 0.5 m. The path gain results with people located at different positions are compared with the results for without people and shown in Fig. 3. The results show that the presence of people in the LOS path will produce the excess attenuation that is 5-8 dB. The influences are severe when the person is close to the transmitter or receiver and this may be because of the propagation loss absorbed by people and the disappearance of some reflected paths.

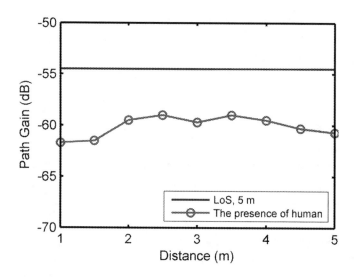

Fig. 3. The measured data for the presence of human in the LOS path at 2.45 GHz

4   Conclusion

The propagation characteristics of short-range wireless links were studied. The propagation loss caused by human body blocked the LOS path is investigated. The results show that the site-specific model is not applicable for the propagation model in body-centric communication due to the need of the precise information of environment. The conventional path gain model can express link budget when taking account of the shadowing effect of the human body. It is also found that there is no significant power absorption observed by the human body in the gigahertz frequency range. Instead, the radio waves are diffracted around the body and lead to the attenuation.

Acknowledgment

This work is partially supported by the National Science Foundation of China (No: 60688101), National "111" Project (No: Y02000010201006) and a grant from Science Fund for Young Scholars in UESTC (No: JX0610).

References

1. Park, C., Rapparpot, T.S.: Short-Range Wireless Communications for Next-Generation Networks: UWB, 60 GHz Millimeter-Wave WPAN, and ZigBee. J. IEEE Trans. Wireless Commun. 14, 70–78 (2007)
2. Omeni, O., Wong, A., Burdett, A.J.: Energy Efficient Medium Access Protocol for Wireless Medical Body Area Sensor Networks. J. IEEE Trans. Biomed. Circuits Syst. 2, 251–259 (2008)

3. Fettweis, G., Zimmermann, E.: Challenges in Future Short Range Wireless Systems. J. IEEE Veh. Technol. Mag. 1, 24–31 (2006)
4. Obayashi, S., Zander, J.: A Body-Shadowing Model for Indoor Radio Communication Environments. J. IEEE Trans. Antennas Propag. 46, 920–927 (1998)
5. Gao, X., Zhang, J., Liu, G., et al.: Large-Scale Characteristics of 5.25 GHz Based on Wideband MIMO Channel Measurements. J. IEEE Antennas Wireless Propag. Lett. 6, 263–266 (2007)
6. Yazdandoost, K.Y., Kamran, S.P.: Channel Model for Body Area Network (BAN) IEEE P802.15-08-0780-02-0006
7. Welch, T.B., Musselman, R.L., Emessiene, B.A., et al.: The effects of the human body on UWB Signal Propagation in an Indoor Environment. J. IEEE J. Sel. Areas Commun. 20, 1778–1782 (2002)
8. An Internet Resource for the Calculation of the Dielectric Properties of Body Tissues, http://niremf.ifac.cnr.it/tissprop/

A New Efficient Multiple Messages Signcryption Scheme with Public Verifiability

Hassan Elkamchouchi[1], Mohammed Nasr[2], and Roayat Ismail[2]

[1] Faculty of Engineering, Alexandria University, Egypt
[2] Faculty of Engineering, Tanta University, Egypt
helkamchouchi@yahoo.com, mnasr@yahoo.com, roaayat@yahoo.com

Abstract. Signcryption is a cryptographic primitive first proposed by Zheng in 1997 to combine the functionality of a digital signature scheme with that of an encryption scheme. Public verifiability is very important requirement for a signcryption scheme to settle a repudiation in case of a dispute. Recently in [1], a new efficient public key multi-messages signcryption scheme was introduced. This scheme is based on the intractability of Discrete Logarithm Problem (DLP) and used a multi-key generator to simultaneously signcrypts multiple messages in a logical single step, but it doesn't achieve public verifiability. In this paper we introduce a new multiple messages signcryption scheme which achieves the same efficiency as that of the scheme in [1] but with the following advantages: (i) It is publicly verifiable. (ii) It uses a simple and dynamic multiple keys generation routine (MKGR). (iii) Its security is based on the intractability of three hard problems: DLP, Diffie-Hellman Problem (DHP) and reversing a One-Way Hash Function (OWHF).

Keywords: Signcryption, multiple messages signcryption, public verifiability, multiple keys generation routine, DLP, DHP, OWHF.

1 Introduction

Confidentiality and non-repudiation of transmitted information are important requirements in many applications of cryptography. The conventional approach to achieve these goals is signature followed by encryption, namely before a message is sent out, the sender of the message would sign it using a digital signature scheme, and then encrypt the message using a private key encryption algorithm under a randomly chosen message encryption key. The random message encryption key would then be encrypted using the recipient's public key. We call this two–step approach "signature-then-encryption". With the current standard signature then encryption approach, the cost for delivering a message in a secure and authenticated way is essentially the sum of the cost for digital signature and that for encryption. Signcryption is a cryptographic primitive first proposed by Zheng [2] to combine the functionality of a digital signature scheme with that of an encryption scheme. A signcryption scheme consists of a pair of (poly-nominal time) algorithms (S, U), where S is called the signcryption algorithm, and U the unsigncryption algorithm. S in general is

L. Qi (Ed.): FCC 2009, CCIS 34, pp. 193–200, 2009.

probabilistic, but U is most likely to be deterministic. Basically a signcryption scheme should satisfy the following properties:

(1) *Correctness*: A properly formed signcrypted ciphertext by the signcryption algorithm (S) must be accepted by the unsigncryption algorithm (U).

(2) *Unforgeability*: Without the knowledge of the sender private key, it should be computationally infeasible for an adaptive attacker to masquerade the sender and to create a signcrypted ciphertext which will be accepted by the unsigncryption algorithm.

(3) *Confidentiality*: Without the knowledge of the sender or the designated receiver's private key, it should be infeasible for an adaptive attacker to gain any partial information on the contents of the signcrypted ciphertext.

(4) *Efficiency*: The computational cost which include the computational time involved both in signcryption and unsigncryption, and the communication overhead or added redundant bits of the scheme, is smaller than that required by the best currently known signature-then-encryption scheme with comparable parameters.

(5) *Non-repudiation:* The receiver of a message should have the ability to prove to anyone that the sender indeed sent the message. This ability ensures that the sender of a message cannot later deny having sent this message.

(6) *Public verifiability:* A signcryption scheme is publicly verifiable if, given a message m, a signcrypted ciphertext, and possibly some additional information provided by the receiver, a third party can verify that the signcrypted ciphertext is a valid signature on the message without having the knowledge of the receiver's private key [3].

Zheng's scheme has a disadvantage in the way it achieves non-repudiation since the signature cannot be verified publicly and in the case of multiple message signcryption, the signcryption algorithm is used multiple times to signcrypted all messages from A to B which causes a large computation time and communication overhead due to the multi-modular exponentiation for multi-message signcryption. Elkamchouchi et al in [1] introduced an efficient signcryption scheme which simultaneously signcrypts multiple messages in a logical single step by using multi-key generator. But this scheme didn't achieve public verifiability. In this paper we introduce a new multiple messages signcryption scheme which has the same efficiency as that of the scheme in [1], but achieves public verifiability. Also our scheme uses a simpler dynamic MKGR. The security of our scheme is based on three hard problems: DLP, DHP and reversing a OWHF. . The paper is organized as follows: section 2 introduces some preliminaries to the proposed scheme, section 3 discusses the proposed scheme; Finally, security analysis and discussion of the proposed scheme are given in section 4.

2   Preliminaries

The proposed multiple messages signcryption scheme is based on the intractability of the following problems:

- *Definition* 1. Discrete Logarithm Problem (DLP): given a prime p, a generator α of Z_p^* and an element $\beta \in Z_p^*$, find the integer x, $0 \le x \le p-2$, such that $\alpha^x = \beta \bmod p$ [4].

- *Definition* 2. Diffie-Hellman Problem (DHP): given a prime p, a generator α of Z_p^*, an element α^a mod p and α^b mod p and, find α^{ab} mod p [4].
- *Definition* 3. Intractability of reversing a one-way hash function (OWHF): it is computationally infeasible to derive x from a given hashed value Hash(x), or to find two different values x and x* such that Hash(x) = Hash(x*), (collision-free property) [4].

3 Proposed Signcryption Scheme

The proposed scheme consists of six phases: setup phase, key generation phase, multiple keys generation phase, signcryption phase, unsigncryption phase and non-repudiation and public verifiability phase.

3.1 Setup Phase

In this phase the system parameters are setup. The main parameters used in the proposed signcryption scheme are:

p : a large prime with length at least 512 bit
q : a large prime factor of p – 1
g : an integer in the interval [1,....., p – 1] with order q modulo p
H(.): *Secure Hash Algorithm (SHA) [5]:* a one-way hash function which maps arbitrarily long inputs into a string of length |H| bits.
E(.) , D(.): a symmetric block cipher algorithm consists of encryption algorithm E(.) and its matching decryption algorithm D(.).

3.2 Key Generation Phase

The keys of user A and user B are as following:

x_A : User's A secret key which is a random number in the interval [1,....., q – 1].
y_A : User's A public key which is given by:

$$y_A \equiv g^{x_A} \bmod p. \tag{1}$$

x_B : User's B secret key which is a random number in the interval [1,.., q – 1].
y_B : User's B public key which is given by:

$$y_B \equiv g^{x_B} \bmod p. \tag{2}$$

y_{AB} : User's A and user's B shared-secret key computed using Diffie-Hellman key exchange method [4] by user A as:

$$
\begin{aligned}
y_{AB} &\equiv y_B^{x_A} \bmod p \\
&\equiv (g^{x_B})^{x_A} \bmod p \\
&\equiv g^{x_A x_B} \bmod p.
\end{aligned}
\tag{3}
$$

and by user B as:

$$y_{AB} \equiv y_A^{x_B} \bmod p$$

$$\equiv (g^{\,x_A})^{\,x_B} \bmod p$$
$$\equiv g^{\,x_A\,x_B} \bmod p. \tag{4}$$

3.3 Multiple Keys Generation Phase

In this section, we will use the following basic notations:

+ : addition mod 2^{32}.

$\oplus$: XOR, $\wedge$: AND , $\vee$: OR.

$A^{<<<s}$: s-bit left shift rotation a 32-bit string

The proposed scheme uses a simple MKGR which expands the SHA output (k =256 bits) to generate random t keys of 256-bits by using non-linear logical functions operating on 32-bits words. The proposed MKGR uses only two shift rotation operation as compared with 8 shift rotation operation in [1].

Multiple keys generation routine (MKGR)

Suppose that the user A wants to send t secret messages $(m_1, m_2, ..., m_t)$ to B, then he will do the following to obtain two different sets of t-keys: one for the keyed hash algorithm and another for symmetric block cipher.

(1) Choose a random integer x in the interval $[1,....., q-1]$.

(2) Compute with using SHA-256:

$$k = H(\,g^{\,x} \bmod p). \tag{5}$$

(3) Parse k into eight 32-bit words $(w_0, w_1, w_2, w_3, w_4, w_5, w_6, w_7)$ and use these words as an initial value to the MKGR . The MKGR performs a key expansion routine to generate a key schedule. The initial 8 words $(w_0, w_1, w_2, w_3, w_4, w_5, w_6, w_7,)$ represents the key of the message m_1 and each of the $t-1$ messages $(m_2, ..., m_t)$ requires 8 words of key data. The resulting key schedule consists of a linear array of 8t 32-bit words denoted w_i, with i in the range $0 \le i \le 8t-1$.

For $8 \le i \le 8t-1$, w_i is given by:

$$w_i = w_{i-1}^{<<<s_1} + w_{i-8}^{<<<s_2}. \tag{6}$$

where $s_1 = (w_{i-2} \oplus w_{i-3}) \wedge w_{i-4}.$ \hfill (7)

and $s_2 = w_{i-5} \vee (w_{i-6} \oplus w_{i-7}).$ \hfill (8)

The generated t-keys are:

$$k_1 = w_0, w_1, w_2, w_3, w_4, w_5, w_6, w_7. \tag{9}$$

$$k_2 = w_8, w_9, w_{10}, w_{11}, w_{12}, w_{13}, w_{14}, w_{15}. \tag{10}$$

$$k_t = w_{8t-8}, w_{8t-7}, w_{8t-6}, w_{8t-5}, w_{8t-4}, w_{8t-3}, w_{8t-2}, w_{8t-1}. \tag{11}$$

(4) Compute with using SHA-256:

$$k^{`} = H((g^{\,x} \cdot y_{AB}) \bmod p). \tag{12}$$

(5) As in step 3, parse k ` into eight 32-bit words $(w_0`, w_1`, w_2`, w_3`, w_4`, w_5`, w_6`, w_7`)$ and use these words as an initial value to the MKGR. The generated t-keys are:

$$k_1` = w_0`, w_1`, w_2`, w_3`, w_4`, w_5`, w_6`, w_7`. \qquad (13)$$

$$k_2` = w_8`, w_9`, w_{10}`, w_{11}`, w_{12}`, w_{13}`, w_{14}`, w_{15}`. \qquad (14)$$

$$k_t` = w_{8t-8}`, w_{8t-7}`, w_{8t-6}`, w_{8t-5}`, w_{8t-4}`, w_{8t-3}`, w_{8t-2}`, w_{8t-1}`. \qquad (15)$$

In the proposed MKGR, the amount of shift rotation is not constant as in [1], instead it changes as the algorithm moves forward as a function of the previously generated words. This achieves a faster data diffusion and therefore increases the redundancy in the generated keys.

3.4 Signcryption Phase

To send t secret messages $(m_1, m_2, ..., m_t)$ to user B, user A do the following:

(1) Compute encrypted messages $C_1, C_2, ..., C_t$ using the keys $k_1`, k_2`, ..., k_t`$ as follows:

$$C_i = E_{k_i`} (m_i) \qquad \text{for} \quad 1 \le i \le t. \qquad (16)$$

(2) Compute $r_1, r_2, ..., r_t$, the keyed hash algorithm values of the messages using the keys, $k_1, k_2, ..., k_t$ as follows:

$$r_i = H (m_i, k_i) \qquad \text{for} \quad 1 \le i \le t. \qquad (17)$$

(3) Compute the multi-message signature using the random number x, the keyed hash values and A's secret key x_A, as follows:

$$s \equiv (x - x_A \sum_{i=1}^{t} r_i) \bmod q \qquad (18)$$

The signcryption of the multiple messages consists of the encrypted messages $C_1, C_2, ..., C_t$, the keyed hash values $r_1, r_2, ..., r_t$ and the signature s. Then user A sends the signcrypted ciphertext: $\{ C_1, C_2, ..., C_t, r_1, r_2, ..., r_t, s \}$ to user B.

3.5 Unsigncryption Phase

User B unsigncrypts and verifies the given signcrypted ciphertext $\{ C_1, C_2, ..., C_t, r_1, r_2, ..., r_t, s \}$ as following:

(1) Compute:

$$k = H ((g^s . y_A^{\sum r_i}) \bmod p). \qquad (19)$$

(2) Parse k into eight 32-bit words $(w_0, w_1, w_2, w_3, w_4, w_5, w_6, w_7)$ and use these words as an initial value to the MKGR to obtain the keys, $k_1, k_2, ..., k_t$.
(3) Use the shared-secret key y_{AB} to compute:

$$k` = H((y_{AB} \cdot g^s \cdot y_A{}^{\sum r_i}) \mod p). \tag{20}$$

(4) Parse k` into eight 32-bit words ($w_0`$,$w_1`$, $w_2`$, $w_3`$, $w_4`$, $w_5`$, $w_6`$, $w_7`$) and use these words as an initial value to the MKGR to obtain the keys: $k_1`$, $k_2`$,...., $k_t`$.

(5) Compute the decrypted multiple messages m_1, m_2, ..., m_t using the keys $k_1`$, $k_2`$,...., $k_t`$ as follows:

$$m_i = D_{k_i`}(C_i) \qquad \text{for} \quad 1 \le i \le t. \tag{21}$$

(6) Compute the keyed hash algorithm values $r_1`$, $r_2`$, ..., $r_t`$ of the decrypted messages m_1, m_2, ..., m_t using the keys k_1, k_2,...., k_t as follows:

$$r_i` = H(m_i, k_i) \qquad \text{for} \quad 1 \le i \le t. \tag{22}$$

(7) Compare the values r_1, r_2, ..., r_t and $r_1`$, $r_2`$, ..., $r_t`$.

(8) User B accepts the decrypted messages m_1, m_2, ..., m_t as a valid messages originated from the user A only if: r_1, r_2, ..., $r_t = r_1`$, $r_2`$, ..., $r_t`$.

3.6 Non-repudiation and Public Verification Phase

If user A denies the signature of the multiple messages m_1, m_2, ..., m_t , user B after decrypting and verifying the signcrypted ciphertext can prove the dishonesty of the signer by passing the public verifiability data ,{m_1, m_2, ..., m_t , r_1, r_2, ..., r_t, s} ,to a trusted third party (TTP) who can be convinced that it came originally from A as follows:

(1) Compute: $k = H((g^s \cdot y_A{}^{\sum r_i}) \mod p)$

(2) Parse k into eight 32-bit words (w_0 ,w_1, w_2, w_3, w_4, w_5, w_6, w_7) and use these words as an initial value to the MKGR to obtain the keys: k_1, k_2,...., k_t.

(3) Compute the keyed hash algorithm values $r_1`$, $r_2`$, ..., $r_t`$ of the messages m_1, m_2, ..., m_t using the keys k_1, k_2,...., k_t as follows:

$$r_i` = H(m_i, k_i) \qquad \text{for} \quad 1 \le i \le t. \tag{23}$$

(4) Convince that it came originally from A by verifying: r_1, r_2, ..., $r_t = r_1`$, $r_2`$, ..., $r_t`$.

The non–repudiation of our scheme is done publicly. To speak more precisely, in our scheme, with {m_1, m_2, ..., m_t , r_1, r_2, ..., r_t, s}, anyone can verify the origin of the signature.

4 Analysis of the Proposed Scheme

4.1 Security

Correctness. The multiple messages m_1, m_2, ..., m_t can be recovered successfully by the receiver if the signer produced the signcrypted ciphertext honestly, since the right-hand side of Eqn. (20) is:

$$H\left(\left(y_{AB}\cdot g^{s}\cdot y_{A}^{\sum r_i}\right)\bmod p\right)$$

$$=H\left(\left(y_{AB}\cdot g^{(x-xA\sum r_i)}\cdot y_{A}^{\sum r_i}\right)\bmod p\right) \text{ (substitute for } s \text{ from Eqn. (18))}$$

$$=H\left(\left(y_{AB}\cdot g^{(x-xA\sum r_i)}\cdot g^{xA\sum r_i}\right)\bmod p\right) \text{ (from Eqn. (1))} = H\left(\left(y_{AB}\cdot g^{x}\right)\bmod p\right)$$

$$= k` = \text{ the left-hand side of Eqn. (20)} \quad \text{(from Eqn. (12))}$$

Then parse k` into eight 32-bit words $(w_0`, w_1`, w_2`, w_3`, w_4`, w_5`, w_6`, w_7`)$ and use these words as an initial value to the MKGR to obtain the keys, $k_1`, k_2`, ...., k_t`$ which are used to decrypt the multiple message $m_1, m_2, ..., m_t$ as in Eqn. (21).

Confidentiality. The only way to decrypt the multiple ciphertexts $C_1, C_2, ..., C_t$ and obtain the multiple messages $m_1, m_2, ..., m_t$ is to have the shared-secret key y_{AB}. But it is difficult to obtain this key from the public keys due to the intractability of DHP. For a passive adversary, the information available is only $(C_1, C_2, ..., C_t, r_1, r_2, ..., r_t, s)$. From this data he can only obtain $k = H\left(\left(g^{s}\cdot y_{A}^{\sum r_i}\right)\bmod p\right) = H(g^x \bmod p)$ but he cannot guess the corresponding multiple messages $m_1, m_2, ..., m_t$. Also it is difficult to obtain x from k due to the intractability of both reversing OWHF and DLP. Assume an intruder intends to reveal the secret parameters x_A and x from Eqn. (18). This will be difficult because there are two unknown variables (x_A, x) in one equation.

Unforgeability. For successful signature forging attack, an attacker must find another message m_{io} and k_{io}, $1 \le i \le t$, such that: $H(m_i, k_i) = H(m_{io}, k_{io})$.

This is impossible due to the randomness and the collision-free property of OWHF. Even if an attacker can generate m_{io} and k_{io} satisfying the above equation, he cannot generate the corresponding s as he doesn't know secret key of the signer, x_A which is protected due to the DLP. Assume an intruder intends to reveal the secret parameters x_A and s from Eqn. (18). Then this will be difficult because there are two unknown variables (x_A, x) in one equation as we previously mentioned.

Non-repudiation and Public Verifiability. Passing the multiple messages $m_1, m_2, ..., m_t$ and the signature$\{r_1, r_2, ..., r_t, s\}$ to any third party convinces him that the ciphertext is the signcrypted version of a given multiple plaintext messages made by the sender, so the proposed scheme satisfies public verifiability. This passing doesn't affect the confidentiality of the scheme because an adversary cannot get the shared-secret key, y_{AB}, due to the intractability of the DHP even if he gets once the multiple messages $m_1, m_2, ..., m_t$ and its corresponding signcrypted ciphertext.

4.2 Efficiency

The computational cost of the proposed signcryption scheme is one modular exponentiation for signcryption and two for unsigncryption while the length of the signcrypted data in bits is $[t \cdot (|r| + |C|) + |s|]$ where $|x|$ refers to the size of a binary string. So the efficiency of the proposed scheme is the same as that of the multi-messages signcryption scheme in [1].

5 Conclusions

In this paper, we have presented a new multiple messages signcryption scheme that is based on the intractability of three hard problems: DLP, DHP and reversing a OWHF. Our scheme is publicly verifiable. This means that after a transmitted signcrypted ciphertext is decrypted and verified by the recipient, the decrypted signature can be verified publicly. Therefore, non-repudiation is easily achieved. We have achieved this important property with using a simple and dynamic MKGR which generates multiple secret keys for both block cipher and keyed hash algorithms simultaneously. The MKGR uses non-linear logical functions which are much faster than the multiple modular exponentiation. It requires one modular exponentiation for signcryption and two for unsigncryption. So it is as efficient as the multi-messages signcryption scheme in [1] which is based on DLP, but it has the advantage of public verifiability and the simpler and dynamic MKGR.

References

1. Elkamchouchi, H., Emarah, E., Hagras, E.: Public Key Multi-Message Signcryption (PK-MMS) Scheme For Secure Communication Systems. In: Fifth Annual Conference on Communication Networks and Services Research (CNSR 2007) (2007)
2. Zheng, Y.: Digital Signcryption or How to Achieve Cost (Signature & Encryption)< < Cost (Signature) + Cost (Encryption). In: Kaliski Jr., B.S. (ed.) CRYPTO 1997. LNCS, vol. 1294, pp. 165–179. Springer, Heidelberg (1997)
3. Tso, R., Okamoto, T., Okamoto, E.: An Improved Signcryption Scheme and Its Variation. In: International Conference On Information Technology (ITNG 2007) (2007)
4. Menezes, A., Oorschot, P., Vanstone, S.: Handboock of Applied Cryptography. CRC Press, Boca Raton (1997)
5. National Institute of Science and Technology: Secure Hash Standard. USA, Federal Information Processing Standard (FIPS) 180-2 (August 2002)

Research and Implementation of Reconfigurable Multiplier over Galois Field Targeted at Stream Cipher

Xueying Zhang, Zibin Dai, Wei Li, and Longmei Nan

Institute of Electronic Technology, The Information Engineering University,
Zhengzhou 450004, China
zhxy727@163.com

Abstract. Multiplication over Galois field is the core operation in stream cipher. Based on the conversion of polynomial basis over different finite fields, a reconfigurable hardware architecture for multiplier over Galois field is presented. The multiplier can perform multiplications over $GF((2^8)^4)$, $GF((2^8)^2)$, $GF(2^{32})$, $GF(2^{16})$, $GF(2^8)$ with one single hardware architecture. The design has been realized using Altera's FPGA of the family of Stratix II, the result indicates that the hardware spending is saved with one single multiplier. And when the multiplication over $GF(2^{32})$ is performed, the clock frequency is up to 70.22Mhz, the data throughput can achieve 4.83Gbps, and the area only takes 586 ALUTS.

Keywords: Reconfigurable, Multiplication over Galois Field, Composite Filed Stream Cipher.

1 Introduction

The performance of the LFSR (liner feedback shift register) influences the throughput of the stream cipher directly. Based on the different types of the feedback function, there are two groups of the stream ciphers: the SSC-like ciphers (based on the SSC family of ciphers) which use bit rotations to update the elements in LFSR, they could be performed in a higher speed but worse in security, the SOBER-like stream ciphers which use some arithmetic operations over one Galois field, the hardware complexity is higher but better in security, they are the mainstream. Multiplication is the most important and complexity operation, so the design of the multiplier over the Galois field of stream ciphers explicitly significant.

Previous published multipliers over Galois field can be classified into there categories to achieve the trade off between the speed and area: the bit-serial, the bit-parallel and the hybrid. Another classification can be considered based on the basis representation, the dual multiplier which consumes little areas by using only shift and XOR operations, but conversion between different bases is inevitable and it's hard to implement. The normal multiplier was more simply, but consumes more area. The polynomial multiplier which is been used widely as the polynomial basis is the most directly representation of the element over the finite field. The multiplier hardware

L. Qi (Ed.): FCC 2009, CCIS 34, pp. 201–209, 2009.

complexity can be reduced if the irreducible polynomial is an All-One Polynomial (AOP) or a trinomial, but this method is not suitable for all finite fields.

Combined with the multiplication in stream cipher, a reconfigurable hardware architecture for multiplier over Galois field is presented, which based on the architecture of multiplier over composite field.

2 Applications Analysis

Multiplication over finite field is the most important department of the feedback functions for LFSR, the generating polynomial and the multiplier had been gave by the designer of the arithmetic, the multiplicand changing while the arithmetic running. The characters multiplication in Galois field of 9 word-oriented stream ciphers which were appeared in NESSIE Project an ECRYPT Project were shown in Table 1.

Table 1. Characters multiplication in Galois filed of 9 word-oriented stream ciphers

Stream Ciphers	Field Degree	Generating Polynomial	Fixed Multiplier
Snow1.0	32	$x^{32} + x^{31} + x^{22} + x^{17} + x^{12} + x^3 + 1$	$A = 0X20108403$
Snow2.0	32	$x^4 + 0XE1x^3 + 0X9Fx^2 + 0XCFx + 0X13$ Subfield: $x^8 + x^7 + x^5 + x^3 + 1$	α (Primitive element)
Sober	8	$x^8 + x^6 + x^3 + x^2 + 1$	$A1 = 0XCE$
Sober-t16	16	$x^{16} + x^{14} + x^{12} + x^7 + x^6 + x^4 + x^2 + x + 1$	$A1 = 0XE382,$ $A2 = 0X67C3$
Sober-t32	32	$x^{32} + \left(x^{24} + x^{16} + x^8 + 1\right) + \left(x^6 + x^5 + x^2 + 1\right)$	$A = 0XC2DB2AA3$
Sober-128	32	$x^4 + 0XD0x^3 + 0X2Bx^2 + 0X43x + 0X67$ Subfield: $x^8 + x^6 + x^3 + x^2 + 1$	α (Primitive element)
Sosemanuk	32	$x^4 + 0XE1x^3 + 0X9Fx^2 + 0XCFx + 0X13$ Subfield: $x^8 + x^7 + x^5 + x^3 + 1$	α (Primitive element)
Sss	16	$x^2 + 0X50x + 0X0F$ Subfield: $x^8 + x^6 + x^3 + x^2 + 1$	α (Primitive element)
Yamb	32	$x^{32} + x^{27} + x^{24} + x^{20} + x^{19} + x^{17} + x^{16}$ $+ x^{12} + x^{10} + x^9 + x^8 + x^7 + x^6 + x^3 + 1$	$A = 0X40000000$

Obviously, there were two methods for generating the Galois field $GF(2^k)$ in stream ciphers, the first one, $GF(2^k)$ is generated from an irreducible polynomial of degree k over $GF(2)$. The second one, if $k = n \times m$, $GF(2^n)$ is generated from an irreducible polynomial of degree n over $GF(2)$, then $GF((2^n)^m)$ is generated from an irreducible polynomial of degree m over $GF(2^n)$.

3 Design of the Reconfigurable Galois Field Multiplier

3.1 Introduction of Composite Field Multiplier

The implementation of the multipliers over binary extension field had been described above. For composite field $GF((2^n)^m)$, its generate polynomial is $g(x)$, β is its root.

Element $A, B \in GF((2^n)^m)$, could be represented as:

$$A = A_{m-1}\beta^{m-1} + \ldots + A_1\beta + A_0 \; ; \; B = B_{m-1}\beta^{m-1} + \ldots + B_1\beta + B_0 \; , \quad A_i, B_i \in GF(2^n) \; . \tag{1}$$

If B is the root β of $g(x)$:

$$
\begin{aligned}
AB = A\beta = \left(A_{m-1}\beta^{m-1} + \ldots + A_1\beta + A_0\right)\beta &= A_{m-1}\beta^m + \ldots + A_1\beta^2 + A_0\beta \\
&= A_{m-1}\left(g_{m-1}\beta^{m-1} + \ldots + g_1\beta + g_0\right) + A_{m-2}\beta^{m-1} + \ldots + A_1\beta^2 + A_0\beta \\
&= \left(A_{m-1}g_{m-1} + A_{m-2}\right)\beta^{m-1} + \left(A_{m-1}g_{m-2} + A_{m-3}\right)\beta^{m-2} + \ldots + \left(A_{m-1}g_1 + A_0\right)\beta + A_{m-1}g_0
\end{aligned}
\tag{2}
$$

The implementation architectures of the operation is shown in **Fig.1.**The product of whichever element of $GF((2^n)^m)$ and β could been obtained in one clock, $\otimes$ represent the multiplication in field $GF(2^n)$, and $\oplus$ represent XOR-operator.

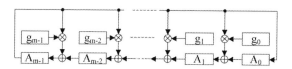

Fig. 1. Hardware architecture of $A\beta$

If B isn't a root of $g(x)$, the product :

$$Z = A \bullet B = A(B_{m-1}\beta^{m-1} + \ldots + B_1\beta + B_0) = (((B_0 A) + B_1 A\beta) + \ldots) + B_{m-1}A\beta^{m-1} \; . \tag{3}$$

The implementation architectures of the operation is shown in **Fig. 2.** The product of two $GF((2^n)^m)$ elements could been obtained in m clock.

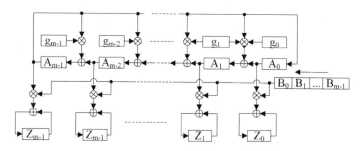

Fig. 2. Hardware architecture of multiplier over composite field

The multiplier over composite field $GF((2^n)^m)$ is composed of 2m multipliers over $GF(2^n)$, it can complete any multiplication for any element in m clocks. Especially, if the multiplier is the root of the generate polynomial, it can complete the multiplication in one clock, and the frequency was equal to the frequency of multiplication over $GF(2^n)$. Obviously, the multiplication over $GF((2^n)^m)$ has more efficient performances than $GF(2^k)$. If the multiplication over binary extension field $GF(2^k)$ can be conversed to composite field $GF((2^n)^m)$, it's implementations would be improve greatly.

3.2   The Theory of Conversion of Basis

In order to represent a composite field, we must know the general polynomial $g(x)$ of the composite field $GF((2^n)^m)$, the general polynomial $p(x)$ of the subfield $GF(2^n)$, and the conversion matrix T and it's reverse matrix T^{-1}. Which are used to conversion two different representations of the single element.

Generate polynomial of composite field: $GF((2^n)^m)$ **:** If α is a root of $f(x)$, the generate polynomial of $GF(2^k)$, the conjugates of α with respect to $GF(2^n)$ is $\left\{\alpha, \alpha^{2^n}, \alpha^{2^{2n}}, \dots \alpha^{2^{(m-1)n}}\right\}$, the polynomial $g(x)$ which is called the minimal polynomial of α is the generate polynomial of composite field $GF((2^n)^m)$, α is also a root of $g(x)$:

$$g(x) = (x+\alpha)(x+\alpha^{2^n})(x+\alpha^{2^{2n}})\dots(x+\alpha^{2^{(m-1)n}}) . \tag{4}$$

Generate polynomial $p(x)$ of subfield: $GF(2^n)$ **:** For γ is a root of $p(x)$, the generate polynomial of $GF(2^n)$, so $\gamma^{2^n-1}=1$, the conjugates of γ with respect to $GF(2)$ is $\left\{\gamma, \gamma^2, \gamma^{2^2}, \dots \gamma^{2^{n-1}}\right\}$, for α is the root of $f(x)$, so $\alpha^{2^k-1}=1$, $\alpha^{2^k-1}=\gamma^{2^n-1}$, $\gamma=\alpha^r, r=\dfrac{2^k-1}{2^n-1}$, the polynomial $p(x)$ which is called the minimal polynomial of γ is the generate polynomial of subfield $GF(2^n)$:

$$p(x) = (x+\gamma)(x+\gamma^2)(x+\gamma^{2^2})\dots(x+\gamma^{2^{n-1}}) = (x+\alpha^r)(x+\alpha^{2r})(x+\alpha^{4r})\dots(x+\alpha^{2(n-1)r}) . \tag{5}$$

Conversions matrix T: In binary field $GF(2^k)$, element A could be represented by using $B_1 = \{1, \alpha, \alpha^2, \dots, \alpha^{k-1}\}$ as:

$$A = \sum_{i=0}^{k-1} a_i \alpha^i, a_i \in GF(2), i = 0, 1, \dots k-1 . \tag{6}$$

In composite field, α is also the root of $g(x)$, element A could be represented by using $B_1 = \{1, \alpha, \alpha^2, \dots, \alpha^{m-1}\}$ as:

$$A = \sum_{i=0}^{m-1} A_i' \alpha^i, A_i' \in GF(2^n), i = 0, 1, \dots m-1 . \tag{7}$$

Any sub-vector A_j' could be represented by using $B_2 = \{1, \gamma, \gamma^2, \ldots \gamma^{n-1}\}$ as:

$$A_i' = \sum_{j=0}^{n-1} \overline{A_{ij}} \gamma^j, \overline{A_{ij}} \in GF(2), j = 0, 1, \ldots n-1 \tag{8}$$

So we can derive the binary representation of A from its composite representation as equation (9), t_{ijh} are the elements of the conversion matrix.

$$A = \sum_{i=0}^{k-1} a_i \alpha^i = \sum_{i=0}^{m-1} A_i' \alpha^i = \sum_{i=0}^{m-1} \sum_{j=0}^{n-1} \overline{A_{ij}} \alpha^{rj+i} = \sum_{i=0}^{m-1} \sum_{j=0}^{n-1} \overline{A_{ij}} \sum_{h=0}^{k-1} t_{ijh} \alpha^h = \sum_{i=0}^{m-1} \sum_{j=0}^{n-1} \sum_{h=0}^{k-1} t_{ijh} \alpha^h \overline{A_{ij}} . \tag{9}$$

On the basis of theory that the conversion above, we can conversion the element in $GF((2^n)^m)$ to $GF(2^k)$, and the same in reverse. Then the multiplication in large Galois field could be implemented in terms of a smaller, intermediate Galois field.

3.3 Design of the Reconfigurable Galois Field Multiplier

After the analyzing the characters of the multiplication over Galois field, comparing the performances of multipliers over different fields, and using the theory of conversion between two representations, in this design, a reconfigurable multiplier over Galois field is presented, the architecture of the multiplier is show in **Fig.3.**

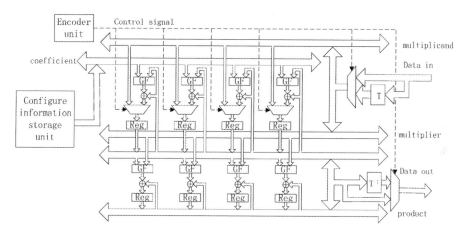

Fig. 3. Hardware architecture of the reconfigurable multiplier

In this design, the reconfigurable multiplier must had been configured before it was used to implement the multiplication configure information. Such as the generate polynomials of composite field and subfield, the conversion matrixes and so on, must be kept in the configure information storage unit while the multiplier was running.

The conversion matrixes T and T^{-1}, matrix T^{-1} could conversion the multiplier and multiplicand from the binary to composite representations, matrix T was inverse. The circuit of row conversion circuit of the matrix T^{-1} is shown in **Fig.4.**

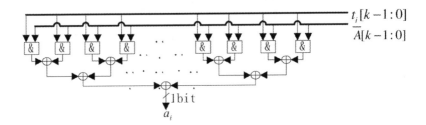

Fig. 4. Row conversion circuit of the matrix T^{-1}

The circuit is a XOR-net with tree-like structure, the input signal t_i is the i-th row vector of the matrix T^{-1}, the output is the i-th bit of the vector which represent element A in $GF(2^k)$. In the whole circuit of the matrix T^{-1}, there are k rows in matrix T^{-1}, they have the same structure but different input vectors. The matrix T is same.

In this design, the reconfigurable multiplier is based on the composite field multiplier, this methodology requires that construct the composite field by suitably selecting n and m. Combined the characters of the other departments in stream cipher, we selected $n = 8$, $m = 4$. It means that we used $GF(2^8)$ as the subfield, constructed reconfigurable multiplier over composite field $GF((2^8)^4)$. The multiplier could implement all multiplications which were shown in **Table.1.**, and its frequency, throughput and performance is better to connect with other departments of the arithmetic. The unit used shift-add arithmetic to implement the multiplication with arbitrary generate polynomial and arbitrary operand. The theory and performance had described in[7].

When the multiplication is over composite field, multiplier and multiplicand could be inputted directly. Control by the signals, the architecture can implement one multiplication over $GF((2^8)^4)$, two multiplications in parallel over $GF((2^8)^2)$, eight multiplications in parallel over $GF(2^8)$. Especially if the multiplier is a root of generate polynomial of the composite field, it could implement two multiplications in parallel over $GF((2^8)^4)$, four multiplications in parallel over $GF((2^8)^2)$.

When the multiplication is over binary field $GF(2^k)$, multiplier and multiplicand must through the matrix T^{-1}, and the product through matrix T, output to next department. Under the control signals, the architecture can implement one multiplication over $GF(2^{32})$, two multiplications in parallel over $GF(2^{16})$. Especially, if the multiplier is a toot of the generate polynomial, it can implement two multiplications over $GF(2^{32})$, four multiplications over $GF(2^{16})$ in parallel.

4   Performance and Analysis

4.1   Performance of This Design

Based on the analysis above, the prototype has been accomplished RTL description using Verilog language. And the design continues with the synthesis using QuartusII 6.0 from Altera Corporation. The prototype has been verified successfully based on Altera's stratix EP2S180F1508C3. The performance is shown in **Table. 2.**.

Table 2. The performance of the reconfigurable multiplier

	Shift-add arithmetic			The design in this paper	
Degree of the field	8	16	32	16	32
ALUTS	78	342	1759	277	586
Frequency(Mhz)	80.57	57.75	28.65	75.22	70.22
Memory(bits)	0	0	0	512	2048
clocks	1	1	1	2(1)	4(1)
Reconfigurable	×	×	×	√	√
parallel	1	1	1	1(2)	1(2)

When the multiplier is a root of the generate polynomials of the field, the performances of the reconfigurable multiplier are the dates in brackets.

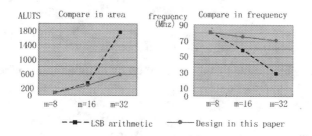

Fig. 5. Compare Sihft-add arithmetic and this design

It obviously that, when using shift-add arithmetic to design the multiplier, the factor k increases one time, the area of circuit will increases four or five times, and the frequency only half. In area limited application is unsuitable. Use the methodology of this paper, when factor k double, the area of the circuit increase one times only, and the frequency is as same as before. Especially, if the multiplier is the root of the generate polynomial, the whole multiplication could be completed in one clock, its performances of the circuit would be improved greatly.

4.2 Compare with Other Designs

The multiplier architecture in this paper was designed modularization, can implement multiplication over different fields with different parameter n , m , compared with other designs it has great optimization on area, frequency and generality.

Reconfigurable multiplier for given type of the polynomial. The reconfigurable multiplier in Ref[3] could reconfigure fields which have the same type of the polynomial, AOP and required the most degree of the variable is odd. The circuit who could implement two types of the polynomials such as AOP and trinomials in Ref[4], it can reconfigure more multiplications, but the area is too large. The architecture in this design could implement all types of the field, and doesn't require more logic circuits. The results of the compare with this design has shown in **Fig.6.(a)**.

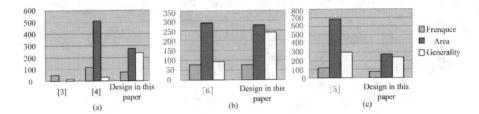

Fig. 6. Compare with other designs

Reconfigurable multiplier for any degree of the field . The reconfigurable multiplier in Ref[5] was designed based on the improved serial multiplier, could implement all types field. The architecture equally divides the multiplier and multiplicand of field multiplication into two sub-polynomials, and reconfigurable implement respectively. The speed is two times faster than the traditional serial multiplier, but the area is one point five times lager than the serial multiplier, the optimization is not obviously. The results of the compare with this design has shown in **Fig.6.(b)**.

Reconfigurable multiplier for composite field by using KOA arithmetic . The multiplier which used composite filed to implement multiplication is described in Ref[6], it's frequency and area are equal to the multiplier in this design. When divided the polynomial of the composite field, it use Krartsuba-Ofman (KOA) arithmetic, the method was more complex and required the factor n and m is prime, it can't suitable all field too. The results of the compare with this design has shown in **Fig.6.(c)**.

5   Conclusion

Combined with the multiplication in stream cipher, a reconfigurable hardware architecture for multiplier over Galois field is presented in this paper, by selecting the values of the vector n and m, the architecture could implement multiplication over any field whose degree isn't prime. The multiplier was designed modularization, could be extend easily.

Acknowledgments

This research is supported by 863 Project of China (Grant No. 2008AA01Z103).

References

1. Sunar, B., Savas, E., Eetin, K.K.: Constructiong Composite Field Representations for Efficient Conversion. IEEE Trans.On Computers 52(11), 1391–1398 (2003)
2. Cho, Y.S., Park, S.K.: Design of GF(2m) multiplier using its subfields. IEEE, electronics letters 34(7), 650–651 (1998)

3. Imana, J.L.: Reconfigurable Implementation of Bit-Parallel Multipliers over GF(2m) for Two Classes of finite Fields. In: ICFPT 2004, pp. 287–290 (2004)
4. Dan-shou, Y., Meng-tian, R., Chen, B.: A Fast Finite Field Multiplier Architecture and Its VLSI Implementatio. Microelectronics 35(5), 314–317 (2005)
5. Dan-shou, Y., Meng-tian, R.: Reconfigurable and Fast Finite Field Multiplier Architecture. Journal of Electronic& Information Technology 28(4), 717–720 (2006)
6. Lu, J.-S., Zhang, W.-X., Wang, X.-H.: A Fast Multiplier Design and Implication over Finite Fields. Journal of Computer Research and Development 41(4), 755–760 (2004)
7. Yang, X., Dai, Z., Yu, X., Su, J.: A Design of General Multiplier GF(28) and FPGA Implementation. In: 2006 1st Internationl Symposium on Pervasive Computing and Applications, pp. 503–507 (2006)

Research of Grey Relation Theory Algorithm for Customer Classification of Manufacturing Enterprise

Laihong Du and Ping Kang

Xi'an University of Finance and Economics, Xi'an, ShaanXi, 710061, China
dlh06@163.com, kangpingxinxi@126.com

Abstract. The paper puts forward customer classification method based on grey relation theory for customer classifying problem of manufacturing enterprise. Customer classifying comprehensive evaluation index system is introduced on the basis of analyzing research result about qualitative or quantitative customer classification at present. What's more, customer classification grey relation evaluation model is discussed, and the method and step based on grey relation theory are also introduced in detail. The process and result of customer classification are lastly discussed by taking one manufacturing enterprise as instance, and the customer type of enterprise is determined by utilizing ABC taxonomy.

Keywords: customer classification method; comprehensive evaluation index system; grey relation evaluation.

1 Introduction

With the development of information technology application, manufacturing mode changed from mass customization to scalable batch production, and small-and-medium-sized enterprises are faced with the same question, that is how to rapidly respond market requirement and manufacture product for various customer requirement. For current complicated market environment, how to correctly, efficiently and soundly manage customer relation is one of key problems for networked manufacturing.

Customer classification is one of the vital tasks for customer relation management (CRM). Customer set is classified according to customer attribute, and customer consumed mode is analyzed and forecasted by acquiring customer class [1]. After customers have been classified, manufacturing enterprise may analyze it easily and provide corresponding marketing strategy and service to attract primary customer and prevent customer loss. From previous literature about customer classifying method, we can draw a conclusion: If customer is individual, customer category is usually analyzed by clustering approach, such as demography and artificial neural network [2]; If customer is enterprise, category of customer is often discussed at the aspect of profit and value [3]. The paper mainly discusses customer classifying problem for manufacturing enterprise by considering qualitative and quantitative in terms of gray relation theory.

L. Qi (Ed.): FCC 2009, CCIS 34, pp. 210–217, 2009.

2 Evaluation Index System for Customer Classification Management

The paper considered each factor that is related to customer classification, including customer profit index, customer credit level, and customer loyalty degree and so on, and each index is consist of different influence factors. The evaluation index system for customer classification is following as Figure 1.

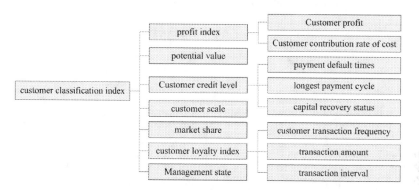

Fig. 1. Customer classification evaluation index system

(1) Profit index (L_1)

Profit index mainly emphasizes on classifying and sorting customers in terms of their bringing profits to enterprises. According to reference [3], customer quantitative classification is realized by customer profit taxonomy method and customer cost contribution rate approach, and it considers comprehensively product price, cost, sales volume and other indirect expense in nature.

● Customer profit(L_{11})

During calculating customer profit, how to allocate indirect expense (such as operating expenses, management expenses) to each customer is the un-ignored problem, and customer profit considering indirect expenses can be gotten by equation 1. Moreover, *CProfit* represents customer profit, *RPrice* is real price, *PCost* is product cost, *Quantity* represents sales volume and *OCost* is indirect cost for customer.

$$CProfit=(RPrice-PCost)\times Quantity-OCost . \qquad (1)$$

● Customer contribution rate of cost(L_{12})

Customer contribution rate of cost is the ratio of profit from customer to indirect expense, and it can be calculated by equation 2. Moreover, *CRatio* represents customer contribution rate of cost, *RPrice* is real price, *PCost* is product cost, *Quantity* represents sales volume and *OCost* is indirect cost for customer.

$$CRatio=(RPrice-PCost)\times Quantity/ OCost-1 . \qquad (2)$$

(2)Customer loyalty index (L_2)

Customer loyalty index is the degree of repeating transaction with preference enterprise, and it includes customer transaction frequency (L_{21}), transaction amount (L_{22})

and transaction interval (L_{23}). Customer transaction frequency is the times of exchange within one year, and transaction amount is annual total expenses.

(3) Customer credit level (L_3)

According to international current credit grade standard, customer credit level can be discussed from payment default times (L_{31}), longest payment cycle (L_{32}) and capital recovery status (L_{33}).

Table 1. Quantification standard of customer loyalty index

Quantification grade	Payment default times	Longest payment cycle(day)	Capital recovery status (%)
1	>5	>270	<30%
2	4~5	255~270	30%~60%
3	2~4	105~255	60%~75%
4	1~2	75~105	75%~90%
5	0	<45	>90%

(4) Potential value (L_4)

Potential value is the influence coefficient of customer to enterprise about profit and development in the future, and it is classified into five grades: AAAAA, AAAA, AAA, AA and A. The higher of grade, the influence degree is bigger, and its quantification standard is shown as Table 2.

Table 2. Quantification standard of potential value

L_4	A	AA	AAA	AAAA	AAAAA
Value	1	2	3	4	5

(5) Customer scale (L_5)

Customer scale [4] can be considered in different view. The paper emphasizes on enterprise capital, and divides it into large customer (its capital is more than 5 million Yuan), medium customer (its capital is between 1 and 5 million Yuan), small customer (its capital is between 0.5 and 1 million Yuan) and sundry customer (its capital is lower than 0.5 million Yuan).

(6) Market share (L_6)

Market share is the ratio of product quantity provided by enterprise to purchase quantity from market. Market share of steady customer exceeds 70%, basically steady customer is between 50% and 70%, unsteady customer is between 10% and 50% and market share under 10% is extremely steady customer.

(7) Management state (L_7)

Management state impacts on enterprise's profit and development to a large extend. It can be divided into four grades: AAAA (management state is good, profit is stable), AAA (management state is general, and profit is slight), AA (management state is general, and there are losses. However, general performance of enterprise is on the rise) and A (management state is poor, and there are losses. Moreover, it shows no tendency to improve), The quantification standard is shown as table 5.

3 Model and Method of Customer Classification Grey Relation Evaluation

Grey relation analysis belongs to grey system theory put forward by Professor Deng Ju-long in 1982, and it mainly researches quantification analysis problem of system state development. In grey relation theory, the geometry curve constructed by several stat. data is more similar, the relation degree is bigger. As Figure 2, the similarity degree of curve one and two is greater than similarity degree of curve one and three, and the relation degree of curve one and two is more than curve of one and three.

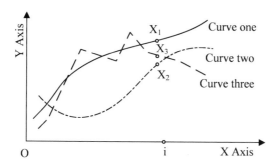

Fig. 2. The thought of grey relation

The relation sequence reflects approximate sequence of each project to objective project, and the project of maximal grey relation degree is best one. For standard reference sequence $x_0=[x_{01}, x_{02}, ..., x_{0n}]$, $x_i=[x_{i1}, x_{i2}, ..., x_{in}](i=1,2,...,m)$ is regarded as compared sequence, and the grey relation coefficient matrix is defined as following:

$$\xi_i^{(k)}=\frac{\Delta\min+\sigma\Delta\max}{\Delta ik+\sigma\Delta\max} . \tag{3}$$

$$\Delta\min=\min_i\min_k|x_{ik}-x_{0k}| . \tag{4}$$

$$\Delta\max=\max_i\max_k|x_{ik}-x_{0k}| . \tag{5}$$

$$\Delta ik=|x_{ik}-x_{0k}|(i=1,2,...,m ; k=1,2,...,n) . \tag{6}$$

σ is distinguishing coefficient, and it shows importance degree of unity in relation space. According to grey relation literature research, grey relation coefficient $\xi_i^{(k)}$ is monotone increasing function, and its principle is shown as following:

The comparison mean of relation space is defined as $\overline{\Delta}$, and $\overline{\Delta}=\sum_{i=1}^{m}\sum_{k=1}^{n}|x_{0k}-x_{ik}|\bigg/(n\cdot m)$. The scale coefficient of mean is $\gamma=\overline{\Delta}/\Delta\max$.

The relation coefficient for each comparison sequence can be determined by Equation 7, and ω_k is weight of each item in comparison set. What' more, ψ_i is grey relation coefficient for each comparison sequence.

$$\psi_i = \sum_{k=1}^{n} \omega_k \zeta_i^{(k)} \ . \tag{7}$$

The method and step of grey relation evaluation model for customer classification is described as following:

(1) Determine optimal index set

The optimal index set $x_k = [x_{k1}, x_{k2}, \dots ,x_{kn}]$ is determined from customer classification index set, and x_{ki} is the maximal/minimum value of corresponding index i (If index i belongs to benefit type, x_{ki} is maximal value of index i. Otherwise, x_{ki} is minimum value of index i).

(2) Standardization disposal of index data

For cost type index, the smaller value is, the better it will be. For example, transaction interval belongs to cost type index, and it can be standardized by Equation 8. For benefit type index, the larger value is, the better it will be. For example, market share is benefit type index, and it can be standardized by Equation 9. x_{ij} is evaluation index j of customer i, and variable m indicates enterprise customer quantity.

$$\overline{\delta}_{ij} = \left[x_{ij} \left(\sum_{k=1}^{m} x_{kj}^{-1} \right) \right]^{-1} \ . \tag{8}$$

$$\overline{\delta}_{ij} = x_{ij} \bigg/ \sum_{k=1}^{n} x_{kj} \ . \tag{9}$$

(3) Determine weight of each hierarchy index

By sorting importance degree of each hierarchy index, we can construct evaluation index judgment matrix, and get eigenvector of evaluation index based on power algorithm by Equation 10.

$$AW = \lambda_{max} W \ . \tag{10}$$

(4) Determine grey relation coefficient of grade I

Grey relation coefficient matrix for customer classification can be acquired according to Equation 3 and step I.

(5) Calculate comprehensive grey coefficient, and get the final evaluating result

According to Equation 7 and result of step 3 and 4, grey relation coefficient of each hierarchy is determined, and custom is classified according to calculating result and ABC taxonomy.

4 Case Study

One machinery plant mainly produces shaft-disc type components, and its mode of production is multi-type and small-batch production. For the sake of argument, the paper selects 5 customers randomly to discuss the classification of customer, and relevant evaluation data is qualified as Table 3. L_{11} add L_{12} is calculated by Equation 1 and Equation 2. The data of evaluation index set is standardized by Equation 5 and 6, and data pretreatment matrix is show as Table 4.

Table 3. Customer classification evaluation index set

	L_{11}	L_{12}	L_{21}	L_{22}	L_{23}	L_{31}	L_{32}	L_{33}	L_4	L_5	L_6	L_7
Customer I	5785.9	521.5	13	34.5	3.6	4	3	5	3	3	3	2
Customer II	2458.3	342.7	5	126.9	4.2	3	4	3	3	4	3	1
Customer III	1365.2	254.9	1	56.4	14	5	3	2	2	3	2	2
Customer IV	4783.8	135.2	7	12.6	5.9	2	1	1	2	1	1	1
Customer V	6743.6	423.5	8	3.2	12.7	2	3	4	4	3	4	4
X^*(Optimum set)	6743.6	521.5	13	126.9	3.6	5	4	5	4	4	4	4

Table 4. Standardization disposal matrix of customer classification

	L_{11}	L_{12}	L_{21}	L_{22}	L_{23}	L_{31}	L_{32}	L_{33}	L_4	L_5	L_6	L_7
Customer I	0.27	0.31	0.38	0.15	0.33	0.25	0.21	0.33	0.21	0.21	0.23	0.2
Customer II	0.12	0.20	0.15	0.54	0.29	0.19	0.29	0.20	0.21	0.29	0.23	0.1
Customer III	0.07	0.15	0.03	0.24	0.09	0.31	0.21	0.13	0.14	0.21	0.15	0.2
Customer IV	0.23	0.08	0.21	0.05	0.20	0.13	0.07	0.07	0.14	0.07	0.08	0.1
Customer V	0.32	0.25	0.24	0.01	0.09	0.13	0.21	0.27	0.29	0.21	0.31	0.4
X^*(Optimum set)	0.27	0.31	0.38	0.15	0.33	0.25	0.21	0.33	0.21	0.21	0.23	0.2

After investigation and analysis, the importance sequence of each hierarchy evaluation index for customer classification: $L_1>L_3>L_2>L_4>L_7>L_5>L_6$, $L_{11}>L_{12}$, $L_{22}>L_{21}>L_{23}$, $L_{33}>L_{32}>L_{31}$. The judgment matrix E_1, E_2, E_3, E_4 can be gotten by AHP method. According to Equation 7, weight vectors W_1, W_2, W_3, and W_4 for each judgment matrix are shown as following: W_1= {0.349, 0.159, 0.237, 0.105, 0.046, 0.032, 0.072}, W_2= {0.75, 0.25}, W_3= {0.26, 0.633, 0.106}, W_4= {0.106, 0.26, 0.633}. First-order coefficient vector of comparison sequence is gotten by Equation 7: ψ^1= {0.934, 0.505, 0.417, 0.412, 0.764}, ψ^2= {0.936, 0.844, 0.482, 0.715, 0.715}, ψ^3= {0.707, 0.64, 0.845, 0.399, 0.504}. According to solving process of first-order correlation coefficient, second-order coefficient vector can be calculated by Equation 7: ψ={0.862, 0.664, 0.645, 0.527, 0.767}.

Palette analytical method (ABC taxonomy) emphasizes on classifying and sorting problem according to its technology or economy main feature, and determines correspond management method. The paper simulates and analyzes grey relation coefficient for customer classification, and its simulation curve is shown as Figure 3. From the figure, we can draw a conclusion: 60% of grey relation coefficient comes from 20% of customer, and another 60% of customer only provides 40 of grey relation coefficient. Thus, the customer of enterprise can be divided into three parts: A type customer, whose grey relation coefficient range is $\xi \in (0.7,1]$, should be given priority to the development. B type customer, whose grey relation coefficient range is $\xi \in (0.4, 0.7]$, need to maitain or reduce. C type customer, whose grey relation coefficient range is $\xi \in (0, 0.4]$, should be given up. In terms of ABC taxonomy and second-order coefficient vector ψ, the classification of above five enterprises is: customer I and V belong to A type, customer II, III and IV are B type customer.

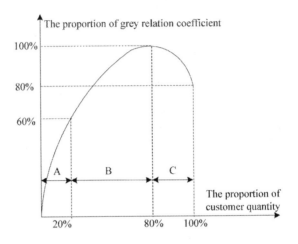

Fig. 3. Palette curve for customer classification

5 Conclusions

Customer classification is the key problem of customer relation management. The paper breaks through the tradition customer classification of only thinking about enterprise profit, and analyzes and explains evaluation index that impact customer classification management in detail on the basis of other scholar's research. Besides, the paper applies grey relation theory on customer classification for the first time, and discusses application process of grey relation algorithm for customer classification by instance. In the future, the paper will extend to customer clustering and data mine for realizing soft customer classification of manufacturing enterprise.

Acknowledgement

It is a project supported by Shaanxi Province Natural Science Foundation-funded projects (SJ08ZP14) and ShaanXi Province Education Department Natural Science Project (07JK244).

References

1. Xiangbin, Y., Yijun, L., Qiang, Y.: Research on customer segmentation based on purchase behaviors. Computer Integrated Manufacturing Systems 11(12), 1769–1774 (2005)

2. Natter, M.: Conditional Market Segmentation by Neural Networks: A Monte Carlo study. Journal of Retailing and Consumer Services 6(4), 237–248 (2006)
3. Meijing, C., RongFang, Q.: Application of customer classification in wholesale trade. Market Modernization (10), 78–79 (2005)
4. Guoqin, Z.: Customer Classification in Custome Relationship Management. Journal of Anhui Institute of Mechanical and Electrical Engineering (4), 51–55 (2001)
5. Yadong, F.: Research and Realization of Partner Selection System in Cooperative Manufacturing Based on Web. Systems Engineering 23(7), 118–123 (2005)
6. Kaijun, W.: Research of Customer Classification Method. Industrial Technology & Economy (6), 95–96, 99 (2003)

General Structural Model and Application of Intelligent Decision Support System Based on Knowledge Discovery

Faguo G. Zhou[1], Fan Zhang[1], and Bingru R. Yang[2]

[1] School of Mechanical Electronic and Information Engineering,
China University of Mining and Technology Beijing, Beijing 100083 China
[2] School of Information Engineering, University of Science and Technology Beijing,
Beijing 100083 China
{zhoufaguo,zhangfansailor}@sina.com, bryang_kd@yahoo.com.cn

Abstract. This paper mainly discusses the general structure model of IDSSKD (Intelligent Decision Support System Based on Knowledge Discovery) and describes the function of each of its sub-systems. IDSSKD has perfected and extended the function of conventional IDSS, and revised the running mechanism of conventional IDSS. Knowledge acquiring of domain experts, reasoning mechanism, KDD* mining and Web mining are efficiently fused into IDSS. Consequently, IDSSKD is a new type of intelligent decision support system that covers two networks and six bases. Furthermore, it is synthetically integrated, multi-tiered, and model-driven. It is promising that IDSSKD would play an important role in promoting the mainstream development of IDSS and become a new generation of intelligent decision support model.

Keywords: Intelligent Decision Support System, Knowledge Discovery, Data Mining.

1 Introduction

Decision Support System (DSS) [1], [2] is an information system that participates and supports the decision-making process of human beings. Through a series of human-machine conversations, it can provide a variety of dependable programs and check the decision-makers' requirements and assumptions, thus achieving the aim of supporting decision-making. Until now, people have not reached an agreement upon the definition of DSS. Generally speaking, it is an interactive computer information system [3] that can help decision-makers make use of data and models and solve the problem of non-structures. It makes full use of suitable computer techniques and through the interactive human-machine model, helps and enhances the effectiveness of decision-making about semi-structures and non-structures [4].

The rest of this paper is organized as follows. Section 2 describes the structure and limitation of traditional decision support system. Section 3 discusses new type intelligent decision support system based on knowledge discovery. The application of intelligent decision support system based on knowledge discovery is introduced in section 4. Section 5 concludes the paper and prospects future work.

L. Qi (Ed.): FCC 2009, CCIS 34, pp. 218–225, 2009.

2 Structure and Limitation of Traditional Decision Support System

DSS is a system that utilizes a large amount of data synthetically, combining numerous mathematics models and data processing model, through human-computer interaction and assisting with the policymakers at all levels to realize the science decision. DSS is formed of the following 3 parts mainly: (1) problem resolving and human-computer interaction system (consist of language system and problem-solving system); (2) model base system (consists of model administrative system and model base); (3) database system (consists of database management system and database).

Intelligent DSS is a kind of new decision support system that integrates expert system [2] in artificial intelligence research fields on the basis of ordinary DSS. The expert system among it is mainly formed of knowledge base, reasoning machine and knowledge base management system. The general systematic structure of intelligent DSS is as Fig. 1 shown:

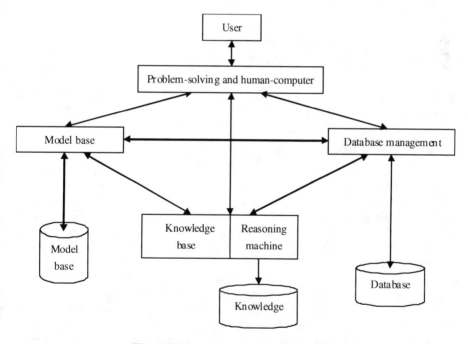

Fig. 1. Structure diagram of intelligent DSS

Intelligent DSS has not only given full play to the expert system's characteristic of solving the qualitative analysis problem with the form of knowledge reasoning, but also given full play to the DSS's characteristic of solving the quantitative analysis problem with the core of model computer. And it has the organic integration between qualitative analysis and quantitative analysis, which greatly develops the ability and range in computer system.

Though intelligent DSS has been greatly improved compared with ordinary DSS, there still exist a lot of unsatisfactory factors, shown in the following several aspects mainly:

(1) Traditional intelligent DSS is a non-embedded system. It can't interact with the environment directly. And it gets information from user not from sensors. So it can't complete the task with its own ability;

(2) Traditional intelligent DSS does not provide the real-time operational function, so in the circumstance with urgent time, it can not make timely response to help people with decision, thus loses its efficiency;

(3) Traditional intelligent DSS can't predict the changes in most situation and environment in its design, thus it can't obtain more information in resolving the environmental problem to adjust its behavior to solve the problem with high efficiency;

(4) Traditional intelligent DSS generally adopts a direct manipulation interface and with the increase of the task's complexity, the user's manipulation will be more and more complex, which will influence the systematic effect finally.

3   New Type Intelligent Decision Support System Based on Knowledge Discovery (IDSSKD)

In recent years, the organic integration problem of theoretical research and practical intelligence system of knowledge discovery, is one of the key problem that must be settled in enterprise information management, assisting decision support, and intelligent predict support area etc. The practical intelligence system based on knowledge discovery is a young and spanning science research area, full of potential commercial future. It is applied in commerce and finance market with the analysis, prediction and decision support. And it can also be used in other fields [5], [6].

With the increasing speed of enterprise information, more and more resource including information flow, fund flow, human resource and so on is greatly restricted with existing information framework. Every kind of useful information has become a detached information island. All kinds of enterprise businesses (such as ERP, CRM, SRM and DRP, etc.) need urgently integrating in order to realize the sharing and interaction of information resources. However, how to utilize knowledge discovery to find a large amount of knowledge contained in countless information resources, has become the key point whether various kinds of integration information could play an important role. So, the organic integration of data mining systems and the other intelligent systems (such as DSS), especially of the enterprise business, which some users have already acquainted with, is very important for system to exert full functions.

3.1   Theoretical Foundation of IDSSKD

To further analyze the hidden relationships among different attributes, KDD*, which is a software designed by us, is used for discovering association rules from massive trading data [7]. The main ideas of this paper used for association rule mining were described as follows.

We regard knowledge discovery as cognitive system, study the knowledge discovery process from cognitive psychology perspective, and our emphasis is self-cognition. Two important features of cognitive psychology was adopted, i.e. "creating intent" and "psychology information maintenance", to deal with two important issues of knowledge discovery. (1) Making the system find knowledge shortage automatically by simulating "creating intent". (2) Performing the function of real-time maintenance of knowledge base by simulating "psychology information maintenance". To accomplish the above two functions, database and knowledge base were used at the same time and 1-1 mapping between them was constructed under the condition that they are specifically constructed. Meanwhile the knowledge discovery process model was improved and some new mining methods were derived.

The theoretical foundation of double base cooperating mechanism and structure correspondence theorem firstly was constructed in order to the above two important functions. Our goal is to accomplish the function of "directional searching" and "directional mining" which can reduce the searching space and complexity of algorithms. To achieve this goal, the key technology is to construct certain mapping between database and knowledge base. This kind of mapping is named as double bases cooperating mechanism. It can discover potential essences, principles and complexity of knowledge discovery to certain extent from a special perspective.

Then, based on double bases cooperating mechanism, KDD* which is a software for association rule mining was developed. The main advantage of KDD* is that it can avoid multiple scans of database in a certain extent.

3.2   Overall Structural Model of IDSSKD

We have formed IDSSKD—Intelligent Decision Supporting System based on Knowledge Discovery, whose overall structural model is shown as Fig. 2(Next Page).

3.3   The Core Components of IDSSKD

Generally speaking: IDSSKD = DM + WM + KAS + RM

In this formula, DM, namely data mining, mainly represents traditional structural data mining, in another word, KDD* system;

WM (Web Mining) mainly includes text mining based on web, user access log mining and web structure mining;

KAS (Knowledge Acquirement System with Intervention) is mainly used to acquire the knowledge of domain expert through induction;

RM (Reasoning Machine) is mainly used when IDSS is carrying on reasoning.

These four parts are combined through synthetic knowledge base and web knowledge base.

3.4   Main Modules of IDSSKD

(1) Structural data mining module, namely KDD* system, mainly realizes data mining process for structural data, which we explain in two parts:

(a) The new structural model of data mining --KDD*. Simply said, KDD* = KDD + double bases cooperating mechanism. And the implementation of double-base cooperating mechanism depends on heuristic components and maintaining components.

(b) The integrated algorithm base in the course of data mining: We have designed an integrated base algorithm in data mining, which is integrated into the model base of DSS. And for several kinds of main knowledge types among them, we gather the corresponding effective mining algorithms. Meanwhile this algorithm base has scalability. Algorithm base is connected to an interface engine, which chooses the suitable mining method according to the user's needs under the function of system controller to make corresponding progress and put the knowledge mined out into derived knowledge base.

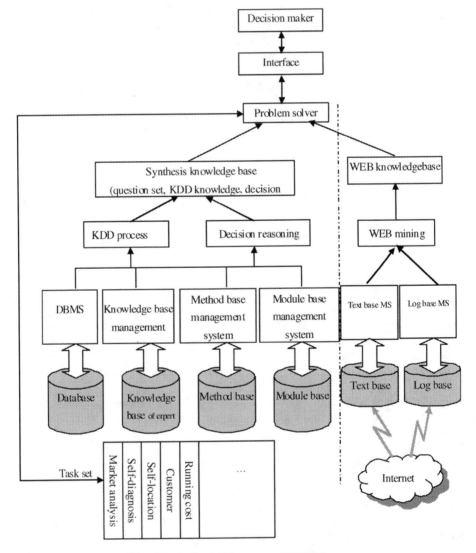

Fig. 2. Overall Structure of IDSSKD

(2) Web mining module. It mainly realizes mining non-structural (or semi-structural) complicated information (including text information, user access log information);

It mainly includes two major parts: First, text information mining; Second, user access log information mining. For text information mining, we integrate it with the methods, such as wavelet analysis, the potential semantic index, concept grid, etc.; For user access log information mining, we utilize sequence pattern to mine.

In addition, considering that the knowledge mining of Web information needs to obtain the complicated type information from Web network timely. So we will get the initial data set from Internet with intelligent search engine technology, and form data mining set through pretreatment in order to prepare for successor data mining processing.

(3) Interactive knowledge acquisition module. It brings friendly interaction interfaces to user, and makes it convenient for system to obtain expert knowledge.

(4) The module of reasoning machine. It will form the corresponding decision tree according to different question set, in order to use the decision tree to carry on the reasoning process. It will integrate various kinds of effective reasoning mechanisms (such as reasoning based on case.) during the process that the reasoning machine is realized, to produce the corresponding solution by resolving different decision problem.

On the basis of the above modules, the promotion and integration of the knowledge base will run through the whole course. In this course, for internal data mining, the knowledge base experience a constant promotion process, from basic knowledge base, deriving knowledge base, synthesis knowledge base, to expanding knowledge base. The basic knowledge base stores initial knowledge and domain expert knowledge into the basic knowledge base. In this knowledge base expert can add new domain knowledge at any time with a knowledge acquisition component connected to the man-machine dialogue component. So this knowledge base is a dynamic one; the deriving knowledge base stores new knowledge found in KDD*, and deriving knowledge base and basic knowledge base forms a synthesized knowledge base through processing redundancy.

As far as web information mining is concerned, we will construct a web knowledge base, and finally integrate the synthesis knowledge formed by the process of internal knowledge discovery in the intelligent decision system. The knowledge, with different form of representation, non-isomorphism and non-resource, is integrated to form the final knowledge base of knowledge mining.

4 Application of IDSSKD

The Intelligent Decision Support System (IDSS) is based on the knowledge discovery system of double bases cooperation mechanism (KDD*) and the WEB data mining process that we have proposed. It is characterized by the structure of multi-knowledge-sources, multi-abstraction-nodes and different knowledge layers and the coordinated operation of the six bases including database, knowledge base, method base, module base, text base and log base. Thus, a very rich dynamic knowledge base and a relevant integrated inference mechanism are formed, providing an effective solution for the core knowledge of the decision-making system and promoting the application of the decision support system.

In the process of cooperation with the International Commerce Center of the Ministry of Commerce of China, the IDSS Which is Oriented to Processing Trade and Based on Competitive Intelligence is established on the basis of our patented technology.

In the analysis of domestic purchasing and supply chain in foreign trade processing through data mining, web mining, case inference and OLAP, etc., some rules that cannot be found by our intuition and experience are mined. And new knowledge is discovered. This provides a certain value of reference for leaders' strategies and firms' managerial and operating strategies.

The research and development work is based on the data collected by International Commerce Center of the Ministry of Commerce of China on foreign processing and trade and the creative information processing technology and data mining technology. Now the work has been examined and it will exert a big influence on China's foreign trade and commercial activities. The influence can be summarized as follows:

1). Provide decision-making support for foreign trade enterprises to go outside and invite foreign capital.

2). Provide decision-making support for leaders concerning hot issues.

3). Provide consultations for foreign merchants.

4). Provide scientific advise for China and local regions to invite foreign merchants and foreign capital.

In the field of the content of the purchasing value chain, data mining will be carried out. The focus is put on the current situation of domestic purchasing and relevant rules will be sampled to provide decision-making information for leaders.

5   Conclusions

In the intelligent decision support system based on knowledge discovery (IDSSKD) that we have proposed in this article, the diversity and dynamicity of the information sources are paid enough attention to.

The core of the system is a knowledge discovery system that is integrated and has multi-abstraction-nodes and different knowledge layers. It has more diversified information sources and richer decision-making technology than traditional decision-making system. Therefore, it can make the decision-making process more accurate and timely.

There is a huge amount of structured data and web data. So the data and model mined are also tremendous and differently structured. The future focus of research will be the automatic technology evaluation method based on subjective evaluation, objective evaluation and comprehensive evaluation and the visibility of knowledge and models.

Acknowledgements

This work is partially supported by National Nature Science Foundation of China (Grant No. 60675030).

References

1. Yang, B.R.: Knowledge Engineering and Knowledge Discovery. Metallurgy industry Press, Beijing (2001) (in Chinese)
2. Power, D.J.: Decision Support Systems: Concepts and Resources for Managers. Greenwood, Quorum (2002)
3. Yang, B.R., Tang, J., Yang, Y.Y.: General Structural Model of Applied Intelligent System Based on Knowledge Discovery. Computer Engineering 19(17), 42–45 (2003) (in Chinese)
4. Zhou, X.Q., Li, M.L., Xiao, S.W.: Study for setting up the decision-support system based on KW, MW and DW. Journal of Computer Applications 27(4), 1027–1029 (2007) (in Chinese)
5. Zhou, X.Y., Zhang, J., Liu, Y., et al.: The Intelligent Decision Support System Model of SARS. Engineering Sciences 2(2), 88–89 (2004)
6. Yang, M.H., Huang, J.G., Zang, T.G.: Research on an Intelligent Maintenance Decision-making Support System. International Journal of Plant Engineering and Management 9(2), 85–90 (2004)
7. Yang, B.R.: Knowledge Discovery Based on Inner Mechanism: Construction, Realization and Application. Elliott & Fitzpatrick Inc., USA (2004)

Application of Improved GA in System of Public Vehicle Dispatching

Wang Bing, Yang Xianfeng, and Liao Haode

School of Computer Science, Southwest Petroleum University,
610500, Chendu, SiChuan, China
wangbing20090101@163.com

Abstract. The system of public vehicle dispatching is a daily grind in the management of public vehicle company. In this paper method about how to build models for public vehicle dispatching model with computer is presented .The method about how to build models for system of public vehicle dispatching is detailed in this paper. To improve the solution of the dispatching problem, a multi—objective optimization model was proposed. The adaptive genetic algorithm based on entropy was improved and was used to solve the dispatching problem to attain the best solution. Simulation results show that the algorithm is reasonable. The correctness and advancement of this model and algorithm were tested by solving public vehicle dispatching problem.

Keywords: Public vehicle system; Multi-objective optimization; Adaptive genetic algorithm; Public vehicle dispatching model.

1 Introduction

What is called vehicle dispatching [1], in fact is a process to find the best result for the function of aim under satisfactions some restriction condition and to make sure the best sequence of behave base on finites resource. When behave will be make sure, this problem will change for the optimize problem of combination. A fair and reasonable dispatching system plays a very important role in arousing worker's enthusiasm and setting work productively, and it also brings great economic benefit for company.

Advanced Public Transportation System (APTS) is importing that status and function. The Public vehicle dispatching is the keys problem of APTS. In our country, especial big city, the average speed of public vehicle is descending for public vehicle increasing, road extending, road block and frequency of public vehicle increasing. The average speed of public vehicle of the period of "65 programming", "75 programming", "85 programming" is 19 km/h, 17 km/h and 15 km/h respectively. The average speed in period of "95 programming" is keep up descending [2]. The traffic transportation, management department and city layout department will face to a important problem that how to effective superintend, dispatching and management public vehicle between cantonal of city and city.

L. Qi (Ed.): FCC 2009, CCIS 34, pp. 226–234, 2009.
© Springer-Verlag Berlin Heidelberg 2009

The design and realization of algorithm of public vehicle dispatching always be attention in department of academic and industry [3,4]. Algorithm of public vehicle dispatching is typical NP-Hard problem when station of public vehicle is increasing and size of operation increasing like exp. The effect of traditional mathematic layout method which application research of Public vehicle dispatching is not perfect with improves of computer hardware. Genetic algorithm, Simulated annealing Algorithms and nerve network were proposed by many scholars nowadays. There is an important research direction by using above algorithms in problem of public vehicle dispatching.

2 Related Works

The earliest paper about Vehicle Routing Problem (VRP) was written by Danzig and Ramer in 1959. VRP has extensive application in goods transportation, traffics transportation and airmail etc since paper has been public [5]. According to relation of vehicles and park, VRP will include two kinds as following: Routing close problem [6] (vehicle must return jumping-off place) and Routing open problem (vehicle may not return jumping-off place).Public vehicle dispatching problem belong to routing close problem, namely vehicle will return jumping-off place.

The earliest paper about routing close problem was written by Schrage [7].He descripts some actually routing problem, but detailed model and algorithm is not present. The paper which was written by Bodin[8] descript about US airmail transportation problem and solve it by using C-W algorithm, but model and algorithm is only base on routing open problem. The paper which is written by Sariklis and Powell's [6] present a new heuristic algorithm by two stages. The first stages, we will get minimum number of group and restrict condition by considering restrict of vehicles weight and passenger grouping. The second stages, making sure at last vehicle routing by finding minimum resultant tree in every groups. Different dispatching methods in allusion to three kind scales are confirmed with one-point crossover and two-point crossover of GA in paper which was written by Zhang Feizhou etc [9].The method can effectively improve the optimizing effect of operation on dispatching of public vehicle, so that operation efficiency, traveling safety and service level of public vehicle are enhanced. Effective method is provided for intelligent dispatching management of urban public vehicle, but alternation of public vehicle and work number of public vehicle in vehicle dispatching is not considering in this paper.

The aim of problem of public vehicle dispatching is finding dispatching method which is form by dispatching expert, dispatching experience and repository of dispatching forecast. Meanwhile, we will illation and assistant decision-making by model and optimize intelligent algorithm under promise the best dispatching. The public vehicle dispatching management make by three stages: plan, dispatching and controlling. (See fig 1).

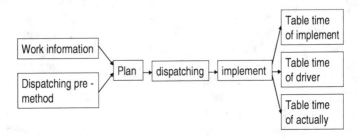

Fig. 1. Plan flow of public vehicle dispatching

Dispatching is keys flow. The problem of vehicle dispatching is like compositor or resource distributing problem in theory. But in fact, problem of vehicle dispatching is worked which planning of transaction of vehicle and company management [10,11]. So it's necessary to save optimize problem of vehicle dispatching by using intelligent algorithm.

In this paper method about public vehicle dispatching model base on Genetic Algorithm is presented. The method of vehicle dispatching which will consider vehicle configure, time, resource using, alternation of public vehicle and work number of public vehicle. Meanwhile, VRP mathematic model base on basic of vehicle is presented. The adaptive genetic algorithm based on entropy was improved to solve the dispatching problem. Simulation results show that the algorithm is reasonable. Model and algorithm of public vehicle dispatching problem is correctness and advancement.

3 The Establishment and Analysis of Public Vehicle Dispatching Model

3.1 Dispatching Principle Analysis

In this paper method about public vehicle dispatching model base on Genetic Algorithm is presented which is typical multi-objective optimization problem. Two functions base on minimum pay of public vehicle company and minimum wait time of passenger will propose which will be optimize to more approach actually numbers. Dispatching ideal will be showed in figure 2.

Base on above discuss. The system of public vehicle dispatching should have restriction as follows:

(1)Routing has been made sure and between routing is complete independence;

(2)Number of the passenger in routing is known in every period of time;

(3)Public vehicle spent is fixation;

(4)Alternation and work number of public vehicle is equivalent in single period of time;

(5)Satisfactions minimum and maximal of routing of public vehicle starting;

(6)Satisfactions alternation of public vehicle and number of public vehicle in every period of time;

(7)Consider time, resource using, worker pay and oil using of vehicle;

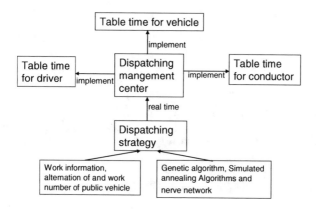

Fig. 2. Vehicle dispatching principle flow

3.2 Time of Vehicle Arriving

Time of public vehicle arriving will establish the model as follows [12]:

$$
t_j^k = \begin{cases} t_j^k + \sum_{i=1}^{j-1}(Q_{i,j+1} + q_i^k * t_q + t_g) & j > 1, \\ t_s^k & j = 1 \end{cases} \tag{1}
$$

Where:

t_j^k Represents time j station of arriving of k vehicle;

t_s^k Represents starting time of k vehicle;

$q_{i,j+1}$ Represents fixation time of public vehicle between station i and $i+1$;

q_i^k Represents number of passenger in i period of time of arriving of k vehicle;

t_q Represents get up of unit number of passenger;

t_g Represents delay time of speed-down and acceleration of vehicle in station.

3.3 Time of Passengers Waiting

Time of passenger waiting and work pay of public vehicle company will be influence by alternation and work number of public vehicle. If alternation of public vehicle is more min, the passenger will wait least time. Suppose the passenger is symmetrical arriving in between alternation of public vehicle, the paper will establish model as follows [16]:

$$
T_w = \sum_{k=1}^{N_F} \sum_{i=1}^{M} \frac{1}{2} q_i^k * t_i^{k-1,k} \qquad \begin{matrix} j > 1 \\ j = 1 \end{matrix} \tag{2}
$$

$$t_i^{k-1,k} = \begin{cases} t_i^k - t_i^{k-1} \\ t_i^k - t_b \end{cases} \tag{3}$$

Where:

T_w Represents sum of passenger wait time;

q_i^k Represents number of passenger in i station of k arriving;

M Represents sum of stations;

N_F Represents number of public vehicle every day;

$t_i^{k-1,k}$ Represents alternation of vehicle starting in i station of k vehicle;

t_b Represents time sum of every day of public vehicle.

4 Optimize of Public Vehicle Dispatching Model

4.1 The Analysis of Public Vehicle Company Model

Public Vehicle Company model required alternation of public vehicle starting and stop is min. The costs of public vehicle will less if time of public vehicle starting and stop is less. Now we give costs function of $F1_{min}$ as follows:

$$F1_{min} = a*(t_j^k + \sum_{i=1}^{j-1}(Q_{i,j+1} + q_i^k * t_q + t_g) +$$

$$b\sum_{k=1}^{N_F} \max(0, t^{k-1,k} - T_{max}) + c\sum_{k=1}^{N_F} \max(k, T_{min} - t^{k-1,k}) \tag{4}$$

Where:

$F1_{min}$ Represents cost of public vehicle;

T_{max} And T_{min} Represents max and min of alternation of public vehicle starting;

$t^{k-1,k}$ Represents alternation of public vehicle starting;

a,b,c Represents constant will make sure.

4.2 The Analysis of Passenger Optimize Model

The aims of model of passenger are satisfaction requirement as follows:

(1)Time of passenger waiting is least in stations;
(2)Time of passenger in public vehicle is least;
(3)Alternation of time of passenger is least;

According to level of public vehicle server which is rule of public vehicle starting, alternation convenience and veracity of arriving stations. There are corresponding three variables as follows:

(1)After alternation, passenger waiting time in stations is $E\Delta WT$;

(2)Alternation of passenger time is $E\Delta TT$;

(3)Sum of passenger time in public vehicle is $E\Delta RT$.

There is an object function which is by plus power is made by using above three variables. Object function will be optimizing to maximal values. Object function as follows:

$$f(\min) = \alpha * E\Delta WT + \beta * E\Delta TT - \gamma * E\Delta RT \tag{5}$$

There into: The values of variables α、 β、 γ is positive and represents different levels. If considering benefit of alternation of passenger in dispatching, then the condition $\beta > \alpha$ is satisfaction. But in fact, we will consider feeling of passenger time under different conductions because the passengers will more care for waiting vehicle time and not care for time in public vehicle. According to analysis, the condition of $\alpha > \gamma$ $\beta > \gamma$ will be satisfaction in this paper.

It is get (6) by using (2) take into (5) as follows:

$$F2_{\min} = (\alpha * E\Delta WT + \beta * E\Delta TT - \gamma * E\Delta RT) * T_w \tag{6}$$

Namely: $F2_{\min} = (\alpha * E\Delta WT + \beta * E\Delta TT - \gamma * E\Delta RT)$

$$* \sum_{k=1}^{N_F} \sum_{i=1}^{M} \frac{1}{2} q_i^k * t_i^{k-1,k} \tag{7}$$

5 Application of Improved GA in $F1_{\min}$ and $F2_{\min}$

Genetic Algorithm is an adaptive global optimization algorithm formed when simulating biological genetic evolution [13, 14]. Its essence is a group iterative process. While GA achieving optimization operation of population genetics through operation of population genetics based on the "survival of the fittest".

This paper used some methods to find a satisfactory solution of public vehicle dispatching and seek an optimal solution [15]. It can be taken as a solution to arrange public vehicle dispatching with the cast of public vehicle company and time of passengers in station. Take an the city public vehicle management whose appointment is based on double criterions for example, to prove many standards method that is used to solve the problem of public vehicle dispatching.(define value is about $F1_{\min}$ and $F2_{\min}$).It is reasonable to use algorithm and settle issue in more aim.

1) Coding

Coding mode of individual should adopt group of vector of ternary operator under the adaptive genetic algorithm based on entropy was improve. Every an individual represented a possible results of public vehicle dispatching. The time of work of public vehicle in one day will divide up N_r period of time. The arriving of passenger in station is fixation in every N_r. The length of chromosome is N_r, the i gene represents starting times of public vehicle in i period of time. Sum of genes is starting times of public vehicle in a day.

The value of initialization will depend on starting times of public vehicle at first. Starting times of public vehicle in i period of time as follows:

$$NS_i = N_F * \frac{Q_i}{\sum_{j=1}^{N_r} Q_j} \tag{8}$$

Where:

NS_i Represents starting times of public vehicle in i period of time;

N_F Represents sum of starting times of public vehicle;

N_r Represents period of time in a day;

Q_i Represents number of passenger in all station in i period of time.

2) make sure of adaptive function

The multi-objective function of directly choice will be as algorithm of the adaptive function and will use reciprocal of multi-objective function. The adaptive function as follows [16]:

$$\overline{F1}_{min} = 1/F1_{min} \tag{9}$$

$$\overline{F2}_{min} = 1/F2_{min} \tag{10}$$

Using of GA will avail to master the best value in seek proceed and avoid to convergence before mature. Meanwhile it does can improve the speed of convergence.

3) Variation

The aims of intercross operation is gene changing in each chromosomes, but will not bring in new gene. Variation operation will not limit in this method. The chromosomes will bring new gene in group by suing variation operation. Variation method in this paper will implement steps as follows:

(1) Two genes will be choice in chromosomes by random method, the value of genes are a, b respectively;

(2) Random choosing $r \in \{1, 2, 3\}$;

(3) $a := a - \vec{r}$, $b := b + r$;

(4) if $a < 0$, then (1) ; if not, it's over.

6 Results and Discussion

In order to investigate the feasibility and accuracy of algorithm, data of a city of Sichuan is used: The company of public vehicle in this city has 400 vehicles, which including 30 routings.

Now we will simulate the function of $F1_{min}$ and $F2_{min}$ by using MATLAB. According to optimize model, Entered into the modeling process in the following parameters: total temperature (number of public vehicle) is 400, the initial temperature (routing of public vehicle) is 30; the rules to change temperature is: The expression of the variable value $\Delta t'$ to calculates heat balance for $T_i = 0.7T_{i-1}$ $i = 1,2,3,......400$ is $\Delta t' = 0.06$ and the power of t of the stand deviation is 5, the deviation of he function of $F1_{min}$ and $F2_{min}$ distribution is gained, the results are particularly satisfied, as shown in figure3.

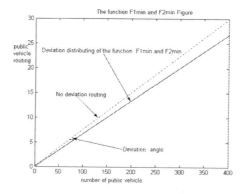

Fig. 3. Deviation distributing of $F1_{min}$ and $F2_{min}$

7 Conclusion and Future Work

In this work, we have method how to resolve a public vehicle dispatching and time allocation is lucubrated. Public vehicle dispatching will limit in vehicle resource, driver, conductor and routing etc. the keys problem of public vehicle dispatching is less cost of public vehicle company and waiting time of passenger. The method is based on two multi--objective functions and its algorithm model of follows strategy is present in my paper. Simulation results show that the algorithm is reasonable. Model and algorithm of public vehicle dispatching problem is correctness and advancement. My model which is present in paper is base on research of static routing dispatching. So the next step, we will research of dynamic routing dispatching and dynamic areas problem in intelligent.

Acknowledgments

The authors would like to thank the anonymous reviewers for their helpful suggestions and comments. This work was supported by emphases projects of education department of Sichuan in 2009 "Research and application of ultrasonic medical image base on differential coefficient equation" whose project number is "08ZA005".

References

1. jitao, T., feizhou, Z.: GA research for vehicle dispatching problem in intelligent traffic system. Journal of Beijing University of Aeronautics and Astronautics 29(1), 12–16 (2003)
2. Jing-liang, S., shi-feng, T.: Intelligent Dispatch for Public Traffic Vehicles Based on Genetic Algorithm. Computer knowledge and technology 2(12), 1679–1681 (2007)
3. xueqin, N., qian, C., et al.: Dispatching frequency optimize model for city public routing. Journal of transaction and engineering 3(4), 68–69 (2003)
4. jin, T., xiaoguang, Y.: Real time dispatching method research for public vehicle in APTS. Theory and practice of system engineering 30(2), 138–139 (2006)
5. Brandao, J.A.: Base on Genetic algorithm research for open vehicle routing problem. European Journal of Operational Research 157, 552–564 (2004)
6. Sariklis, D., Powell, S.: A heuristic method for the open vehicle routing problem. Journal of the Operational Research Society 51, 564–573 (2000)
7. Schrage, L.: Formulation and structure of more complex/realistic routing and scheduling problems. Networks 11, 229–232 (1981)
8. Bodin, L., Golden, B., Assad, A., et al.: Routing and scheduling of vehicles and crews: the state of art. Computers&Operations Research 10, 63–211 (1983)
9. feizhou, Z., Yanlei: Public vehicle dispatching research for intelligent traffic system. China Journal of Highway and Transport 16(2), 83–87 (2003)
10. Sun-huip, S.: Vehicle scheduling problems with time-varying speed. Computers & Industrial Engineering 33(3-4), 853–856 (1997)
11. shaoli, Y., jin, T.y.: System research for produce dispatching method. System engineering 17(1), 41–45 (1999)
12. Feizhou, Z., Dongkai, Y., Xiuwan, C.: Intelligent scheduling of public raffic vehicles based on hybrid genetic algorithm. In: Intelligent Transportation Systems Proceedings, vol. 2, pp. 1674–1678. IEEE, Los Alamitos (2003)
13. Talluri, K.T.: The four-day aircraft maintenance routing problem. Transportation Science (1), 43–53 (1998)
14. Haidi, L., Yi, Y.: A Grid Task Scheduling Strategy Based on Hierarchical Genetic Algorithm. Journal of Computer Research and development 45(z1), 35–39 (2008)
15. Xian-qiong, F., Dai-qun, X.: Investigation about carry out condition of nursing arrangement. Chinese journal of practical nursing 23(32), 37–39 (2007)

Design and Implementation of Chat Room Based on UDP

Zhao-na Zheng and Peng Sun

School of Information science and Engineering, University of Jinan,
Jinan 250022, P.R. China
zzn0805@163.com

Abstract. As a common technology used in modern computer network communication, Socket network programming is one of the most popular technology to develop based on TCP/IP because it can customize packets communicate with each other effectively [1]. Network communication uses the interface which provided by operating system at different levels of communication to implement the secure communication in the process of network. Socket communication belongs to the bottom level of network communication, and API is used to program for network communication. This paper provides a method about a chat room using socket based on UDP (User Datagram Protocol). This design includes two parts, Server and Client. After client and server set up to connect, you can achieve many machines to communicate. It is equivalent to a dedicated chat server, a simplified WWW server. This system designed with C++ achieves a satisfying effect by experimental verification.

Keywords: Network Communication; Socket; UDP; Chat Room.

1 Introduction

As a common technology used in modern computer network communication, Socket is a technology for bidirectional communication between two procedures running on the network [2]. It can accept request and send request. And it is more convenient to carry out data transmission on the network. Socket communication belongs to the bottom communication of network. It is the commonly used network programming concepts and tools [3]. In the TCP / IP network, using socket can handle complex data in the network, so we use socket in a variety of network applications related to data transmission and reception [4].

Internet in the transport layer has two main types of protocol: one is connection-oriented protocol (TCP) and other is a connectionless protocol (UDP). [5] TCP is a connection-based communication protocol, when two computers required for reliable data transmission, they establish a stable and reliable network connection. Such connections are point-to-point. The communication parties transmit data back and forth through this data connection. The difference between UDP and TCP protocol is that the UDP is not a connection based on the stability of the communication protocol. UDP uses Datagram to transmit data do not need to first establish a connection before. UDP does not retransmit the request of assembly and function, it is only to transmit data packets, but neither guarantee that the recipient can receive the packet, nor

L. Qi (Ed.): FCC 2009, CCIS 34, pp. 235–239, 2009.

guarantee that the receive data and the send data is entirely consistent in the content and sequence. Its main job is following: it partitions the data transmitted application into blocks and give them to the network layer to confirm packet information was received. So when the application does not communicate a large amount of data immediately, the development based on UDP makes the application more efficient.

This paper introduces a implementation process concerning a chat room using socket based on UDP. The system designed by above-mentioned way achieves a satisfying effect by experimental verification.

2 The Basic Principles of Socket

2.1 The Definition of Socket

As a matter of fact, socket provides an endpoint for communication between processes. Before the communication of processes, both sides must first create a respective endpoint, otherwise there is no way to establish contacts and communicate mutually. As before the call, the two sides must each have a phone. Each socket described by a semi-related: (protocol, local address, local port), a complete socket has an exclusive local socket number distributed by the operating system.

The most important thing is that socket is a client / server model designed for client and server to provide a different socket system calls. Clients randomly applied for a socket (It equals that a person can dial a number at any network phone). System assigned a socket number to it and server has a global recognized socket. Any client can send out connective and information request. client / server model was used by socket to subtly solve the problem of establishing connection between processes.

2.2 Two Types of Operation of Socket

Socket has two main types of operation: connection-oriented and connectionless. Connection-oriented sockets operate like a telephone, and they must set up a connection to call one person. The order arrived is the same as things set out. Connectionless sockets operate like a mail delivery with no guarantee. The order of arriving is not the same as Multi-mail set out.

(1) The operation of the connectionless use datagram protocol. A datagram containing all of the delivery information is an independent unit. Image it as an envelope with destination and content. Socket under this mode need not to connect a purpose socket, just send datagram. Connectionless operation is fast and efficient, but poor data security.

(2) Connection-oriented operation use TCP protocol. Once the link acquired by socket under this mode with purpose socket before sending data is established, a stream interface can be used by socket: Open - Reading - Writing - turn off. All information will be received with the same order at the other end. Connection-oriented operation is less effective than connectionless but higher data security than it.

As it can be seen, setting up connection means establishing an access of information transmission to both sides that need communication. After the sender sent the request to connect the receiver and obtain the response, receiver can receive message completely because it transmit information only after the response of receiver and transmit at the same access. It means that the reliability of information transmission is relatively high. The spending of resources increases because of the need of establishing links (It must wait for the response of receiver and must be confirmed whether the information is conveyed or not), it monopolize a access and should not set up another connection before disconnection. Connectionless is a one-off transmission which sends information at the beginning and need not wait for the response of receiver. To some extent, it can not guarantee the reliability of the information transmission. It likes writing a letter, so we will only mail the letter, but can not guarantee that the receiver will be able to receive.

3 The Mechanism of Chat Room

UDP is a non-connection-oriented and unreliable communications protocol. Compared with TCP, UDP is less reliable but higher transmission efficiency. Therefore UDP is much useful in the network. In this design, the server of chat room accepts information from each connected client and broadcast to each client. It primarily includes the following two parts.

3.1 The Part of Server

The server end is that ChatSer automatically monitors the default port after start: DEFAULT_PORT 5000 wait for the connection of clients and display connection information in the text domain. At server end, clicking the closure of windows and the exit button of window can close the server.

Part of server-end code is following:

```
BOOL CChatSrvDlg::InitControls()
    {
    gethostname(name,  128);//获得主机名
    pHost  =  gethostbyname(name);//获得主机结构
    srvaddr  = inet_ntoa(*((in_addr  *)pHost->h_addr)) ;

if(GetPrivateProfileString(_T("PORT"),_T("LastSrvPORT"),NULL,srvport_t,6,
NULL)>0)
    {srvport = atoi(srvport_t);}
    else
    {srvport = 5000;}
    return 0;
}
    DWORD WINAPI CChatSrvDlg::RecvProc(LPVOID lpParameter)
    {
    SOCKET sock = ((RECVPARAM *)lpParameter)->sock;
    HWND hwnd = ((RECVPARAM *)lpParameter)->hwnd;
    .........
}
```

3.2 The Part of Server

The client end is that ChatClient displays client interface after start. Click the "setting" button on top of the windows to set the server address and click "ok" to connect the serve. After the success of connection, clients can enter the message in the text at the bottom of windows and click "send" to send the message. The information received by clients will be displayed in text at the central of windows, and then many users can chat in the chat room.

Part of client-end code is following:

```
BOOL CChatClientDlg::InitControls()
{
    hostent*  pHost;
    if(GetPrivateProfileString(_T("ADDR"),_T("LastSrvaddr"),NULL,srvaddr_t,
20, NULL)>0)
    {srvaddr = srvaddr_t;}
    else
    {
        gethostname(name,  128);//获得主机名
        pHost = gethostbyname(name);//获得主机结构
        srvaddr = inet_ntoa(*((in_addr  *)pHost->h_addr)) ;
    }
    if(GetPrivateProfileString(_T("PORT"),_T("LastSrvPORT"),NULL,srvport_t,
6, NULL)>0)
    {srvport = atoi(srvport_t);}
    else
    {srvport = 5000;}
    return 0;
}
void CChatClientDlg::OnSysCommand(UINT nID, LPARAM lParam)
{
    if ((nID & 0xFFF0) == IDM_ABOUTBOX)
    {.......}
}
```

Fig. 1. Client Send a Message

4 The Final Effect of Design

Firstly, client-end sends a message, we can see from the Fig. 1.

This procedure based on the UDP protocol has the same principle with chat software called QQ. If you test the procedure used several computers, only need to set up the server IP address.

And then server-end write back a message. As shown in the Fig. 2.

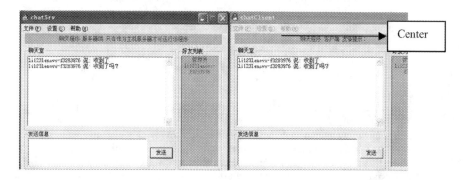

Fig. 2. Server Return a Message

5 Conclusion

Chat room based on socket is relatively rare. Unlike the chat room called CGI where the screen will be refreshed from time to time in spite of nobody speaking, the content of chat will be display on the screen only when someone speaks in the chat room based on socket. Also unlike CGI where client browser request chat content regular, it send messages to client browser by software of chat server. This chat room can accommodate many people and the capability will not be significantly reduced, so socket-based chat rooms have a great advantage compared with traditional chat rooms. The design is developed based on UDP. We have achieve a satisfying effect after tested online used several computers.

References

1. RFC 2292, Advanced Sockets API for IPv6, 1998.2
2. Wang, F., Luo, J.-R.: The Research and Application of Multi-threaded Communications. Computer Engineering and Applications (16), 42–45 (2004)
3. Liu, J., Yan, G.-f.: Network Programming Technique and Its Realization Based on Socket. Journal of Jiangnan University (3) (2002)
4. Clark, D.D.: An Analysis of TCP Processing Overhead. IEEE Communication Magazine, 23–29 (June 1989)
5. Richard Stevens, W.: UNIX Network Programming, 2nd edn. Networking APIs: Sockets and XTI, Perntice, vol. 1 (1998)

Emotion Recognition in Modern Distant Education System by Using Neural Networks and SVM

Qi Luo[1,2]

[1] School of Computer Science and Engineering, Wuhan Institute of technology,
Wuhan 430205, China
[2] Department of Information Engineering, Wuhan University of Science and Technology
Zhongnan Branch Wuhan 430223, China
ccnu_luo2008@yahoo.com.cn

Abstract. Modern distant education (or e-Learning or eLearning) is a type of Technology supported education/learning (TSL) where the medium of instruction is through computer technology, particularly involving digital technologies. Aiming at emotion deficiency in present modern distant education system, a lot of negative effects were analyzed and corresponding countermeasures were proposed. Basing on it, we combined affective computing with the modern distant education system. The model of modern distant education system based on affective computing was constructed by using speech emotion and facial emotion, which took speech feature and facial emotion as input data. The key technologies of Speech Emotion Recognition based on Neural Networks and Facial Emotion Recognition based on SVM have been proposed.

Keywords: SVM, Affective Computing, Emotion recognition, Neural Network, Modern Distant Education System.

1 Introduction

Modern distant education (or e-Learning or eLearning) is a type of Technology supported education/learning (TSL) where the medium of instruction is through computer technology, particularly involving digital technologies. Modern distant education has been defined as "pedagogy empowered by digital technology" [1]. In some instances, no face- to- face interaction takes place. Modern distant education is used interchangeably in a wide variety of contexts. In companies, it refers to the strategies that use the company network to deliver training courses to employees. In the United States, it is defined as a planned teaching/learning experience that uses a wide spectrum of technologies, mainly Internet or computer-based, to reach learners. Lately in most Universities, Modern distant education is used to define a specific mode to attend a course or programs of study where the students rarely, if ever, attend face-to-face for on-campus access to educational facilities, because they study online.

Although the current Modern distant education have many merits, many of them only treat advanced information technology as simple communication tools, and release some learning contents and exercises in the network [2]. This kind of movable textbook or electronic textbook is indifferent to the learners, which lacks of the

L. Qi (Ed.): FCC 2009, CCIS 34, pp. 240–247, 2009.

interaction of emotion. Besides, this kind of learning materials without using of the superiority of interactive multimedia technology and displaying the function of network effectively, which leads to the phenomenon of emotion deficiency in the current Modern distant education system system.

Emotion deficiency refers to the separation among students and teachers, students and students, which make students and teachers, students and students can't carry on face to face communicating promptly like conventional education. Thus, some learning problems of the learners in the learning process can't be solved and perplexity of the psychology can't get help. If students gaze at indifferent computer screens for a long time, they do not feel the interactive pleasure and emotion stimulation, and they may have antipathy emotion.

The network institute of Central China Normal University (CCNU) has carried out an investigation on learning conditions for 203 distance education learners in 2006. The author took out two results that are related to emotion deficiency form the investigation results. Two results are shown in table1 and table 2.

From tables 1 and table 2, the influence that is caused from the separation among teachers and students or students and students is obvious (obvious influence and great influence occupy 56.5%. The influence that is caused from the interaction deficiency of teaching contents is obvious too. (Obvious influence and great influence occupy 63.8%).

Table 1. The influence is caused from the separation among teachers and students or students and students

Influence degree	Great influence	Obvious influence	A little influence	No influence
Student number	33	81	62	27
percent	16.3%	40.2%	30.3%	13.2%

Table 2. The influence is caused from the interaction deficiency of teaching contents

Influence degree	Great influence	Obvious influence	A little influence	No influence
Student number	42	87	42	32
percent	20.8%	43.0%	20.6%	15.6%

How to measure cognitive emotion of learners in the Modern distant education system and realize harmonious emotion interaction becomes an important research topic in the distance education [3]. Aiming at the problem of emotion deficiency in Modern distant education system, domestic and abroad scholars bring forward some strategies as follows:

(1) Designing the emotional network curriculums. The emotional mark is added to interactive network curriculums.

(2) Implementing exploring and cooperative learning. The learning groups are constructed, which is advantage to the communication among students and teachers.

(3) Implementing blended learning. The superiority of traditional learning and Modern distant education system is combined to display the leading role of teachers and the main-body function of students.

(4) Improving learning supporting service system. Comprehensive, prompt, and convenient learning of support service is provided to maintain learners' positive emotion.

The application of above strategies have avoided emotion deficiency in certain degree, but learner's emotion state cannot be tracked accurately, the corresponding emotional encouragement and compensation also cannot be provided according to specific emotion state, which cannot help the learner to solve emotion deficiency fundamentally.

2 Affective Computing

Affective computing is a branch of the study and development of artificial intelligence that deals with the design of systems and devices that can recognize, interpret, and process human emotions. It is an interdisciplinary field spanning computer sciences, psychology, and cognitive science. While the origins of the field may be traced as far back as to early philosophical enquiries into emotion, the more modern branch of computer science originated with Rosalind Picard's 1995 paper on affective computing.[4][5] A motivation for the research is the ability to simulate empathy. The machine should interpret the emotional state of humans and adapt its behavior to them, giving an appropriate response for those emotions.

Technologies of affective computing are as follows:

(1) Emotional speech
Emotional speech processing recognizes the user's emotional state by analyzing speech patterns. Vocal parameters and prosody features such as pitch variables and speech rate are analyzed through pattern recognition. Emotional inflection and modulation in synthesized speech, either through phrasing or acoustic features is useful in human-computer interaction. Such capability makes speech natural and expressive. For example a dialog system might modulate its speech to be more puerile if it deems the emotional model of its current user is that of a child.
(2) Facial expression
The detection and processing of facial expression is achieved through various methods such as optical flow, hidden Markov model, and neural network processing or active appearance model.
(3) Body gesture
Body gesture is the position and the changes of the body. There are many proposed methods to detect the body gesture. Hand gestures have been a common focus of body gesture detection, apparentness methods and 3-D modeling methods are traditionally used.

Basing on it, affective computing is applied in the Modern distant education system, while the model of Modern distant education system based on affective computing is proposed in Figure 1. Speech emotion recognition is used to construct affective computing module. Then, the emotion state is judged and understood. The corresponding emotion encouragement and compensation are provided according to the specific emotion state. Teaching strategies and learning behaviors are adjusted according to learners' emotion state. Thus, the system could help the learners to solve emotion deficiency in Modern distant education system essentially.

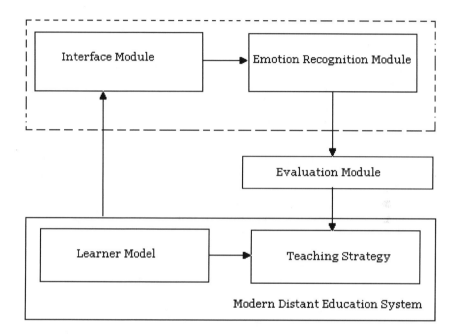

Fig. 1. The Model of Modern Distant Education System based on Affective Computing

Interface Module: affective computing input (final expression input and speech emotion recognition input)is added to human machine interface of traditional Modern distant education system, which collects learners' emotion feedback information primarily, thus emotion compensation is realized.

Emotion Recognition Module: emotion recognition module is composed of input, pre-processing, feature extraction, feature selection, emotion recognition and output. Basing on it, the appropriate evaluation of learning is obtained.

Evaluation Module: it collects evaluation results and transforms into a corresponding evaluation parameters. Simultaneously, Learning records are extracted from learners' model.

Teaching Strategy Adjusting Algorithm Module: teaching strategies are adjusted according to the evaluation parameters and learning records of learners' model. Appropriate teaching contents and teaching mode are provided to learners. Simultaneously, emotional encouragement and compensation is provided.

Expanding Learner's Model: it records personal information mainly, including learning background information, cognitive style information, emotional information, and so on.

3 Speech Emotion Recognition Based on Neural Networks

The processing flow of speech emotion recognition is illustrated in Figure 2. The process is divided into two main parts: speech processing and emotion recognition.

A speech input (an utterance) is input into the speech processing part. First, the speech features for that utterance are calculated. Next, the utterance is divided into a number of speech periods. Finally, for each speech period the speech features are extracted, and features for the utterance are compiled into a feature vector. The feature vector is then input into the emotion recognition part. In the training stage, the feature vector is used to train the neural network using back propagation. In the recognition stage, the feature vector is applied to the already trained network, and the result is a recognized emotion. These steps are explained further in the following sections.

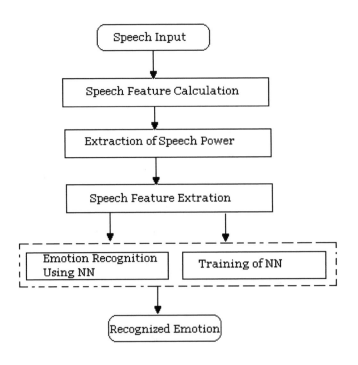

Fig. 2. The Processing Flow

The emotion recognition stage of the processing flow is shown in Figure 3. The network is actually composed of eight sub-neural networks, with one network for each of the eight emotions that are examined. This type of network is called a One-Class-in-One Neural network (OCON). The feature vector (300 speech features for each utterance) is input into each of the eight sub-neural networks. The output from each sub-network is a value ($v_1, v_2, v_3 \cdots v_8$), representing the likelihood that the utterance corresponds to that sub-network's emotion. Decision logic selects the best emotion based on these values.

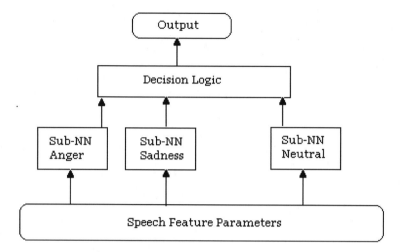

Fig. 3. Emotion Recognition Stage

4 Facial Emotion Recognition Based on SVM

Support vector machines are based on the structural risk minimization principle and Vapnik-Chervonenkis (VC) dimension from statistical learning theory developed by Vapnik, et al [6]. Traditional techniques for pattern recognition are based on the minimization of empirical risk, that is, on the attempt to optimize performance on the training set, SVM minimize the structural risk to reach a better performance.

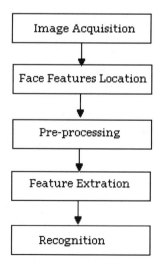

Fig. 4. Steps of Facial Expression Recognition

Support vector machine for classification can be seen as the application of perception. When classification problem is linearly separable, a hyper plane that makes two categories of separable data more close to the plane is set up; usually the plane is called optimal separation hyper plane. Regarding to nonlinear problem, original data is mapped from a low dimensional space to the new data sets of a higher dimensional space (feature space) through a nonlinear mapping (nuclear function).New data sets are linearly separable in feature space, thus the classification in higher dimensional space is completed.

Basing on it, we can put the question of nonlinear separable and linear separable into a unified formula. Regarding to the sample space:

$\Omega = \{(x_i, y_i) \| i = 1, 2, \cdots, N\} \subset R^n \times \{-1, 1\}$ and the function $\{\Theta(x_i), \Theta(x_j)\} = K(x_i, x_j)$

Standard support vector machine can represent as follows

$$\min Q(w, \varepsilon) = \frac{1}{2} \| w \|^2 + C \sum_{i=2}^{l} \varepsilon_i \tag{1}$$

$$s.t. y_i [\{w \bullet \Theta(x_i) + b\} - 1 + \varepsilon_i \geq 0, \quad \varepsilon_i \geq 0, i = 1, \cdots, l \tag{2}$$

(a). When $K(x_i, x_j)$ is linear transform, especially when $K(x_i, x_j)$ is linear invariant mapping, and C=O, $\forall \varepsilon_i = 0$, (1) (2) is correspond to linear separable condition.

(b). $K(x_i, x_j)$ is nonlinear mapping that transforms Ω to a higher dimensional space H, and $K(x_i, x_j)$ satisfies Mercer theorem. If $K(x_i, x_j)$ is Kernel Function, (1) (2) is correspond to nonlinear separable condition. C>0 is a constant, which control the punishment degree of misclassification. Loss function $\sum_{i=1}^{l} \varepsilon_i$ is an upper bound of misclassification. In fact, $\sum_{i=1}^{l} \varepsilon_i$ can represent as

$$F_\sigma(\varepsilon) \sum_{i=1}^{l} \varepsilon_i^\sigma \tag{3}$$

$\sigma = 1$ is corresponding to support vector machine of one time loss function, $\sigma = 2$ is correspond to support vector machine of twice time loss function.

(1)- (3) can be summarized to solve the problem of quadratic programming.

$$Min \quad W(a) = -\sum_{i=1}^{l} a_i + \frac{1}{2} \sum_{i,j=1}^{l} a_i a_j y_i y_j K(x_i \bullet x_j) \tag{4}$$

$$s.t : 0 \leq a_i \leq C, i = 1, \cdots, l; \sum_{i=1}^{l} a_i y_i = 0; \tag{5}$$

That is corresponding to decision functions of the broadest and optimal classification

$$f(x) = \text{sgn}(\sum_{S.V.} y_i a_i K(x_i \bullet x) + b) \tag{6}$$

In fact, a classifier is a judge function, which makes variable D in definition domain divide to inconsistent range subspaces $C = \{C_1, C_2, C_3, \cdots, C_n\}$ though certain principles, $C_i \cap C_j = \varnothing$ the input variables is the most approach to another defined category according to some testing degree σ.

$$f_\sigma = (x_0) = \arg \max_{c_i \in C}(c_i, x_0) \tag{7}$$

The steps of facial expression recognition are divided into five parts, which is shown in Fig.4

5 Conclusion

In the paper, affective computing is applied in the modern distant education system, while the model of modern distant education based on affective computing is proposed in the paper. Speech emotion recognition and facial emotion recognition are used to construct affective computing module. Then, the emotion state is judged and understood. The corresponding emotion encouragement and compensation are provided according to the specific emotion state. Teaching strategies and learning behaviors are adjusted according to learners' emotion state. Thus, the system could help the learners to solve emotion deficiency in modern distant education system essentially.

Acknowledgment

The Research Work in this paper was supported by Hubei Provincial Department of Education science and technology project: Research on Multimode Emotion Recognition Algorithms for Distant Education Learners.

References

1. Anderson, D.M., Haddad, C.J.: Gender, voice, and learning in online course environments. Journal of Asynchronous Learning Networks 9(1) (2005)
2. Jijun, W.: Emotion deficiency and compensation in distance learning. Chinese Network Education (2005)
3. Xirong, M.: Research on harmonious man-machine interaction model. Computer Science (2005)
4. Picard, R.W.: Affective Computing. MIT Press, Cambridge (1997)
5. Picard, R.W.: Affective Computing, Challenges. Cambridge. International Journal of Human Computer studies 59(1), 55–64 (2003)
6. Vapnik, V.N.: Statistical learning theory. Wiley, New York (1998)

Author Index